EDUCATING
FOR AN
ECOLOGICALLY SUSTAINABLE
CULTURE

Morris Graves Archive. University of Oregon Museum of Art. [Sketch for Painting *Crane with Void*] ca. 1945–46. Pen and Ink on Paper. Reprinted by permission of the University of Oregon Museum of Art.

Educating
for an
Ecologically Sustainable Culture

RETHINKING MORAL EDUCATION, CREATIVITY, INTELLIGENCE, AND OTHER MODERN ORTHODOXIES

C. A. Bowers

State University of New York Press

SUNY Series in Environmental Public Policy
David W. Orr and Harlan Wilson, Editors

Other books by C. A. Bowers
The Progressive Educator and the Depression: The Radical Years
Cultural Literacy for Freedom
The Promise of Theory: Education and the Politics of Cultural Change
Elements of a Post-Liberal Theory of Education
The Cultural Dimensions of Educational Computing: Understanding the Nonneutrality of Technology
(with David J. Flinders) *Responsive Teaching: An Ecological Approach to Classroom Patterns of Language, Culture, and Thought*
Education, Cultural Myths, and the Ecological Crisis: Toward Deep Changes
Critical Essays on Education, Modernity, and the Recovery of the Ecological Imperative

Published by
State University of New York Press, Albany

For information, address State University of New York
Press, State University Plaza, Albany, N.Y., 12246

Production by E. Moore
Marketing by Dana E. Yanulavich

Library of Congress Cataloging-in-Publication Data

Bowers, C. A.
   Educating for an ecologically sustainable culture : rethinking
moral education, creativity, intelligence, and other modern
orthodoxies / C.A. Bowers.
      p.   cm. — (SUNY series in environmental public policy)
   Includes bibliographical references and index.
   ISBN 0-7914-2497-9. — ISBN 0-7914-2498-7 (pbk.)
      1. Environmental education. 2. Environmental ethics—Study and
teaching. 3. Sustainable development—Study and teaching.
I. Title. II. Series.
GE70.B68 1995
304.2′07—dc20   94-22747
                                                              CIP

10   9   8   7   6   5   4   3   2

To my brother
Al Bowers (1932–1994)

CONTENTS

ACKNOWLEDGMENTS

Educational institutions are now joining corporations in the rush to make information highways the primary basis of human interaction and learning. One promise of the current cyber-hype is that the sense of community will be electronically expanded on a global scale. Another promise is that the information highways will democratize information and thus empower people to make decisions based on the vast storehouse of data that is now available to them. The spread of this latest form of technological change is now reframing how other aspects of cultural experience are being understood—from educational restructuring to the globalization of a technological/consumer-based form of modernization.

Writing a book that brings into question the cultural assumptions that many educators take for granted in their efforts to align educational reforms with the new electronic infrastructure now being designed and put into place has often seemed like an activity radically out of step with the times. Suggesting that the future decades are not likely to be the golden age that is supposed to mark the transition from human to cyberculture also seems to go against the grain of current thinking. Indeed, keeping the human/environment relationship in focus has required maintaining a skeptical attitude toward the radical cultural experimentation being promoted by every person who is working alone or as a member of a corporate effort to reduce the knowledge of cultural groups to what can be put on a computer disk. This skeptical stance toward what others regard as the latest expression of progress makes writing about these issues a very solitary activity—particularly when many professional colleagues across the country have built their careers on the cultural assumptions that have contributed to environmentally destructive practices.

While this book represents the continued development of an ecologically oriented critique of cultural and educational practices, as well as reform proposals, that goes back to the 1974 book, *Cultural Literacy for Freedom*, it also reflects the influence of a number of colleagues who have given constructive suggestions for improving the clarity of my arguments. I particularly want to thank Maggie McBride, Kathryn Ross Wayne, and David A. Gabbard who read all except the final chapter. Their comments helped in the framing of certain themes, and their encouragement made the writing seem a less solitary activity. David Clarke Burks offered valuable editorial suggestions that were incorporated into chapter 5. Joseph Kiefer's comments helped to ensure the accuracy of my discussion of the Common Roots curriculum in chapter 7. Dolores LaChapelle provided both encouragement and special insights relating to earlier efforts in this country to lay the foundations for a deep ecology way of thinking. Having a dean and department chairperson who respected my need to spend uninterrupted hours at my writing desk in Eugene by not scheduling meetings that I would have to attend in my off-teaching days in Portland made it possible to turn a number of disconnected intellectual concerns that were becoming an increasingly prominent feature of my class discussions into a book manuscript. Thus, a special thanks is owed to Robert Everhart and Carol Mack. For the constant encouragement and continual discussion of how my analysis could be framed more effectively, as well as for her tenacious approach to proof reading all of the chapters, I want to acknowledge a special indebtedness to my wife, Mary Katharine Bowers. With each succeeding book she has become a more indispensable part of the writing process.

The author gratefully acknowledges the following for granting permission to quote from copyrighted material: "Postmodern Environmental Ethics: Ethics as Bioregional Narrative," by Jim Cheney, *Environmental Ethics*, Vol. II, Summer, 1989; "The Foxfire Approach: Perspective and Core Practices," The Foxfire Fund, Inc. 1990; "Artist Profile: Ross Sheakley," *Journal of Alaska Native Arts*, January-March, 1992; "Principles of Ecology/Principles of Education," *Guide to Ecoliteracy*, The Elmwood Institute, 1993. Chapter Four appeared earlier in *Holistic Education Review*.

ONE

INTRODUCTION

The consequences of abusing the environment with the waste products of a technological/consumer-oriented culture are becoming part of the consciousness of an increasing number of citizens. But their political activities mostly are limited to addressing the dangers of deadly toxins that are being released into the air, soil, and ground water in their neighborhoods. Aside from the more focused and energized environmentalists and supporters of the deep ecology movement who study, write, and, in general, devote their lives to raising consciousness about the threatened condition of various ecosystems, most citizens appear not to recognize the connections between the Western ideas and values they were inculcated with in schools and universities, their consumer-oriented life style, and the depletion of fish stocks, aquifers, old growth forests, petroleum reserves, and the accumulation of toxic wastes at all levels of the biosphere. In effect, the cultural message systems that sustain the images and values upon which the consumer-oriented society rests continue unchallenged to reinforce the taken for granted attitudes toward material progress and individual opportunity—even as the evidence mounts that the destruction of the environment now puts the entire technological/economic infrastructure at risk. The schizophrenic condition that now characterizes people's lives, where concern about the immediate impact of degraded environment on health and economic well-being is kept separate from the critically important existential and cultural questions relating to "how much is enough?," to quote Alan Durning's fundamental question (1992), may very well continue until it is too late to affect the necessary cultural changes.

This pessimistic prognosis is based on an awareness that people's thought processes and value frameworks are deeply embedded in the taken for granted patterns of everyday life. In effect, the locus of deep and long lasting change is at the preconscious level of a culture's symbolic foundations that provide answers to how human purposes and relationships are to be understood. Yet the primary agent of political action is the person whose experience and thought/ value processes are at odds with some aspects of these otherwise taken for granted cultural patterns. Individual members of a culture may make explicit certain cultural patterns, such as gender discrimination in schools and the work place, but continue to reinforce other taken for granted patterns—such as the belief that change is progressive and that the individual is the basic social unit. It is this deeper level of shared, taken for granted, cultural knowledge that makes addressing the ecological crisis so problematic. The deepest assumptions of the culture, in effect, often go unrecognized even in the face of the most radical political action. The result is that well intentioned efforts at political reform may actually strengthen the deeper and more hidden traditions of the culture. For example, recent efforts to win greater equality of opportunity for various minority groups, while successful in terms of transforming certain aspects of taken for granted patterns, did not alter the deepest levels of cultural knowledge that drive us collectively to develop certain forms of technology over others, and to continue to reward people whose economic behavior degrades the environment—to cite just two examples. Similarly, the recent rethinking of the hierarchical and deskilled nature of the work place, which was prompted by the more cost effective Japanese approach, has not altered the deeper held assumptions about the need for expanding the cycle of economic/ technological development in order to raise the consumption level of the entire population of the world.

The awareness that the ecological crisis is, in part, a crisis in cultural values and beliefs leaves us with some difficult questions. How fast can a culture change itself? What are the leverage points for affecting fundamental changes that are needed if we are to achieve the goal of an ecologically sustainable culture? What is the nature of an ecologically sustainable culture? Do the changes have to be evenly orchestrated? That is, how do we reconcile certain specific changes where the sources of injustice seem obvious (such as providing for economic opportunities for otherwise excluded social groups) with the need to change ecologically destructive economic values and practices? If we look at the length of time it has taken to alter cultural beliefs relating to gender and racist attitudes, the answer to questions relating to the culture's ability to change itself in the time span that may be necessary to avert ecological disaster may be disheartening indeed. But doing nothing in the face of the glacial pace of cultural change does not seem to be a viable alternative.

Formal education appears both very powerful in terms of conserving the deepest and largely unconsciously held patterns of modern culture and, at the same time, as one of the few public forums we have for developing a critical understanding of the crisis we are now in. Both the civil rights and feminist movements focused attention on the need to change the content of the curriculum at all levels of education, as well as the taken for granted attitudes of teachers and professors. Public schools and universities are again being singled out as a critical leverage point for affecting changes in America's ability to compete in the global economy. And to a lesser extent public schools are being viewed as sites for learning about recycling and other environmentally sound practices. While the ability of public schools and universities to fulfill the social missions assigned to them over the last few decades is still not fully determined, it is nevertheless safe to assume that their conserving role in other areas of culture continues unchallenged.

The irony is that the ways of thinking and valuing reinforced (conserved) by public schools and universities are still viewed by most educators as expressions of the most enlightened and progressive aspects of modern culture. But as I shall develop the argument in this book, this would be a totally incorrect way of understanding the nature of these beliefs and practices. The ecological crisis, for most people, is experienced directly in terms of economic dislocations, toxins that are changing the chemistry of our bodies, and changes in the carbon cycle that alter weather patterns. These direct experiences, in diverging from the expectations that people have been culturally conditioned to accept, now force us to confront more directly the mythical foundations of mainstream cultural beliefs and values. In effect, the ecological crisis forces us to confront the problematic aspects of culture that would otherwise remain part of our taken for granted background knowledge. But it has not yet brought into question the core beliefs and values taught directly and indirectly at all levels of the educational process. The progressive and modernizing nature of beliefs and values promoted in public schools and universities make sense only within the context of the myth of social progress. This myth, as we are now beginning to understand, is predicated on an anthropocentric view of the universe and the further assumption that our rationally-based technology will always enable us to overcome the breakdowns and shortages connected with the natural world. Given the scale of ecological disruption, it is becoming increasingly difficult to maintain the interlocking set of myths that represent the primacy of human interests and technological empowerment. Beliefs and values once regarded as basic aspects of a modern and progressive form of consciousness, when viewed against the devastating impact that modernization has had on natural systems, now appear as reactionary and as contributing to deepening the crisis. This is the double bind that most educators have not yet recognized.

Part of the statement presented to the General Assembly of the United Nations by the Union of Concerned Scientists (which was signed by 1600 scientists from 70 countries, including 100 recipients of the Nobel Prize) will put the discussion of the conceptual foundations of current educational theory, research, and classroom practices in the proper perspective. The joint statement included the following warning: "A great change in our stewardship of the Earth and life on it is required if vast human misery is to be avoided and our global home on this planet is not to be irretrievably mutilated. The Earth is finite. Its ability to absorb wastes and destructive effluent is finite. Its ability to provide food and energy is finite. And we are fast approaching many of the Earth's limits" (1993, p. 2). The amount of time the scientists estimated we have for changing destructive cultural values and practices is a mere forty years. Given the slow pace of deep cultural changes, as opposed to the rapid rate of the more surface level technological changes, their warning has to be taken seriously—even if they are grossly underestimating the number of decades it will take us to reach critical thresholds in the life sustaining capacities of natural systems. Indeed, the need to reconstitute the deep foundations of cultural beliefs and behavior would be just as great if their estimate had been one or even two hundred years. This sense of urgency is also reflected in Vice President Al Gore's appeal to "make the rescue of the environment the central organizing principle of civilization" (1993, p. 269).

Before identifying the bedrock educational beliefs that have been overtaken by recent advances in understanding the influence of culture on what previously were regarded as individually-centered processes of rational thought, creative expression and moral decision making (now made reactionary ways of thinking by the evidence of ecological disruption) it would be useful to clarify how the phrase "ecologically sustainable culture" is being used. While it is possible to identify non-Western cultures as examples of ecologically sustainable cultures (e.g., traditional Hopi and other American Indian cultural groups, Australian Aboriginal tribes, indigenous cultures in various regions of the world prior to the impact of Western modernization), their traditions, technologies, and economic/political systems were based on meta-narratives that were fundamentally different from those of Western cultures. The use of these cultural groups as models for evolving our own ecologically sustainable form of culture is further complicated by the fact that we are largely urbanized and now dependent upon a technologically driven division of labor that has left most people lacking in the basic skills and knowledge essential to a bioregional and community-centered life style.

Yet, for all the unique characteristics of the Western approach to modern existence, it is still necessary to establish a general reference point that can be used to assess whether our own cultural evolution is in the direction of ecological sustainability, or is continuing on the pathway of expanding material expectations that place the Earth's ecosystems under increasing stress. Aldo Leopold, the author of the modern classic on ecologically-centered thinking, provides a moral framework for judging whether human behavior meets the hard test that must be met by all ecologically sustainable cultures. According to Leopold, "A thing is right when it tends to preserve the integrity, stability, and beauty of the biotic community. It is wrong when it tends otherwise" (1972 edition, p. 262). Although Leopold's writings are vague about whether the "land ethic" is to be centered in the rational judgment of individuals (which would make its moral authority contingent upon the personal whim and assessment of self-interest—always an unpredictable situation) or in the symbolic languages that sustain the cultural life of the group, he is very clear and precise about what constitutes the fundamental basis of moral judgment. Whether viewed as individually or culturally centered, behaviors are wrong in every sense—morally, politically, educationally, economically, and ecologically—if they threaten the "integrity, stability, and beauty of the biotic community." In effect, behaviors that undermine the viability of the energy and information webs upon which humans and other members of the biotic community are absolutely dependent are to be judged as ecologically unsustainable. The shift implicit in Leopold's land ethic, as George

Sessions and other deep ecology supporters have pointed out, is from an anthropocentric to an ecocentric way of understanding how humans relate to the rest of the world (1992, p. 64).

Alan Durning uses a slightly different vocabulary for articulating the essential criterion for judging the pathway of culture development. The new Golden Rule, as he puts it, "is simple: each generation should meet its needs without jeopardizing the prospects of future generations to meet their own needs" (1992, p. 136). Like other profound moral templates, the basis for determining whether the Golden Rule has been transgressed is simple, clear, and free of ambiguity about competing interests. But it does shift the emphasis away from the traditional liberal concern with using the well-being and self-determined interests of the individual as the basic social unit for determining the moral tenor of social life.

The straightforward simplicity of these moral dictums has not been matched by our efforts to address the many dimensions of the ecological crisis. Our first steps to locate an ecologically sustainable pathway, particularly efforts by the federal government, threaten us with a new form of fascism now made increasingly possible by the marriage of the panopticon potential of computer technology (in collecting data on people's behavior) with the progressive centralization of political power in federal and state bureaucracies. With this danger in mind, I would like to use the sparsely formulated criteria of Leopold and Durning as the moral/political/educational reference point for suggesting areas of cultural transformation that may help put us on a less fascist pathway for dealing with the ecological crisis. This change in the foundations of taken-for-granted beliefs will require us to develop the same sense of a natural attitude toward ecologically sustainable cultural practices that now characterizes our natural attitude toward a consumer/technologically driven life style.

The need to reconstitute the deep foundations of culture in ways that make possible more ecologically oriented taken-for-granted beliefs and values should not be interpreted to mean that this should be the only focus of attention. Reforms such as those recently urged by the Worldwatch Institute, and echoed in the recommendations of other national and international groups, must also be pursued. The Worldwatch Institute's list of essential reforms include: "Reestablishing climate stability, protecting the stratospheric ozone layer, restoring the earth's tree cover, stabilizing soils, safeguarding the Earth's biological diversity, and restoring the traditional balance between births and deaths" (1993, p. 17). Efforts to shift from fossil fuels to solar energy, to introduce more energy efficient technologies into all levels of human activity, and to develop more sustainable ways of using fresh water are also essential to matching future economic/technological infrastructures with what natural systems can sustain over the long term. Efforts to achieve these ends will bring about changes in other areas of the world's cultures, with the biggest changes occurring in those cultures that have abandoned folk community oriented traditions for the more individually-centered consumer lifestyle. But the changes in cultural beliefs and values will not be automatic, or free of reactionary developments—as we witnessed in the case of how federal civil rights legislation introduced changes that were not matched by changes in people's taken-for-granted beliefs and behaviors.

Although a strong case can be made that fundamental cultural changes occur more slowly in public schools and universities than most social reformers would like to acknowledge, they remain arenas in which the problem of evolving an ecologically sustainable culture needs to be addressed. Regardless of whether public schools and universities are viewed as on the leading edge of cultural change or as institutions that help perpetuate ecologically destructive traditions associated with modernism, they are not without influence—particularly when teachers, professors, and curriculum materials are working at cross purposes with the direction of reform that is now needed. Socializing the next generation to understand the nature of cultural changes decided upon through the political process, and to developing taken-for-granted attitudes toward behavioral patterns that are consistent with the agreed upon changes, is vitally important to ensuring that these political agreements are not continually reopened and contested. For example, much of recent environmental legislation is based on the recognition of the dependency of humans on the viability of natural systems. The purpose of the legislation, whether it has to do with protecting salmon migration patterns, protecting fresh water from contamination and other misuses, or curbing pollution in urban areas, is undermined when public schools and universities reinforce the old set of cultural beliefs that represent the individual as the epicenter of the universe. Similarly, as we begin to recognize that a more ecologically-centered form of existence will require more attention to the storage and sharing between generations of knowledge that has proven over time essential to group survival (such as agriculture and forestry techniques that have evolved in response to the characteristics of local ecosystems) the current emphasis on students learning from their own direct experience (which is more a feature of public schools), and learning to associate experimental forms of knowledge with social progress, will be recognized as contributing to yet another double bind.

The following chapters, in effect, can be viewed as an attempt to initiate a discussion about the nature of a series of double binds that characterize the relationship between deeply held cultural assumptions that guide the processes of inquiry and theory building, educational goal setting, and classroom practices. Many of these cultural assumptions frame how professors understand the nature and purpose of their own inquiry process, as well as their approach to teaching and curricular decisions. But the main focus will be on how these double binds relate to public education and, more specifically, to the education of teachers. It is at the level of public school education that the most basic schemata of the culture are systematically presented and reinforced. It is hoped that the re-conceptualization of the ways of thinking that create these double binds will contribute to the "greening" process becoming more visible in universities.

The primary focus in chapter 2 will be on the ways in which the educational establishment over the last several decades has understood the problem of moral education. As theorists of moral education, as well as classroom teachers, shifted from a student-centered values clarification approach to the more developmental stages of moral reasoning advocated by Lawrence Kohlberg, the primacy of the individual as the agent of moral decision making remained a constant. A second constant was that moral choices should be the outcome of an individually-centered rational process. A critical issue raised by the rational, individually-centered approach to moral education is whether it can avoid the problem of nihilism where shared moral norms are relativized as individuals decide in accordance with their own reflections and emotive responses. There is also the question of whether this more deliberate approach to moral education, with its accompanying assumptions about the autonomous nature of the individual, corresponds to the multiple ways that the languages of a cultural group encode at a tacit level the shared assumptions about how relationships (human with human, and human with non-human) are to be conducted. Most of human history has involved the use of cultural patterns (analogs) as the primary means of moral education. I shall argue that this process also occurs in the dominant culture, but is fundamentally different from the approaches to moral education found in more ecologically-centered cultures. I shall also argue that since the use of all languages that sustain the patterns of a culture are about relationships, and encode the cultural group's taken-for-granted moral schemata, the entire curriculum reinforces the moral conventions that govern how different relationships are experienced and, in some instances, even understood.

If our approaches to moral education are predicated on overly optimistic assumptions about autonomous individuals being able to reach moral decisions that reconcile their interests with those of the larger community and, now, with the ability of the biotic community to reproduce itself, perhaps we ought to step back in order to ask whether this is a viable approach to evolving a culture where self-limitation for the sake of others (the other beings that make up the ecosystems, nonhuman systems and process, future generations, etc.) can become a taken-for-granted attitude toward existence. Moreover, if our approaches to moral education reinforce other modern assumptions about the efficacy of new (experimental) values and the primacy of individual judgment in relationship to the natural world, we have then even more reason to ask whether the culture taught in schools is reactionary and out of step with evolving a more ecologically, as opposed to anthropocentric, form of culture.

Any relevant discussion of moral education must also address the question of how moral values are communicated to the young in cultures that have evolved along more ecologically-sustainable pathways. Understanding the context in which moral values are taught, how their approaches to moral education incorporate a land ethic and why the youth of these cultures accept the moral teachings of their elders (instead of seeking their own sense of identity and freedom from external authority), may provide insights into the limitations of our approaches to moral education.

Chapter 3 will be used to examine a second sacrosanct goal of educators at all levels of formal education that may now represent, as I shall argue, a reactionary way of thinking. Creativity has been a guiding metaphor both for American educators and modern artists. While postmodern artists now view creativity as a problematic metaphor, and are even beginning to ask about the artist's responsibility for communicating a more ecocentric way of understanding and valuing (Gablik, 1991), mainstream educators continue to think of creativity as a goal that will, if attained, free each student's unique power of origination in the areas of ideas, values, and expression. The cultural assumptions that are at the core of the educational establishment's anthropocentric world view are fully represented in the following statement by two art educators. In a position paper written in 1992 for the National Art Education Association, Cynthia Colbert and Martha Taunton explain that

Through creating art, children understand and experiment with various sources of inspiration for creative work. They develop *their own ideas* for expression and use their understanding of materials, creative problem solving, observation, and imagination skills. Children learn to select, control, and experiment with a variety of art tools, materials, and processes to create two and three dimensional forms. From creating *their own works of art,* children learn how and why other people create art and understand that art has personal meaning to the creator (1992, p.1, italics added).

This set of ideals can be sustained only if other cultural assumptions are still taken for granted, like the assumption that original ideas and forms of expression contribute to the onward march of social progress. There is also the assumption that students must reach deep within themselves to find and activate the nascent powers of original expression. But this image of the creative individual does not take account of the influence of culture on thought, identity, and expression. It also represents the individual as separate from the environment.

Colbert and Taunton's view of the creative individual is widely shared by professors of teacher education, and by most public school teachers who struggle daily against the intrusions of street violence, economic disruptions that affect the home environment, and myriad other social problems in order to educate students to the values and beliefs of modern culture. Developing the student's potential for creative expression has thus become one of the highest goals to strive for. But if we look at this ideal from a historical and cross-cultural perspective, as well as how it relates to the ecological crisis, it suddenly becomes exceedingly complicated—even problematic.

Tracing how the metaphorical image of being "original" has changed over the last two thousand years of Western history, and exploring how educators borrowed their image of creativity from artists who were themselves engaged in an ideological struggle with what they regarded as the stifling and materialistic values of bourgeois culture, would help illuminate how the educator's way of understanding creativity is an expression of modernism. But I shall take a different tack, one that frames the discussion of creativity within a cultural/environmental context where linear progress can no longer be taken for granted. Part of the discussion needs to foreground the culture/individualism connection, and thus expose the mythic image of the student represented in the commonly used phrases as "their own ideas," "creating their own works of art," and so forth. An equally critical part of the discussion must address how modern art, which educators use as an analog for their own understanding of the creative process, encodes cultural assumptions that represent humans in a dominating relationship to the environment.

As the educator's way of understanding the creative individual is an expression of the modern, pre-ecological consciousness, it is necessary to introduce a comparative perspective into the discussion, particularly if we are to escape the limitations of our own ethnocentrism. Among the questions that need to be asked are: How is creativity understood and expressed in cultures where the person, community (as living tradition and future), and all the members of the biosphere are experienced as connected and as sharing a common fate? A second question that may help make more visible the modern ideology of the educator is: How do creative members of ecologically-centered cultures balance the need for individualized expression with the need to deepen and restate the traditional symbolic knowledge that has contributed to the survival of the entire biotic community? One of the great ironies surrounding the modern educator's ideal of creativity is that the type of individualism they wish to foster has not stood out as an exemplar of ecological sensitivity or, for that matter, as a critic of the culture's assaults on the environment. In order to reframe the discussions that are going on within special groups of educators concerned with creativity, giftedness, and art education (which are both separate and interconnected discussions), I will argue that the destruction of the environment confronts us with the need to make a radical shift away from the current emphasis on individually-centered creativity, and toward a greater emphasis on using the arts as a form of cultural storage that enhances communication between generations, and across species, about how to live in ecologically sustainable relationships. As critics are likely to claim that I am submerging individual creativity into group processes, I want to emphasize that a more ecological understanding of creativity should not be interpreted to mean that there would be no individualistic expression, interpretation, and renewal of cultural patterns. Rather, it would represent a form of a rebalancing of the individual's relationship with the larger culture, as well as with the life sustaining characteristics of natural systems that make individual/cultural life possible. The modern idea of the creative individual fails to recognize these interdependent relationships, and thus must be viewed as an example of the dualistic thinking essential to maintaining the idea of an autonomous individual.

While one segment of the educational establishment is urging

more emphasis on fostering creativity, another segment is presenting the argument that computers need to be made a more central part
of the educational process if students are going to be prepared fully
for citizenship in the dawning of the Information Age. Chapter 4 will
examine two characteristics of educational computing largely ignored by educators in the field of educational computing and by
business interests committed to extending the use of computers into
more areas of the educational process. The first characteristic relates
to how the uses of computers for the purposes of doing simulations,
storing and manipulating information, word processing, and so forth,
also mediates the larger experience of culturally embedded existence. The word "mediate" suggests that the cultural/mental processes encoded in the design of computer programs and operations
both selectively amplify and reduce the kinds of knowledge, forms of
communication, and ways of knowing experienced by the student.
But as the amplification and reduction processes involve cultural
patterns often taken for granted by students, the full extent of the
shaping influence of the computer goes unnoticed. In effect, *as the
student uses the computer for specific educational purposes, the
computer is helping to alter the symbolic foundations of the student's culture.*

The critical issue, in terms of the problem of cultural demands
exceeding the Earth's natural resources, relates to which cultural
orientations (ways of knowing, how human/environmental relationships are represented, view of language, etc.) are reinforced through
computer-mediated thinking and communicating. I shall develop
the argument that the cultural orientations amplified through educational computing are the very same cultural orientations that have
contributed to destroying the environment in the name of progress:
an anthropocentric view of the universe, an instrumental way of
knowing, a view of knowledge that maintains the mythic dimensions of modern science where facts are kept separate from values,
the emphasis on individual thought as being based on data, and the
assumption that new and experimental knowledge should have
more authority in people's lives than forms of knowledge that have
evolved over generations. I shall also lay out the argument that computers contribute to the double bind where what we most need to
know is hidden by the increasing amounts of data; that is, the deep
taken for granted cultural assumptions that underlie the cognitive
schemata we use as the basis for relationships with each other and
the environment. To put this another way: if the cultural patterns
formed during that time in Western history when humans under-

stood the primary issues of survival in terms of acquiring power to bring nature under control represent the most critically important educational challenge we face today, the more widespread use of computers in educational settings will contribute more to hiding these patterns (even reinforcing them) than to the process of learning more ecologically sustainable patterns. Indeed, if we do not address the deep cultural foundations of our individualistic/consumer-centered life style (which is now being made an even more critical issue by the expanding world population that is being encouraged to contribute to the growth of the world economy) the information highways that are to serve as the electronic infrastructure of the Information Age are going to be overwhelmed by the collapse of natural systems. Ironically, computers provide us a window (information) for recognizing the early warning signs of over stressed ecosystems, but they also mesmerize us into thinking this is the primary form of knowledge we need for correcting the problem.

Another key building block supporting the edifice of educational orthodoxy is the view of intelligence as an attribute of the individual. Why this is a conceptually inadequate basis for education, even reactionary in light of the ecological crisis, will be the focus of chapter 5. John Dewey located intelligence in the transactions (guided of course by the fusing of the scientific method of problem solving with the principles and values of a participatory democracy) between individuals and the problematic aspects of their social environments. But most theorists, researchers, and classroom teachers who make up the educational mainstream ignored Dewey's partially-correct insights. Instead, some opted for the behaviorist position where the agency of intelligence is replaced by the contingencies of reinforcement in the environment, while others continued to embrace the long-standing myth that locates intelligence as a mental process that occurs in the brain of the individual. The most recent representation of the latter position stresses the individual's activist role in constructing knowledge and, by extension, choosing one's own authentic values. In the early eighties, Seymour Papert's influential book, *Mindstorms*, provided an alternative to the image of the passive individual required by the social engineering orientation of behaviorist psychologists and educators. Papert's view of the individual as a constructor of knowledge is clearly articulated in the following advice to people who design educational software: "When knowledge can be broken into 'mind-size bites,' it is more communicable, more assimilable, more simply *constructable*" (p. 171, italic added). In his more recent book, *The Children's Machine*,

Papert acknowledges that "constructions in the world" may have something to do with "those in the head." But his question, "How can one become an expert at *constructing* knowledge?" indicates his continued belief that intelligence is an individually centered activity 1993, p. 143, italic added). Robert J. Sternberg, a Yale University psychologist who is a leader in the field of cognitive psychology, refers to intelligence as "what goes on inside a person's head when he or she thinks and behaves intelligently" (1987, p. 194). A leader in the field of artificial intelligence, Marvin Minsky, uses a different metaphor to represent intelligence as individually centered: "Our conscious thoughts use signal-signs to steer *the engines in our minds,* controlling countless processes of which we're never much aware" (1986, p. 56, italics added). Even Howard Gardner's seven forms of intelligence are represented as attributes of the individual.

Theorists and reformers who translate cognitive principles into teaching strategies for the classroom tend to fuse this so-called scientific view of the individual's cognitive activity with liberal ideology, thus making it even more difficult to challenge this view of intelligence as excessively narrow and based on outmoded assumptions. Witness the following statement by Barbara Z. Presseisen, which she wrote for the National Education Association's School Restructuring Series: "At the heart of the new view of curriculum *cum* thinking is an acceptance of the constructivist-developmental psychology and an appreciation that, over time, every student can become a more adept *builder of his/her own knowledge system"* (1990, p. 148, last italics added).

As long as social progress and development of the individual's autonomy are the primary social reference points, there will be no reason for challenging the cognitive principles that now guide the most recent educational reform efforts. And even though the cognitivist position, and its variant forms of expression, does not take adequate account of the many ways intelligence is embedded and encoded in the communication/symbolic systems and artifacts that make up the cultural ecology superimposed on natural ecosystems, few educational theorists or classroom teachers possess alternative conceptual frameworks that would allow them to challenge it. The various layers of the educational establishment carry on a highly successful process of socializing classroom teachers with a metaphorical language that sustains the "reality" of the individually-centered view of intelligence, but carefully avoid introducing alternative language/epistemological/ideological frameworks necessary for a different way of understanding. But this orthodoxy must be challenged and replaced if we are to break with the long tradition of ignoring how our current cultural ways of knowing still misrepresent how the fate of humans is dependent upon changes taking place in the environment, and how limited "human intelligence" is when natural systems become stressed and undergo rapid change.

The task of rethinking the nature of intelligence is immense, as it will involve developing a new language that will allow us to think within the framework of less anthropocentric ideologies and to represent more fully the cultural and ecological nature of intelligence. Bateson's "ecology of mind" and what Humberto R. Maturana and Francisco J. Varela refer to as the structural coupling of autopoietic systems will help in this task. Just as who we are depends upon who we are interacting with, how we think, behave, and value depends upon the intelligence immanent within the dynamic patterns of the larger systems within which we find ourselves. This view of intelligence involves abandoning the Cartesian representation of the individual as spectator of an external world and, now, manipulator of data. Instead, we need to adopt a view of the individual as an interactive member of the larger and more complex mental ecology that characterizes the culture/environment relationship. The various interpretations of intelligence as an attribute of the individual leads to educational situations where students' thoughts and behaviors are judged as manifesting "intelligence," even when they contribute to degrading the environment. An ecological view of intelligence introduces a different and more complicated set of criteria for judging the expression of intelligence. Contributing to the long-term sustainability of the ecosystems, and thus to the survival of the culture, should become one of the criterion now missing from current educational thinking. Why this is the ultimate test of intelligence, what the other criteria should be for judging intelligence, and what the implications of an ecological way of understanding intelligence would be for learning in the classroom and elsewhere will be the main themes addressed in this chapter.

The ecologically problematic nature of the current emphasis on students learning from their own experiences (and using their own experience as the primary reference point for evaluating what knowledge and which values will have authority in their lives) will be addressed in chapter 6. The current emphasis on the educational value of the student's own experience has its roots in such diverse thinkers as Locke, Rousseau, and Dewey. It was given further legitimation by the progressive education movement in the early twenties and thirties, and by the more recent open classroom of the sixties. The argument of liberal educational thinkers that the student's immediate experience provides the form of learning necessary to a more democratic society has appealed to many public schools teachers, with the result that the student's direct experience is now taken to be one of the most significant bases for judging the educational value of the curriculum and teaching style. Indeed, this exalting of the student's experience is now part of the conventional wisdom that prevails in most teacher education programs. Even the curricular changes resulting from recent advances in computer technology reinforce this cultural emphasis on the efficacy of the student's own power of judgment and interpretation, and ability to validate what knowledge is relevant (and even how it is to be organized).

As long as the assumptions and values associated with modernity are the only ones that are taken seriously it will be difficult to challenge the wisdom of this position. The march of social progress seemingly advanced by each new technological innovation has the effect of relativizing all traditional forms of knowledge, thus leaving individuals with the sense that everything beyond their own experience is in flux and thus highly expendable. But one of the problems with the ideology that contributed to the development of modern consciousness, and to the progressive forms of education that both reflect and reinforce the nihilistic characteristics of modernism, is that it is pridefully anthropocentric. That is, the emphasis is on the experience of the individual. But the impact on the environment of this narcissistic orientation was not part of the metaphorical constructions that influenced the development of this modern, progressive form of consciousness. Today, professors of education and classroom teachers continue to ignore the possibility that the ecological crisis might have profound implications for rethinking core liberal assumptions that make the student's direct experience the epicenter of the learning process. Teaching students about recycling, the dangers of polluting the environment, and the characteristics of such natural systems as wetlands and primal forests are not seen as being in conflict with also reinforcing the modern view on the primacy of the student's own subjective experience.

One of the challenges of this chapter will be to expand the discussion of educational/cultural issues by bringing back into focus a characteristic of premodern societies obscured by the relatively recent emphasis on the individual as the basic social unit. For many conservative thinkers this essential characteristic has to do with possessing a more complex and respectful way of understanding tradition. But I would like to frame the discussion of cultural continuity in a way that takes account of the ultimate test facing all cultures; namely, the ability to live in relative balance with the ecosystems they are dependent upon. That is, no culture that has met the challenge of long-term sustainability carried on its primary educational processes by instilling in its young a bias against the knowledge of the older generation. Long-term survival cultures still existing in parts of the world not overwhelmed by the centralized power of the state and the other trappings of modernization appear to entrust their younger members at an earlier age with greater responsibility for carrying out tasks essential to the group than we see in modern cultures. They also place more importance on trans-generational communication. The ceremonies, beliefs, values, technologies, mythopoetic narratives essential to living in balance with the habitat are passed on from one generation to the next. It is not left to the chance occurrence that young learners might happen to discover in their own direct experience a technological practice that corresponds to some part of the stock of technological knowledge that has evolved over centuries in response to the characteristics of the local ecosystems, or some other form of knowledge or way of understanding and valuing relationships that may already be part of the accumulated knowledge of the group.

Perhaps the more fundamental issue that needs to be part of future educational discussions is whether a highly experimental culture, one that follows Paulo Freire's advice that each generation should continually rename the world, is better prepared to meet the challenge of adjusting and, when necessary, even radically reconstituting cultural practices in ways that take account of the increasingly rapid changes in the Earth's ecosystems, and to limiting the impact of adverse cultural practices in ways that allow for the recovery of natural systems—which would be an even more desirable development. Whether most modern adults have any special knowledge about how to live in ecological balance is problematic indeed. That the answer might possibly be largely a negative one does not lessen the importance of considering the need for a radical shift in attitude toward trans-generational communication, and the role that elders should play in the vital processes of cultural storage and renewal. With the nascent awareness among the current school age population that we have to change cultural directions, there is always the possibility that they will help to discover, recover, and renew knowledge and practices that are less wasteful and injurious to the environment. It would be desirable that this new generation's contribution to understanding how to live in ecological balance is not lost because of their own children's ideologically driven need to discover their own knowledge and values.

The current privileging of modern forms of knowledge upon which both a highly mobile population and the new technology depend create divisions that are far more complex and critical to the problem of living within the limits of the environment than the old Marxist notion of social class, which critical educators have focused on over the last several decades. Future discussions of how school and university curricula privilege some cultural groups over others need to be framed in terms of the cultural traditions essential to the self-identity and everyday practices of the different cultural groups that make up American society. The current emphasis on how school curricula and approaches to teaching and learning take account of the cultural diversity represented in the classroom is moving the discussion in this direction. But the really critical issue, the one that brings the hubris of the dominant Western cultural/ educational traditions more clearly into view, has to do with the possibility that the wide range of folk knowledge of minority cultural groups may serve as models of survival-oriented communities where the emphasis was not on consumerism and acquiring power through the acquisition of the latest technology.

How the folk traditions of minority cultural groups, including rural descendants of European cultures, may represent a granary of hitherto unrecognized practices that do not impact adversely on the environment, as well as how these traditions are part of the trans-generational communication process essential to maintaining a cultural sense of identity, will also be addressed in this chapter. This area of the ecologically-oriented discussion that we must undertake is potentially open to a variety of misinterpretations that could help set us back in terms of recent advances society has made in providing (at least in terms of the legal infrastructure) for more equal opportunity for minority cultures. Three fundamental points will need to be kept clearly in view: first, any discussion of the folk traditions of minority cultures must be based on the recognition that the consumer-oriented middle class needs to undergo a radical change in the direction of becoming less materialistically oriented; second, that the folk traditions of minority cultures are not being singled out for the purpose of creating further obstacles to their full participation in the social, political, and economic life of the larger society; and third, the primary challenge is beginning the task of recovering, renewing, and sharing community traditions that can become part of an ecologically sustainable heritage for the entire society. But first, there is the challenge of finding our way back to the main pathway of human history where there has been a taken-for-granted attitude toward valuing the complex stock of knowledge (including song, dance, story telling, community-centered games, technologies, sharing of knowledge of place, etc.) of the older generation. The dangers of this discussion fostering the kind of romanticism that educators seem especially vulnerable to, or the knee-jerk criticism that this discussion is part of an unrealistic political effort to return to the harmony of an Arcadia that never was, must both be met by keeping the fundamental issue in focus: namely, *that the upward growth curve that characterizes consumer habits and forms of technological development in modern cultures cannot be reconciled with the downward curve in the viability of natural systems.* The purpose of considering whether trans-generational communication is an essential characteristic of ecologically sustainable cultures, even ones based on modernistic assumptions, is to contribute to a more sane alignment of these trendlines

Some sense of optimism is essential to writing. Even for Franz Kafka, optimism had to outweigh his deep sense of pessimism and futility, otherwise his manuscripts would not have seen the light of day. When it comes to the daunting challenge of affecting fundamental reform in teacher education, which will be part of the focus of chapter 7, optimism is even more difficult to sustain. My own efforts over nearly twenty years to get colleagues at a major university in the Northwest to shift from a behaviorist/technocratic way of thinking about teacher education to a more cultural and linguistic approach proved absolutely fruitless. The suggestion that culture should be made a more central aspect of understanding communication/ learning processes and the appropriateness of curricular content to social and environmental problems we face was met with the kind of blank stare and incomprehension that usually accompany the encounter with someone who speaks a foreign language. Indeed, the prevailing mental ecology in the department, where the schemata of understanding acquired years earlier in graduate schools simply represented the next stage in a succession of encoding and reproduction processes that tied my colleagues together with the mental ecology of their mentors who had received their own education in the thirties, seemed dependent upon metaphorical constructions that could not take account of the possibility that the ecological crisis might have profound implications for the education of teachers. As I witnessed the wheel of theory never quite touch the ground of reality during these years, certain important patterns emerged that have particular relevance to this discussion. Perhaps the most important and recurring pattern had to do with the top-down nature of how change was introduced into the education of teachers. My repeated attempts to initiate a sustained discussion of the conceptual underpinnings of our approach to teacher education was treated as an interruption of the ongoing efforts to fit new techniques and other mandates from the state and federal bureaucracy into the existing teacher education program. I suspect that my experience was not unique.

Although I am not quite willing to give up entirely on the possibility that faculty in teacher and graduate education programs will have a sustained discussion of the educational and cultural implications of the ecological crisis, I am now inclined to see fundamental reform actually occurring in a different way. The indifference of educators, from the first grade teacher to the professor teaching a graduate class, toward cultural expectations that are putting humanity on a collision course with each other over increasingly scarce environmental resources is similar to the educational establishment's record on gender discrimination. Educators did not take seriously the many ways in which they reinforced cultural patterns that were based on assumptions about differential rights and abilities. After these biases became widely recognized in the larger society, educators then became aware of gender discrimination in the curriculum.

Perhaps this pattern will be repeated as environmentalists, Deep Ecology supporters, and others concerned about the consequences of environmental degradation (rising incidence of cancers and other diseases, economic dislocations, loss of biological and cultural diversity, etc.) convince the larger public that their own futures are being increasingly put at risk. But these groups will also need to awaken to the central role that schooling plays in reinforcing in the next generation the pre-ecological form of consciousness that is now contributing to deepening the crisis the Union of Concerned Scientists and others are warning us about. Feminists did not focus on the reactionary nature of schooling until the latter stages of their reform movement. We are witnessing the same pattern in the environmental/Deep Ecology Movement.

If one overlooks the small scale of the ecologically-oriented educational reform efforts occurring outside the educational mainstream, it then becomes possible to see a basis for optimism. But it must be kept in mind that the scale of these reform efforts is analogous to the emergence of a few seedlings in a vast clearcut and devastated landscape. Of the many small scale efforts to find ecologically responsive approaches to education, I have chosen three for discussion here: the Foxfire, Common Roots, and Ecoliteracy programs. Although the Foxfire approach to curriculum is based on a theoretical framework that does not recognize that culture patterns now need to be understood in terms of their impact on natural systems, it is included because of its potential for incorporating this perspective in both rural and urban classrooms. The other two reform efforts—the Common Roots curriculum being developed in rural Vermont and the Ecoliteracy Project being introduced into the San Francisco Bay Area—are based on a clear understanding of how the entire curriculum can be organized around themes relating to the interconnection of community and environmental renewal.

This chapter will be used to consider the strength and weaknesses of these three radical reform efforts. Differences in guiding conceptual principles, which lead to distinctive approaches to curriculum and community involvement, serve as an important reminder that there is no one best approach to an ecologically responsive form of education. Perhaps more important is that while each approach is based on different guiding principles, they all represent a clear break from key assumptions upon which modern consciousness is based. For example, students in a Foxfire classroom address the problem of community renewal by making trans-generational communication a central part of the learning process. The Common Roots schools integrate community and environmental renewal by centering the learning process around the themes of food, community, and ecology. And the Ecoliteracy project uses the principles of ecology as the basis of school governance and the study of the student's social world.

It is also significant that all three approaches to educational reform share nearly identical weaknesses. The two principle weaknesses include a lack of understanding how the languages of culture encode and reproduce at a taken for granted level pre-ecological patterns of understanding, and how technology (such as the computer) reinforces the more ecologically problematic aspects of modern culture. As the languages of a culture and technology are so central to human existence these limitations are not just marginally significant. That these weaknesses have not been taken into account by the theorists chiefly responsible for Foxfire, Common Roots, and Ecoliteracy programs may be due to the fact that a deep understanding of culture, and of the culturally-mediating characteristics of technology, have not been considered as relevant to the advancement of the modernization process. A second reason these limitations have not been addressed is that the teachers who are reeducated to make curricular and pedagogical decisions consistent with the principles that guide each approach to the classroom are graduates of university education programs. These programs failed to introduce them to how classroom decisions, and the different forms of learning, are embedded in cultural/language patterns. The graduates of these programs, even when educated to think in terms of ecological principles, simply reproduce the silences in their earlier professional experience.

The Foxfire, Common Roots, and Ecoliteracy programs thus serve both as a source of optimism and as a reminder that mainstream teacher/graduate education continues to undermine the kinds of educational reform that are most needed. It is hoped that the discussion of these three educational approaches to community and environmental renewal will make more visible the leverage points for introducing radical changes into more mainstream approaches to schooling. The diversity of these three approaches may also serve to demonstrate that nonindividually centered approaches to moral education, creativity, and intelligence are essential aspects of an ecologically responsible approach to education.

Educational changes that reflected the evolving national consensus on gender and racial issues, as encoded into federal and state laws, were not painless; nor did the changes occur evenly. The challenge of transforming our culture in ways that meet the ultimate test of long-term sustainability, while also expanding on the gains made in the area of civil rights, will involve far deeper changes in taken for granted assumptions. It is thus critically important to have a clear sense of the areas of taken-for-granted culture where gains can be achieved, as well as those aspects of the old way of representing the culture/language/thought/behavior connection that now serve as a keystone for holding together other parts of the conceptual edifice upon which formal education now rests.

Hopefully, these chapters will help identify the issues that should be part of the discussion of how to transform the pre-ecological form of consciousness that still characterizes our approach to education, and will not become simply another instance of thwarted communication.

TWO

TOWARD A RADICAL AND ECOLOGICALLY SUSTAINABLE APPROACH TO MORAL EDUCATION

In recent decades public school teachers have been urged to take a variety of approaches to moral education. Values clarification, Lawrence Kohlberg's stages of moral development (and reasoning), William Bennett's appeal for a narrative approach to moral literacy, and now voices reflecting ethnic and religious perspectives, have all competed for the attention of classroom teachers with varing degrees of success. In order to put the issue of moral education in broader perspective, I would like to state in propositional form three fundamental insights I have gained from Alan Durning, David Orr, and Ron Scollon and Suzanne Wong Scollon. They are: (1) cultures that do not evolve a land ethic will perish; (2) all languages are about relationships and thus encode the moral sensitives of the language community; and (3) *"all education is environmental education,"* to quote David Orr (1992, p. 90). These propositions are related to each other; when taken together, they lead to a profoundly different way of understanding the limitations of past approaches to moral education—particularly the values clarification approach that leads to the nihilistic end of moral relativism and Kohlberg's moral/ rational problem solving that leads to equally questionable culture-free universals.

The first proposition seems to be especially important because it provides a reference point (indeed, an absolute that holds for all cultures) for illuminating the moral judgments that are an integral part of all learning and language processes that occur in the classroom. It also provides the basis of a moral imperative that transcends both the momentary flight of emotive judgments and the ever conflicting arguments and perspectives of the rational mind. Alan Durning stated it in the form of a new Golden Rule: "each generation must meet its needs without jeopardizing the prospects of future generations to meet their own needs" (1991, p. 165). Earlier, Aldo Leopold's classic book, *A Sand County Almanac*, expressed the same moral imperative in terms of a somewhat different line of reasoning. By situating the evolution of ethics within an ecological framework that takes account of human dependency upon the "energy flowing through a circuit of soils, plants, and animals," Leopold arrived at the following conclusion: "An ethic, ecologically, is a limitation on freedom of action in the struggle for existence. . . . All ethics so far evolved rest upon a single premise: that the individual is a member of a community of interdependent parts." Finally, a "land ethic" requires adherence to the following guideline for discriminating between moral and immoral behavior: "A thing is right when it tends to preserve the integrity, stability, and beauty of the biotic community. It is wrong when it tends otherwise" (1966 edition, p. 262).

Although their justifications are given a slightly different emphasis, they both arrive at essentially the same way of understanding the moral imperative: namely, that humans have a moral obligation to act in ways that do not degrade the integrity and viability of natural systems. As the rapidly expanding human population and consumer/technologically-oriented modern life style now impact natural systems in ways that seriously threaten their long-term sustaining capacities, the moral imperative articulated by Leopold and Durning represents a position that a wide variety of groups can agree upon: sociobiologists, pragmatists whose time frame extends beyond the sense of immediate self-interest, and people who have a more holistic and spiritual way of understanding the interconnectedness of life's patterns. But not everybody is aware that we face the possibility of ecological disaster, nor is there widespread agreement among the general public on what should be our moral priorities or how moral values should be taught.

One of the problems educational reformers face in translating our current understanding of human dependency upon the viability of natural systems into our moral codes has to do with the cultural tradition reflected in the rational approach taken by Leopold and

Durning. That establishing the basis of belief through propositional arguments laid out for readers to reflect upon is a culturally-specific approach can be seen by comparing this tradition, which goes back to Plato and the introduction of literacy, to cultures based on meta-narratives that represent humans as interdependent with other life forms and as sharing with them a common life force. Indeed, the difference between our rational approach to establishing the author-ity of beliefs and life patterns and that of ecologically integrated cultures like the Australian Aborigines and the North American Indians (before the impact of Western ideas and technology) is im-mense. Traditional cultures such as the Pintupi of Australia and the Kwakiutl of the Pacific Northwest evolved out of their stories of origins an ecological sensitivity that was part of every member's taken for granted attitude toward all aspects of daily life. The kind of moral behavior Leopold and Durning are hoping to bring about through rational persuasion based on scientific evidence was so much a part of the natural attitude of these traditional peoples that alternative ways of understanding were inconceivable. The irony now is that our own progress toward a land ethic is being obstructed by the same cultural pattern of an individually-centered rational process that helped to produce the forms of technology and con-sumer life style that are now subverting the few remaining examples of ecologically sustainable cultures. As J. Baird Callicott points out in, *In Defense of the Land Ethic: Essays in Environmental Philoso-phy,* Leopold's land ethic stirred up a barrage of critical arguments from philosophers around the world. Supportive arguments have been more forthcoming in recent years, but the additional corpus of printed arguments has not moved the cultural mainstream any closer to living in ways that take account of our moral responsibility to unborn generations or to the larger biotic community. Scientific evidence, particularly in areas where environmental abuses can be linked to health problems, seems now to have the greatest influence on developing a more ecologically-oriented form of consciousness. But science can only take us so far, particularly since the scientific method is unable to address moral issues. The development of sci-ence can also be understood historically as being motivated, in part, by the goal of freeing humans from the "irrational" influence of metanarratives, which have been the basis of cultures that have lived in sustainable relationships with the rest of the biotic community.

The study of the characteristics of ecological centeredness of many traditional cultures brings into focus the nature of the double bind in recent approaches to moral education. As these double binds will also undermine future efforts, it is important to understand how our own culture's highest values may now be the chief impediments to the evolution of a land ethic. The chief cause of the double binds, manifested in a form of social progress that degrades the Earth's ecosystems, is rooted in the particular form of intelligence, individuality, way of experiencing happiness, understanding of success and empowerment, we associate with the modern progress. That these defining aspects of modern consciousness have not yet met the test of long-term sustainability has not altered the existing bias against learning from premodern cultures. Indeed, the bias still holds that modern and progressive cultures possess the only knowledge for living fully in the present, and for controlling the future; premodern cultures that survived for thousands of years are seen as having no relevance to living in today's world—except for their folk medical practices that our experts are now beginning to take notice of. Thus, a series of binary oppositions exist: modern cultures are superior to traditional ones, literate-based intelligence is superior to oral-based forms of coding and cultural storage, and individually-centered rational thought is superior to the collective intelligence sustained through long traditions of cross generational communication.

Gary Snyder puts these double binds into a larger time frame by noting that:

> in certain areas of the world, the Neolithic period was a long and stable part of human experience. It represented 8,000 to 10,000 years of relative affluence, stability, a high degree of democracy, equality of men and women—a period during which all of our vegetables and animals were domesticated, and weaving and ceramics came into being. Most of the arts that civilization is founded on, the crafts and skills, are the legacy of the Neolithic. You might say that the groundwork for all the contemporary spiritual disciplines was well done by then. The world of myth and folklore—the motifs of folklore and the main myths and mythic themes distributed universally around the globe—is evidence of the depth of the tradition. So, in that perspective, civilization is new, writing is even newer, and writing as something that has an influence on many people's lives came only during the last three or four centuries. Libraries and academies are very recent developments, and world religions—Buddhism among them—are quite new. Behind them are millennia of human beings sharpening, developing, and getting to know themselves.

The last eighty years have been like an explosion. Several billion barrels of oil have been burned up. The rate of population growth, resource extraction, destruction of species, is unparalleled. We live in a totally anomalous time. It's actually quite impossible to make generalizations about history, the past or the future, human nature, or anything else, on the basis of our present experience. It stands outside the mainstream. It's an anomaly. People say, "We've got to be realistic, we have to talk about the way things *are*." But the way things for now *are* aren't real. It's a temporary situation (1980, pp. 114–115).

But if we consider carefully the double binds that characterize specific aspects of this "realistic" way of thinking, we can recognize how far we have departed from the forms of consciousness Snyder is referring to as having developed a deep spiritual understanding of basic relationships. The current way of understanding the rational process is an example.

Equating the validation of knowledge, as well as discovery of new knowledge, with the rational process of the individual reinforces a number of other cultural patterns that put us on a highly experimental pathway. But it is a pathway that is moving us away from the patterns shared by what could be called "climax" cultures, if we can borrow a term usually associated with mature, stable, and ecologically diverse natural systems like an old growth forest. The dominant forms of rationality, which include both discursive and purposive rationality (the latter involving a procedural pattern of thinking based on data, etc.), reinforce a competitive approach to knowledge. As these two approaches to knowledge are also dependent upon the assumption that ideas and values are individually centered, the individual becomes the ultimate arbitrator of what knowledge and values will have authority—before being displaced by the authority of new knowledge that may have an equally transient existence. As the source of thought and values, individuals thus experience themselves as separate from the world, a condition Martin Heidegger refers to as a "world conceived as a picture" (1977, p. 129).

The social advances associated with these forms of rationality correlate directly with the degradation of natural systems. Our environmental problems have been further exacerbated by the increasing inability to recognize that the form of freedom we have come to associate with individualism has severely limited our development of a sense of identity that incorporates the multiple relationships and memory webs that make up the environment we share with other members of the biotic community. But there is another double bind that the modern individualistic/rationalistic form of consciousness puts us in that is also relevant to the central issue of how to transform the current highly subjectivist (and anthropocentric) ethic into a land ethic. The dominance of rationally-based knowledge, with its emphasis on explicit knowledge that can be represented in propositional form or in a digital code, has put out of focus the multiple ways cultural knowledge is coded, stored, and used as taken for granted experience. To put this another way, the dominant aspects of the modern mind-set reflect a cultural orientation that marginalizes the symbolically constitutive and sustaining role of culture. While culture is both the medium and content of thought and behavior, the myths of the rationally autonomous individual and objective knowledge require either that culture be left entirely out of the picture or acknowledged as an essential aspect of understanding the other. As suggested at the beginning of the chapter, our assumptions about the nature and authority of rationalism has framed our approaches to moral education in a way that Leopold and Durning do not entirely escape. If we are to avoid the double binds that our rationalistic ways of thinking put us in terms of deepening the ecological crisis, it will be necessary to understand the complex nature of culture. This will also help us recognize the multiple and indirect ways moral education is carried out in ecologically sustainable cultures.

The languages of a group of people (their use of speech, dress, architecture, social space, etc. as a means of communicating about the most fundamental aspects of their relationship with each other and the environment) can be understood both as cultural patterns and as modes of expression. Culture also influences our sense of taste, sound, color, touch, pain, pleasure, and so forth. Even something as seemingly individualistic and private as memory is influenced by the cultural schemata, which for us is centered around the events and relationships of our individual experience. By way of contrast, memory for nonindividually centered cultures like Australian Aborigines connects the perceivable world with the Dreamtime events that originally formed the physical landscape and continues to sustain each form of life. The profound differences between the scope, role, and authority of memory (in comparison with other sources of knowledge) in Western cultures and that of the Aborigines can be seen in Robert Lawlor's account of how memory, place, and a moral sense of order are integrated in Aborigine consciousness. As his description illuminates both the culturally constituted nature of consciousness and a fundamentally different way of understanding the geography of personal and natural space than how Western peoples think about it, I shall quote him in full:

> The Aborigine's daily activity of making camp reenacts the same process by which the landscape was formed in the Dreamtime. They believe that in the act of making camp, they again cause the place and surrounding country to come into being. Thus *ngurra* describes both the physical *place* where they return to share food, dance, and sleep and the metaphysical act of "dreaming" the country into existence. The mythic formative events of that place are sung and danced at night by the campfire. Stories about the acts that resulted in the formation of the hills, rocks, water holes, and local animal species are reborn in the swaying, earth-stomping movements of the hunter-gatherers. To the Aborigines, place is inseparable from the original activities that gave it form. Reliving those activities in performance makes *place* inseparable from *meaning.* All experience of place and country is culturalized. Relating to space in this way enables people to establish a home or camp almost anywhere they may be with no sense of dislocation. The question of identity, of *who* I am, is resolved in the Aboriginal consciousness by knowing the full implications of *where* I am. In demarcating a certain place, the Dreamtime Ancestors deposited a particular potency that stimulates the camper's memory of Dreamtime events to guide their rituals. The Dreamtime stories are the only form of information the Aborigines must commit to memory. All moral codes, spiritual beliefs, and social obligations are embedded in the Dreamtime stories. The landscape is thus the externalization of cultural memory as well as the memory of tribal and mythic forebears (1991, pp. 235–236).

Other examples of the formative influence of culture could easily be cited. But what will be most important to our discussion of moral education is an understanding of the characteristics of culture that are related to the argument that moral/ecological education must utilize a variety of systems of cultural coding. This will mean shifting away from the traditional Western approach that represents the individual as the basic social unit and source of moral judgment, and adopting a perspective that represents the "individual" as giving individualized expression to cultural patterns. This individualizing of cultural patterns may occasionally lead to reconstituting received cultural patterns through critical reflection and creative interpretations. The aspects of culture especially important for teachers to understand have to do with how the cultural codes (the embedded knowledge that serves as technique, pattern, and analogue for responding to everyday situations) become part of students' natural attitude. These aspects can be brought out most clearly by introducing a sociology of knowledge explanation of how communication is part of the "reality" constituting process, and serves to sustain the person's natural attitude toward the reenactment of cultural patterns.

The sociology of knowledge tradition of Alfred Schutz, Peter Berger, and Thomas Luckmann explains several processes especially critical to understanding the leverage points in a cultural approach to moral education. In *The Promise of Theory: Education and the Process of Cultural Change* (1984), I summarized the self-identity and social reality constituting processes that teachers are involved in. Although I would now substitute "culture" for "social" in the following statements, and would represent the intentionality of consciousness as being more influenced by language, the statements still provide, it seems to me, an adequate summary of how the codes that influence thought and behavior are sustained through the multiple language systems we oversimplify through the use of the word culture. The key elements of the reality constituting process are: (1) social reality is shared, sustained, and continuously negotiated through communication; (2) through socialization the individual's intersubjective self is built up in a biographically unique way, and serves as the set of interpretational rules for making sense of everyday life; (3) much of the social world of everyday life is learned and experienced by the individual as the natural, even inevitable order of reality; (4) the individual's self-concept is constituted through interaction with significant others: the individual not only acquires the socially shared knowledge but also an understanding of who she/he is in relation to it; and (5) human consciousness is characterized by intentionality; it is the intentionality of consciousness and the imaginative element in metaphorical thinking that insures that socialization is not entirely deterministic (1984, pp. 35–44).

I would now stress that the reality constituted and sustained through communication needs to be understood more in terms of the coding processes of language, particularly how the metanarratives of a culture influence the process of analogic thinking and the subsequent schema that gets encoded in the iconic metaphors that serve as the conventions of everyday thought and speech. This coding process, whereby the schemata is reproduced in the language/thought process, can be seen in the example of how the Pintupi metanarratives (The Dreaming) provides the analogues for understanding place (ngurra), and thus their image (iconic) metaphor for what constitutes an honest and trustworthy person. The schemata reinforced through every aspect of group communication (the songlines sung and danced, the rituals that revitalize the forms of energy associated with the metaphysical prototypes, the patterns of sharing and verbal interaction, etc.) thus lead to judging the honest person in terms of the following criteria: "One's words and thoughts must stand in the same 'place' as one's body; otherwise the mind is crooked and truth destroyed" (Lawlor, 1991, p. 236). Mainstream American culture has many competing meta-narratives, but one of the most increasingly powerful ones involves thinking of the world as a machine (now as a giant computer encoding and transmitting information). This leads to thinking of the body as made up of parts, and of intelligence as processing information. The relationship of meta-narrative (root metaphor) to the encoding and re-encoding processes associated with analogic thinking and iconic metaphors is the same for us as it is for the Aborigines; it's just that the meta-narratives are profoundly different. Both cultural groups are thought by the cultural schemata in their languages as they think within the languages. Self-identity, what is taken for granted (including patterns of interpretation), and the reality constituted and sustained through ongoing communication are an integral aspect of the cultural metaphors made real through thought and action.

This summary brings us back to two of the propositions introduced at the beginning of this discussion: "All languages are about relationships and thus encode the moral sensitivities of the language community"; and *"all education is environmental education."* What does it mean to say that all languages are about relationships and thus encode the moral templates of the language community? The question certainly goes counter to the conventional view that language (propositional language, that is) has to do with representation, meanings, and the truth of knowledge claims. Perhaps the easiest way to get a handle on this statement is to use the example of what is popularly called "nonverbal communication," where facial expression, body posture, tone of voice, and use of social space are used to communicate the attitude one has toward the other person. The nature of the relationship (friend that one is happy to see, person who is source of anger and contempt, stranger whose essential rights as pedestrian or driver are acknowledged) is communicated indirectly through messages that do not have to be made explicit. If we take architecture as another kind of example of a language that communicates about relationships, we can see in the use of materials and design of space how messages are communicated about public and private boundaries, status, wealth, connection with natural surroundings, and so forth. Classrooms without windows (or rooms with one-way windows), fences, and door entry ways are further examples of sign systems that define and regulate relationships. How the relationships are framed through these indirect and implicit languages largely determine, given the taken for granted nature of supporting cultural codes, what will be seen as moral and immoral behavior.

Spoken language is also about relationships, as well as ideas, information, and emotive expression. In building upon Chad Hansen's study of the differences between the use of count nouns in Indo-European languages and mass nouns in Chinese, the Scollons argue that the use of count nouns in English contribute to the kind of relationship where "language is thought of as describing a world independent of language; meanings of words seem to cluster about a proto-typical example, or in the extreme Platonic form, an ideal type." They go on to observe that "this leads to a general sense that reality is an idea or proto-type from which instantiations depart" (1991, p. 34). The reliance on mass nouns, on the other hand, leads to greater contextual "discrimination and prefers definition by example." As the Scollons are dealing with how ways of knowing are expressed in context-independent and context-dependent patterns, they are dealing with the most basic forms of relationship that a language can foster.

The differences between spoken and written language, which also involves important cultural variables, reflect important differences in forms of relationship. Reading and writing bring into being a very different form of relationship than speaking and listening. The former tends to be more abstract, visual, and individualistic while the latter tends to be more participatory, contextual, and to rely upon all the senses as part of the message exchange process. The two types of relationship also involve differences in moral codes and how they are experienced as sources of authority for moral behavior.

I would now like to explore briefly how the metaphorical maps encoded in language frame how we relate to each other and the natural environment. The image or idea that is the focal point of understanding, in effect, influences the person's moral relationship to what is being understood. The metaphorical image of technology as a neutral phenomenon (like a pencil that can be used to write a hate tract or an essay that benefits humans—depending on the intentions of the writer) contributes to a form of relationship with technology that is not likely to involve any reflection about the technology's mediating characteristics. The cultural way of knowing provides, in effect, the template upon which the relationship will be unconsciously patterned. The metaphorical image of the environment as a "natural resource" also frames the nature of the relationship. To take another example of how the metaphorical images and categories for organizing reality influence relationships, we can see in the "man"/nature dichotomy that characterizes much of our public discourse a form of relationship that separates humans from the environment. Gregory Bateson's statement, *"the mental characteristics of a system are immanent, not in some part, but in the system as a whole,"* (1972, p. 316) which is an epistemological/spiritual position held by many ecologically centered cultures, would involve profoundly different relationships—including how one walks on the land and relates to its bounty.

The connection between the culturally acquired schemata for "understanding" the everyday world and the nature of our relationships can be seen from several different perspectives. The preceding examples indicate how cultural metaphors frame the nature of interaction as well as point to the importance of understanding the influence of meta-narratives or root metaphors on the process of analogic thinking. The root metaphors that were part of the conceptual baggage of early Western explorers and settlers brought to the "New World" resulted in relationships characterized by conquest, exploitation, and taming the wilderness. To cite another example, the mechanistic root metaphor underlying Newtonian science led to relationships characterized by detached observation and measurement. The important point for educators to remember is that the iconic (image) metaphor (e.g., "intelligence," "individualism," "data," "nature," etc.) that is a taken-for-granted aspect of thinking encodes an earlier process of analogic thinking, and that this process was framed by the prevailing root metaphor of the cultural group. Thus, the vocabulary and thought patterns that reproduce the cultural schemata are critically important aspects of moral education; that is, if we understand moral education as having to do with the moral quality of relationships. Later, I shall return to the classroom implications of recognizing that language processes are fundamentally about relationships.

A second way of understanding the language/relationship connection is brought out by Jim Cheney's distinction between "contextual discourse" and what is increasingly being recognized as the discourse of the modern individual. This distinction also is related to the formative influence of the cultural metanarratives (root metaphors) that has just been discussed. However, Cheney and others concerned with the epistemological characteristics of modernity emphasize a different set of issues. According to Cheney, the way of thinking of modern people, and thus their use of language, is based on the Western tradition that represents thought as occurring in the head of a culturally autonomous individual. This view of individual autonomy can only be sustained by holding to the view of language as both functioning as a conduit through which individually authored ideas are transmitted and as a way of using words to represent either ideas or objects in the real world. A further implication of the conduit/mentalist representation view of language is that ideas and values represented by words, assuming they meet certain logical criteria for determining truth claims, are to be treated as context independent. That is, ideas, values, and the language used to communicate them are treated as universally valid and applicable. This may sound abstract and remote from the everyday world of teachers, but this pattern of thinking and language use still prevails in most areas of the public school curriculum. It is also basic to how language is used in classrooms involving computer mediated thinking.

Cheney uses the phrases "colonizing discourse" and "totalizing language" to refer to the thought/language processes that involve imposing the too often hidden culturally specific patterns of modern consciousness on other cultural contexts, while representing these other cultural contexts as possessing universal qualities that can be known by rational minds and generalized in one of several common languages. The forms of relationship Cheney considers to be ecologically sustainable are an outgrowth of what he calls a "contextual discourse." The linguistic characteristics of Northwest American Indian cultures are used as examples of contextual discourse, but other ecologically centered cultures could also serve as examples. The following seems to bring out most clearly how the two language patterns frame fundamentally different relationships between humans and the rest of the biotic community:

> The effect of totalizing language is to assimilate the world to it. Totalizing language provides an abstract understanding that cuts through individual differences when these are irrelevant to its purposes. Nested, logically related concepts are employed to

draw the (to it) idiosyncratic up into language and give it a place in its scheme of the real. Contextual discourse reverses this; it assimilates language to the situation, bends it, shapes it to fit. Contextual discourse is not fundamentally concerned with issues of overall coherence. Or, rather, the kind of overall coherence for which it strives is different: a mosaic of language which serves as a tool of many purposes at once. In the life of a tribal community, for example, it must articulate a sense of those processes which bind the community together and to the land; and it must do this in a language which functions effectively to call forth appropriate responses. It must provide a means whereby individuals can come into their own in non-repressive ways; yet, individual identities must be articulated in a language that makes these individuals intelligible to the community. Culturally understood conceptions of self, that is to say, must come to articulate individual experience without being imposed on individuals in a way that sets up psychic splits. The language must also articulate a process of human interaction with the land which ensures the health both of the land and the community. Contextualized language is tuned to quite specific situations and forgoes the kind of totalizing coherence with which we have been so preoccupied in the modern world (1989, pp. 120–121).

If we can connect Bateson's "map/territory" metaphor with our discussion of the cognitive mapping characteristics of language, we might then view a contextual discourse as a mapping process that takes into account the fullness of the territory. That is, it both names relationships that go unnoticed in the more abstract and totalizing discourse of the modern individual, and it encodes the cultural group's knowledge (wisdom) of sustainable relationships as the moral code that defines current relationships.

To the reader concerned with the scope of the ecological crisis, it might seem reassuring to read that in contextual discourses the scope of moral education is co-terminus with the world that can be thought, experienced, and interacted within the group's language. But this also applies to the English language, with its categories for representing vast areas of the natural world as essentially instrumental relationships, and with its limited vocabulary for representing ecologically sustainable relationships. This turn in the discussion (namely, that moral education is an integral part of using and being used by the languages of one's cultural group) brings us to David

Orr's insight that all forms of education involve some form of environmental education.

At the most elementary level, Orr's observation can be interpreted to mean that if we recognize that humans always exist within an environment (that is, that human life is dependent upon the energy exchanges within natural systems) any form of education would involve learning about how to interact within these systems. Education might take the indirect form of learning how to organize natural systems in terms of the cultural categories of private property, wilderness, natural resources and so forth, while explicitly learning about other issues and practices—such as how our legal and economic systems work. Environmental education might also take the extreme anthropocentric form of fostering self-direction and decision making, as was characteristic of some classrooms in the sixties. Both forms of environmental education would involve learning about relationships and the nature of responsibility—but as dictated by the metaphorical thinking embedded in the deep metanarratives of the cultural group. But they would not be the form of environmental education that would lead to the "self limitation for the sake of others" that Orr and Durning envisaged as the basis of an ecologically based moral imperative. To return to the insight of the Scollons, the languages of a cultural group provide a largely unconsciously held schemata that influence how human/environmental relationships are understood.

This connection between language and environmental education (in all its possible forms of expression) leads to a radically different view of the scope of the teacher's responsibility for moral education. Instead of treating moral education as a responsibility of elementary teachers (teachers dealing with older students often feel inhibited about raising moral questions out of fear of being considered old fashioned) and environmental education as a sub-area of science education, or as the ongoing reminders about the need to recycle that characterize the discourse of many classrooms, moral/environmental education becomes the responsibility of all teachers—regardless of grade level and subject area. To put this another way, it is impossible to teach without the use of language. As language encodes the cultural schemata for understanding and modeling the most fundamental relationships between humans and the environment, any use of language involves some form of moral education. The crucial question now becomes, "Is the form of moral/environmental education part of the problem or part of the solution?" Human behavior, even the most conscientious and well intentioned, seldom fits easily into these binary categories; but it is possible to recognize how past cultural ideals may now be part of the problem—which is where the focus should now be. Most educators still take the cultural ideals of progress through technological innovation, increasing autonomy of the individual, and empowerment through data based thinking for granted, and thus use them as the basis for framing how students learn to think about specific content areas of the curriculum.

Although it involves thinking against the grain of current orthodoxies, I would like to develop further the argument that the form of moral/environmental education that contributes to an ecologically sustainable culture must involve a different ideological/ epistemological framework than what has guided the development of Western cultures over the last three hundred years. The word "ideology" usually is associated with a set of assumptions and a social agenda that is supposed to guide political behavior (e.g., Marxism, liberalism, libertarianism, conservatism, etc.), but a more inclusive way of understanding the deeper implications is to associate the word with an epistemological orientation. That is, the vocabulary of an ideology encodes a way of knowing, and it also determines both what can be named and what will be relegated to the domain of silence. By associating ideology with a way of knowing, we see the "language is about relationships" theme emerging again. By extension, we also see that an ideology encodes a complex set of moral prescriptions that govern the relationships that are to be highlighted and given privileged status. In effect, to learn the language of an ideological/epistemological group is to learn, mostly at a taken-for-granted level, what is included in the group's moral ecology—as well as what is excluded. Furthermore, by understanding that the linguistic and epistemological aspects of an ideology may be the most formative on individual consciousness, we can see how the process of moral education occurs concomitantly with other forms of learning. Thus, when a science, art, or social science class introduces students to a vocabulary that encodes an ideological/epistemological orientation, the teacher is engaging in moral education. But it is not the form of moral education that fits the Western model of propositions being carefully articulated and argued, and independent judgments being made about which propositions, that when acted upon, would lead to moral behavior.

I would like to explain the connection between ideology and moral education within the context of the larger argument that most teachers, even those most concerned with the ecological crisis, reinforce an ideological orientation that envisages unlimited growth, freedom, and progress as the ideal for all humanity. To put it more succinctly, most teachers embrace one of the various expressions of modern liberalism (technicist/behaviorist, neo-romantic, emancipatory, or a melange of liberal assumptions relating to creativity, the progressive nature of change, and individual freedom) and thus fail to recognize that this ideological orientation has nothing to do with conserving ecologically sustainable practices and traditions. For example, the liberal ideology is reinforced in the science class where discoveries are represented as part of the cultural narrative of progress; it is also reinforced in the classroom where change and creativity are upheld as positive and progressive expressions. What students are learning, in effect, is that ideas, values, and behaviors associated with a highly experimental culture—in science, technology, art, forms of consumer fulfillment, moral values, family patterns, and so forth—are desirable. By extension, ecologically sustainable traditions that are slow to change are undesirable because they restrain social progress and individual freedom.

During the Industrial Revolution when Western societies were able to use their technological prowess to extract natural resources from all over the world, there was an economic margin of safety that allowed them to survive what were, in effect, large scale experiments with ecosystems that were more narrowly understood as "natural resources." Even though the destruction of an ecosystem (forests, topsoil, fisheries, etc.) led to human suffering and dislocation, there always seemed to be new lands that could be settled and exploited. With no new lands to settle and with the sustaining characteristics of nearly all ecosystems in decline, we no longer have the margin of safety that will allow the unbridled experimental attitude toward life that has prevailed since the rise of modernism. Shopping malls and the media may still communicate the message of plenitude, but we are demanding more from the environment than can be sustained over the long term. This is now the source of the double bind that the ideals of modernization have put us in. The result is that the more our approach to moral education is framed by the liberal/ modernizing ideology the more we put the future of the ecosystems (and by extension, our progeny) at risk. The ecological crisis, in effect, now confronts us with the challenge of reconstituting our guiding ideological and epistemological frameworks.

The land ethic advocated by Leopold, and the ecological reinterpretation of the Golden Rule articulated by Durning, both suggest that the guiding ideals should be to equate the moral good with what is sustainable in terms of human/natural communities. While the full implications of sustainability have to be worked out in terms of how we understand our guiding moral values, there are several key elements that now seem obvious. The first is that the ideals of liberalism should be replaced by a non-anthropocentric form of conservatism. It might be referred to as cultural/bio-conservatism in order to distinguish it from the anthropocentric conservatism articulated recently by Mortimer Adler and Allan Bloom, and from the forms of religious conservatism that became a prominent feature of the political landscape in recent years (Bowers, 1987, 1993). As we can see in the writings of such thinkers as Wendell Berry, Gary Snyder, and Masanobu Fukuoka, cultural/bio-conservatism is concerned with the forms of community, agriculture, work, and art that improve the quality of human life by living more in harmony with natural systems. The valuing and improving of ecologically sustainable cultural patterns are framed in terms of two other concerns that set eco-conservatism off from the individually centered expressions of liberalism. First, cultural/bio-conservatism involves a sense of time that does not begin and end with the expectations of the individual. Rather, it places the person within a continuum where an awareness of past and future generations helps to define what constitutes meaningful knowledge, values, and sense of responsibility. The practice among American Indian cultures of making decisions with the seventh unborn generation in mind captures the sense of life as part of a continuum, as does the person who values and continues to practice forms of folk knowledge that reflect a sensitivity to the characteristics and limits of the bioregion. Second, cultural/bio-conservative cultures, as exemplified by many aboriginal cultures in what we now call North and South America, understood that human life is part of a larger biotic community. Their sense of participatory and interdependent relationships led to forms of interspecies communication where the bear, wolf, salmon, corn, and so forth, provided the analogues for understanding the basic patterns of life—and for clarifying the moral implications of these patterns. This sense of participation in the rhythms of the natural world was celebrated through the development of the spiritual languages of narrative, song, dance, and the visual arts. These languages also served to strengthen the sense of personal connectedness with the moral ecology that encompassed the most fundamental time/space relationships. In effect, these spiritual languages represented a form of cultural storage that made moral education a participatory and transformative experience where, to quote Ellen Dissanayake, "reality is converted from its usual unremarkable state—in which we take it or its components for granted—to a significant or specially experienced reality in which the components, by their emphasis or combination or juxtaposition, acquire a metareality" (1989, p. 95).

As we develop a deeper understanding both of our own approaches to moral education as well as the more indirect and inclusive approaches taken by ecologically centered cultures, perhaps we will begin to recognize that treating moral education as an area of learning separate from the rest of the curriculum is part of the problem. The challenge facing educators concerned with current approaches to moral education in the schools (as well as in the larger society) is identical to the challenge of transforming those aspects of the dominant culture of modernism that threaten the long-term sustainability of the Earth's ecosystems. The argument that the use of language within a content area of the curriculum helps to reproduce and thus normalize the culture's way of representing which relationships have moral significance, and which do not, brings into focus how the entire curriculum is part of the process of moral education. The argument that cultural practices should meet the test of contributing to long-term sustainability suggests that moral education must also be based on a deep comparative understanding of cultures and their relationship to ecosystems. Finally, the argument that the forms of moral/environmental education that are part of the solution, rather than part of the problem, must be grounded in a fundamentally different ideological/epistemological orientation than what now gives legitimacy to the project of modernization suggests that teachers need to address the deepest cultural assumptions reproduced through both the implicit and explicit curriculum. But the biggest challenge is recognizing the false consciousness that now exists; that is, recognizing the many cultural/individual forms of denial that there is an ecological crisis. Only as we begin to recognize the forms of denial, and the accompanying dangers, will our traditional approaches to an individually centered moral education be radically changed.

THREE

RETHINKING THE MODERN IDEAL OF CREATIVITY

The word "creativity" is one of the most over used words in the educator's vocabulary. For classroom teachers, educational reformers, art educators, and teachers of the "gifted and talented," the metaphor serves to express what is regarded as the ultimate goal of education. Connecting education to creativity also functions as a verbal talisman that makes a questioning attitude appear as unnecessary—even perverse. But like all metaphors that simultaneously illuminate and hide aspects of human relationships, and also encode the moral orientations of the language community (which was discussed in the previous chapter), the educator's use of the term reinforces a complex cultural schemata that legitimates a number of important relationships. To put this another way, the use of the iconic metaphor of creativity encodes traces of and even whole analogs that were part of the metaphorical constructions upon which modern consciousness is based. Like all guiding metaphors, its baggage is less visible than its promises; the achievements made on its behalf are less examined than assumed.

However, the uncovering of all the taken for granted assumptions required by the creativity metaphor is not motivated by a nihilistically driven desire to trash other people's ideals. Rather, the justification for asking educators to reconsider one of their most sacrosanct and inspiring images is grounded in the disjuncture between the promises of modernism and the deepening ecological crisis. While the ecological crisis brings every aspect of modern culture into question, it is important to emphasize that questioning should not be interpreted to mean that all currently held beliefs, values, technologies, and so forth, should be automatically rejected. But we must also keep in mind that ideas and values constituted during a period of cultural formation when human activity was not understood as dependent upon the viability of natural systems must not be treated as immune from critical scrutiny. The conceptual baggage associated with the educator's image of creativity, in effect, may have been essential to the cultural journey motivated by the promises of fully realizing the potential of the individual's inner world and material abundance in the outer world. But as we witness the consequences of the impact of modern cultures (as well as environmental damage resulting from the pressure of an expanding world population) the continual search for ever more creative forms of thinking and expression may further undermine our collective ability to live in a sustainable relationship with an already overstressed environment. Like the educator's ideal of individuals who decide their own values, the current ideal of the creative individual now needs to be radically reconstituted in a way that decenters the individual as the primary creative agent of change. Before we consider the possibility of a more ecologically-centered way of understanding creativity, it would be useful to clarify the multiple layered nature of the metaphorical constructions present in the educator's way of thinking about creativity.

Since the sixties, when there was an explosion of interest in fostering creativity in the classroom, creativity has been understood as the polar opposite of conformity. In the article, "Creativity and Conformity," University of California psychologist Richard S. Crutchfield explained that "conformists are inclined toward pronounced feelings of personal inferiority and inadequacy. They lack self-confidence. Moreover, they tend to be less insightful and realistic in their self-conceptions than are the independent persons" (1962, p. 132). The writings of Clark Moustakas echoed the thinking of such other prominent humanistic psychologists as Abraham Maslow and Carl Rogers, and like them he equated creativity with healthy life processes and conformity with the condition of self-alienation where one's potential remains undeveloped. As later in the discussion I want to show the parallel between how contemporary educators think about creativity and the late eighteenth century Romantic thinkers and artists whose emphasis on subjectivity helped to establish the ideological orientation of modern artists, I shall quote more fully Moustakas' way of understanding creativity.

> When the individual is conforming, following, imitating, being like others, he moves increasingly in the direction of self-alienation. Such a person fears issues and controversies. He fears standing out and being different. He does not think through this experience to find value or meaning, does not permit himself to follow his own perceptions to some natural conclusion. He avoids directly facing disputes and becomes anxious in situations which require self-awareness and self-discovery. He becomes increasingly similar until his every act erases his real identity and beclouds his uniqueness. . . . Gradually the conforming person loses touch with himself, with his own feelings. He becomes unable to experience in a genuine way, and suffers inwardly from a dread of nothingness until finally despair nails himself to himself. . . . In conformity life has no meaning for there is no true basis of existence." (1967, pp. 35–36)

Coming from a faculty member of the prestigious Merrill-Palmer Institute of Human Development and Family Life, these were dire warnings indeed. Moustakas' prescription for everybody was to live a continually creative form of existence. As he put it,

> To be creative means to experience life in one's own way, to perceive from one's own person, to draw upon one's own resources, capacities, roots. . . . Only from the *search into oneself* can the creative emerge. The creator must often be a world unto himself, finding everything within himself and in his relations with others to whom he is attached. . . . In the creative experience, every moment is unique, and contains the potentiality for original expression. There are two basic requirements: that the person be direct, honest, consistent in his own feelings and his own convictions; and that he feel genuine devotion to life, a feeling of belonging and knowing. (pp. 27–28)

Today, creativity is still represented by such leading educational thinkers as Maxine Greene in the same binary, culture-free language. At a conference on Artistic Intelligence held in 1989 at the University of South Carolina, Greene's view of creativity went un-challenged by the other presenters, including Howard Gardner, Elliot W. Eisner, and Harold Taylor. As Greene later put it, conformity can be understood as "ordinary petrified reality" (1990, p. 154). The alternative to conformity "is to summon persons, even within the public schools, away from the 'already constituted reason,' to release them to come in touch with their own visions, with their own lived lives in which, after all, their reason originates" (p. 155). The challenge to educators and artists that cannot be compromised by traditions of any sort is summed up by Greene in the following way: "You must change your life." But this must continually be done by students and adults alike without appeal to external sources of authority. Everybody must answer the questions "In what direction? Why and how?" in their own authentic, subjective way. As she put it at the end of her talk: "The problem remains; the mystery pulls at us. How can we create situations that release the young to pay heed?" (p. 157)

Comparing the literature on creativity in the sixties with what has been written over the last three decades suggests an ironic degree of conformity among the advocates of continual creative self-transformation. Indeed, the meaning of creativity and how it is to be fostered in the classroom has become one of the most enduring orthodoxies in a profession generally known for adopting one fad after another. E. Paul Torrance was perhaps one of the most prominent advocates for using every area of the curriculum to foster creativity. His book, *Creativity*, contained list after list of strategies that would, he argued, contribute to creative thinking and behavior. For example, teachers were urged to structure learning situations in ways that would confront students with ambiguities and uncertainties, use analogs to make the familiar strange and the strange familiar, and encourage students to make predications from limited information. During the lesson itself, teachers were to encourage "creative and constructive questioning rather than cynical acceptance of limitations" and to introduce the "juxtaposition of apparently irrelevant and unrelated elements" into the discussion—thus forcing students to deal with the unexpected and novel (1969, pp. 44–45).

Torrence's efforts were given legitimacy in other fields where humanistic psychologists such as Rollo May represented the "bringing something new into being" as the highest expression of human-ness. Earlier, in the forties, Viktor Lowenfeld's writings in the field of art education had made the linkage between the child's natural propensity for creative expression and their general mental development. According to Lowenfeld,

If children developed without any interference from the outside world, no special stimulation for their creative work would be necessary. Every child would use his deeply rooted creative impulse without inhibition, confident in his own kind of expression. We find this creative confidence clearly demonstrated by those people who live in the remote sections of our country and who have not been inhibited by the influences of advertisements, funny books, and "education." Among these folks are found the most beautiful, natural, and clearest examples of children's art. What civilization has buried we must try to regain by recreating the natural base necessary for such free creation. Whenever we hear children say, "I can't draw that," we can be sure that some kind of interference has occurred in their lives. (1947, p. 1)

Although the literature and artistic expressions of post modernism have largely decentered the individual as the agent of autonomous creative expression by foregrounding the constitutive role of the language systems of a culture (thus reducing the objects of creative expression to the status of texts and cultural products), educators continue to embrace the image of creativity that gave modern art its special energy and distinctness. Within a wide number of subfields of education, creativity is still understood as free, natural, and expressive of the individuals' inner powers of origination. In *Approaches to Art in Education*, a book written for students intending to become public school art teachers, Laura Chapman reiterates the canon: "Inspiration for art may come from the very world of subjective experience" (1978, p. 47). In addition, creative self-expression serves the social purpose of challenging (and overturning) the outside forces that inhibit the individual's inner powers of origination (an echo of Lowenfeld's neo-Romantic way of thinking). As Chapman put it, "Visions of alternative life styles have led many artists to create works that challenge the norms, customs, and unquestioned beliefs of their times" (p. 48). But not all beliefs. The connection between art products and the process of valorization in the art market is to be reinforced in the lesson on "Living with Art" that Chapman developed for elementary students. The vocabulary for the lesson includes "Art show, art gallery, mount," and the learning objectives covered such gallery related activities as "a) understand that artists exhibit their best work for many people to see. b) discuss their reasons for selecting a particular piece of artwork for a class or school-wide art show. c) mount and label one piece of art-work for a class art show" (1985, p. 118).

A similarly subjectively-centered, product-oriented view of creativity is held by educators concerned with gifted and talented students. At the Theory Summit Conference on the Optimal Development of the Mind held in 1990 at Timberline Lodge on Mount Hood, LeoNora Cohen outlined the goals of the conference as the development of a "unified theory that combines theories of giftedness or optimal development with theories of intelligence and creativity in order to fully explain the development of gifted and creative individuals and how they should be identified and served. This might be thought of," she suggests, "as somewhat akin to Stephen Hawking's 'Big Bang' theory of the universe" (1990, p. 1). Given these high expectations for the gathering of scholars, which included Howard E. Gruber, A. Henry Passow, and David Feldman, the collective thinking about creativity moved predictably more in the direction of using current research to legitimate continuing educational practices based on assumptions about the linkage between the autonomous individual, creativity, and social progress than in the direction of questioning these assumptions. For example, David Feldman expressed the view that the term creativity should be used "to mean the purposive transformation of a body of knowledge, where the transformation is so significant that the body of knowledge is irrevocably changed from the way it was before" (1989, p. 241). He went on to say that "the central problem in understanding creativity is understanding change—how it is experienced and how it is controlled" (p. 244). In equating genuine creativity with progressive change, he was separating himself from the more subjectively-centered view of creativity held by many art educators. "When creativity occurs," he observed, "it occurs in part because a person is motivated by the belief that, through his or her individual efforts, the world can be changed" (p. 250).

Howard Gruber's contribution to understanding creativity was even more research orientated and cautious. But it was motivated by a sense of caution framed by years of studying exemplary creative figures and not by any doubts about the essential connection between creativity and social progress. Nor did the paper he read to the conferees democratize creativity as Torrance had done in the sixties. For Gruber, creativity involves mental/behavioral processes that can best be understood in terms of the achievement of outstanding individuals—the truly gifted who make up a small segment of society. Indeed, a serious study of a genuinely creative person should occupy the researcher's entire professional career. As Gruber put it:

> If we accept the idea that our starting point in the study of creativity must be the unique person at work, then we must look for the stages of development in the person, and we must consider the person's developmental history as a whole: a belief system and way of working that functions as a transitional state for one person may well be another's life work. (1990, p. 21)

The cautious, even elitist, approach the cognitive psychologists took at the Mount Hood Summit meeting to the prospects of educating for creativity is not typical of the educational mainstream that stretches from the public school classroom to university level teacher education programs. Professors of education in the Dewey/ Freire tradition that uphold critical reflection as the engine of social progress tend to follow Maxine Greene's lead in viewing creativity as an essential quality of humanness. For these educators, who view themselves as marginalized in relation to their technocratic colleagues because of their commitment to the process of continual emancipation, creativity is synonymous with such other context-free metaphors as freedom, equality, progress, and empowerment. While they consider creativity as being facilitated by emancipatory educational practices, they seem unwilling in their writings to make it the central concern—as is the case with art educators and other educators who have been influenced by humanistic psychology.

The educational mainstream also includes a large number of entrepreneurally-oriented professionals who see themselves as bringing the latest teaching techniques and social mission goals to the attention of classroom teachers. Regardless of whether staff development is focused on the educational implications of brain research, the autonomous learner model of teaching and learning, or a variation of an outcome-based approach to teaching, teaching for the ever more creative student is always represented as one of the goals essential to renewing the teacher's dedication and to helping them focus on what is really important in classrooms where the malaise and conflicting forces of the larger society are often visible in the behavior of students. For example, the Autonomous Learner Model for the Gifted and Talented, which is used in many staff development programs, provides teachers with a number of categories that are intended to serve as guides for stimulating (and collecting data on) different student capacities. The categories include "self-acceptance and understanding," "social skills," "creative thinking," "critical thinking," "independent learning," and "evaluative thinking." Under the category of creative thinking, teachers are to assess the degree to which the student "takes risks in thinking and acting," "generates large quantities of ideas," "demonstrates flexible thinking," "explains ideas in detail," "generates original ideas," and "searches for new means of expressing ideas and products" (Betts and Knapp, 1986, p. 4).

Increasingly, voices from the business community, including high technology spokespersons who view educational and business goals as intertwined, are urging schools to foster creative thinking in order to bolster America's economic competitiveness in world markets. While their view of creativity is essentially identical to the democratized interpretation of creativity held by mainstream educators, it is important to see the language they use in writing and speaking about the nature and value of creativity. Alan C. Kay, who is described in the preface to his *Scientific American* article as a fellow of Apple Computers, has a particularly broad understanding of creativity. Quoting Susan Sontag that "all understanding begins with our not accepting the world as it appears" as a basis for legitimating an equally sweeping generalization, Kay goes on to assert that "each of us has to construct our own version of reality by main force, literally to make ourselves" (1991. p. 140). In effect, he is asserting here that individuals create their own "version of reality"; that is, all knowledge and presumably values are an outgrowth of creative thought and expression. Not only is the will to create our own version of reality a basic aspect of our being, but it is essential to escaping from the "barbarism of the deep past." As Kay put it, "To make contexts visible, make them objects of discourse and make them explicitly reshapable and inventable are strong aspirations very much in harmony with the pressing needs and on-rushing changes of our times" (p. 140).

Stephen H. Schneider's proposal for using the classroom to "unlock children's creative thinking" must be placed within the larger social context he uses to frame his appeal for basic educational reform. His affiliation as a senior scientist at the National Center for Atmospheric Research in Boulder, Colorado, as well as his status as being a recipient of the prestigious MacArthur "genius" award, make his comments on the need for school reform especially noteworthy. Schneider's rather modest proposal is based on a recognition that most of the traditional aspects of schools are not likely to change. Thus he urges teachers to devote 10 percent of classroom time and curricular focus to "encouraging individual initiative and creativity." As he put it, "Creative dialoguing is one way to get kids involved again in the educational process. . . . It is the unthinking followers and the don't-make-waves types who keep some of our industrial and governmental agencies in neutral. The most successful, innovative companies (i.e., high tech firms) reward creativity, helping to maintain America's competitive edge" (pp. 33, 35).

While numerous other advocates of fostering creativity in schools could be cited, and ever so slight variations noted in how creativity is understood, Kay and Schneider are important because they have been identified as exemplary thinkers by some of the most prominent institutions in American society. Having an article published in *Scientific American* signals a sense of legitimacy not gained through professional educational journals—even when it restates the same cultural assumptions that framed Kay's way of understanding creativity. And the recipient of the MacArthur Award is not likely to be viewed as reiterating the banalities that are the trade mark of most educational discussions of creativity. Yet their views about the nature and necessity of creativity are so conventional that my task of asking whether the modern form of creativity contributes to the ecological sustainability of mainstream American cultural patterns is made much easier. While the various advocates of creativity differ on minor issues of interpretation (is it a natural propensity of the socially unrepressed individual or does it have to be encouraged through some form of humanistic social engineering?), they all take for granted an interlocking set of culturally specific assumptions. These include equating creativity with social progress, as well as the idea that the problems besetting the country require new and highly experimental forms of knowledge and values. That is, what is needed is a more experimentally oriented (i.e., creative) culture.

The Encoding, Storage, and Cultural Reproduction Function of Metaphor

"Through creating art, children understand and experiment with various sources of inspiration for creative work" (1992, p. 1). This statement by two art educators, Cynthia Colbert and Martha Taunton, represents an optimism in the human condition that should be particularly welcome in an era of increasing violence and senseless behavior. Unfortunately, this form of optimism, when framed against the background of American society, appears both as illusory and a source of self-deception. Indeed, their optimism is not based on any evidence of a life-sustaining, meaning-enhancing sense of community. Both the ironies and double binds hidden in the views of creativity identified earlier make it necessary to take a critical stance toward the modern view of creativity. One of the ironies is that the current use of the word is intended to suggest the possibility of discontinuous thought and expression—that is, thought and expression that are original and thus without any connection to the past. But the word used to express this possibility is itself a carrier of (that is, it encodes and stores) culturally specific forms of analogic thinking framed by a complex set of meta-narratives that go back to the Romantic thinkers of the late eighteenth and early nineteenth century. In effect, the metaphorical image of creativity serves to simplify and largely hide a complex narrative that has taken many twists and turns in response to the technological and social/economic developments propelling the process of modernization. As a legitimating metaphor, its history contradicts the possibilities of originality it is used to proclaim.

The other irony is that the earlier processes of analogic thinking currently encoded in the iconic metaphor of creativity reinforces a cultural schemata that represents humans as ontologically separate from the natural environment. While creativity for the educator (and the modern artist) is the highest expression of human potential, it is basically understood in anthropocentric terms. Creativity, along with all the other cultural promises that accompany its use, leads to the forms of hubris that either ignores or damages the environment. Indeed, as one of the highest human values in recent Western thought, creativity in the areas of technology and even the visual arts has a visible history of contributing to a spectator and manipulating relationship with the environment. In fact, it is difficult to identify examples of how the modern way (as opposed to the postmodern way) of understanding creativity has contributed to ecologically oriented human/environment relationships. The conceptual baggage and contradictions that are part of the educator's view of creativity, as well as the social reformers who want to harness creativity as the engine of technological progress, are thus in need of critical examination.

But the purpose of this criticism must be seen through radically different cultural lenses; that is, lenses that are able to account for creativity within the context of interacting relationships (including natural systems), and an awareness that these relationships have a moral dimension to them. To suggest that the moral relationships should meet the test of contributing to the long term sustainability of ecosystems upon which humans depend requires the adoption of a sense of optimism in human possibilities similar to that of Colbert and Taunton. The difference is that their optimism is grounded in the meta-narratives of the hyper-modernist culture that celebrates whatever is new and experimental. My optimism, on the other hand, is grounded in the expectation that people, in recognizing the signs of danger ahead, will begin to change the direction their culture is moving in. But what threatens to undermine the basis of my optimism is that the student's sense of reality (including the ability to engage in a sustained and informed critical reflection) will be more influenced by the educator's appeal to give expression to their inner sense of spontaneity and intuitiveness.

Before we consider the mix of conceptual baggage encoded in the educator's image of creativity, it would be useful to review briefly how language reproduces in current processes of thinking and communicating the cognitive schemata, including the contradictions and silences, of earlier members of the language community. As the metaphorical nature of language and thought has now been widely written about, I shall summarize the culture/language/thought framework that will be used here to identify the cultural assumptions encoded in the language educators use to explain the nature of *original* thought and behavior. Briefly, as George Lakoff and Mark Johnson explain in their respective books, all thought and language are based on understanding and experiencing the new in terms of the familiar (Lakoff, 1987; Johnson, 1987). But the familiar analog or pattern, what Johnson refers to as the generative metaphor, is not always known directly. Rather, it often represents the re-encoding processes of earlier processes of metaphorical thinking framed by the metanarratives (root metaphors, stories of origins, paradigms, etc.) of the cultural group. For example, the image of the individual as an autonomous being, equal in worth and rights to everybody else, was dependent upon the continuing influence of Biblical narratives that represented each individual as possessing a soul equal in the eyes of God, and a capacity for autonomous choice and action (Bloom, 1985, pp. 292–293). This view of individualism further encodes traces of later thought patterns, such as the Aristotelian/Medieval meta-narrative of a hierarchically organized universe, with each form of life occupying a fixed position within God's creation, and the more modern account that represents individuals as first existing in a state of nature and needing to exercise political judgment in order to establish a civil society. These changes in guiding cultural assumptions are often referred to as a paradigm shift, but they can also be understood as changes in the root metaphors of a culture. But the change in root metaphors that led to the image of the individual being understood as a subject to that of the individual as a citizen with equal political rights did not involve a clean break with the earlier metaphorically based constructions of the philosophers and theologians who helped to constitute the natural attitude of the Medieval mind-set.

Assumptions about the linear nature of time, the privileged status of humans in relation to the natural world, and the notion that individuals are autonomous in terms of being held accountable for their actions (by God in Medieval times and, in the culture of modernism, by society) survived the demise of the root metaphors that sustained the Medieval period. These assumptions were retained as essential aspects of the meta-narratives fashioned by the fathers of modern consciousness—Locke, Descartes, Bacon, and Hobbes. The essential point here is that the process of analogic thinking (which is the primary pattern of thinking in philosophy and political theory) encodes the cultural schemata framed by even earlier metaphorical constructions, even when it leads to a radical shift in the guiding cultural premises (such as in the thinking of Descartes, Darwin, and, more recently, Einstein).

The influence of a cultural root metaphor on the process of analogic thinking is what is being identified here as the cultural baggage that is part of the metaphorical language/thought process. What survives in the process of analogic thinking, where answers are found for such questions as "What does originality mean? What is intelligence and how is it measured? and How do we understand the man/environment relationship?," are the older schemata encoded in iconic metaphors such as "individual creativity," "intelligence scores," and "natural resource"—to stay with the above examples. In effect, earlier processes of analogic thinking are reproduced even as new situations lead to new metaphorical constructions. The storage, and thus reproduction, of earlier metaphorical ("as if") ways of thinking is an integral part of the process of stringing together of image metaphors as the basis of everyday communication,

With this in mind, we now need to ask the following questions: What is the nature of the metaphorical baggage stored in the educator's use of the word creativity? What are the background assumptions that lead to something as complex and potentially wondrous as creativity becoming a part of the educator's taken for granted expectation for nearly every student?

Part of the answer can be found in the way that the analogs that gave definition to the modern expression of the background assumptions about the nature of creativity were not derived from the exploitive experiences associated with the Industrial Revolution, the regimentation and violence associated with warfare, the reestablishment of self-identity and economic well-being as an immigrant, or from the everyday life of family routines and religious practices—which were the main domains of human experiences for Europeans between the late seventeenth and early twentieth century. Rather the analogs for representing creativity in the modern way were derived primarily from intellectuals and artists who were attempting to understand the cultural changes occurring around them. Indeed, it was the Romantic thinkers and artists of the late eighteenth and early nineteenth century, partly as a reaction to the spread of materialistic values and mechanistic ways of thinking that seemed the hallmark of early industrial society, who introduced key elements of a new form of awareness and sensitivity that is now part of the natural attitude of contemporary advocates of creativity.

According to Brandon Taylor, the Romantics represented "Nature" metaphorically in ways that radically altered the connection between subjectivity and the image of interiorized mental activity that had been one of Descartes' contributions to the formation of modern consciousness. Descartes' way of understanding the subjectivity of the individual was predicated on maintaining a series of dualisms (specifically, mind and body, and mind and nature) that led to a calculating and procedural pattern of thought essential to scientifically based technological advances. The Romantics introduced a radically different image of subjectivity, one which subordinated (even diminished) the rational aspect of the person's inner world in relation to other dimensions of experience. As Taylor puts it, " 'Nature' for the Romantic artist thus became a kind of symbol for the interior life; and the artist became a sensitively tuned instrument who was capable of responding and reacting in particular ways, often spontaneously, usually enthusiastically, like a piece of nature herself" (1987, p. 7). Taylor further suggests that the Romantic's connection of nature with the interior world of spontaneity, intuition, authentic feelings, and thus with the experience of free and natural expression, introduced what was to become a central element of modern consciousness—namely, the sense of the creative self as existing outside of, and often in opposition to the historical process.

The association of nature with the culturally and historically autonomous inner world of the person, in effect, provided a new metaphor
for understanding the connection between creativity and the self as
an autonomous being capable of giving expression to the inner world
in ways that would challenge the norms of society. This roman-
tically inspired metaphor also helped to frame the difference between authentic and alienated experience. The following quotation
from *On the Aesthetic Education of Man,* which Friedrich Schiller
published in 1795, typified the Romantic understanding of
creativity:

> The necessity of Nature which governed him with undivided
> power in the condition of mere sensation, abandons him when
> reflection begins; an instantaneous calm ensues in the senses;
> time itself, the eternally moving, stands still while the
> dispersed rays of consciousness are gathered together, and *form,*
> an image of the infinite, is reflected upon the transient founda-
> tion. As soon as it becomes light inside Man, there is also no
> longer any night outside him; as soon as it is calm within him,
> the storm of the universe is also lulled, and the contending
> forces of Nature find rest between abiding boundaries. (1965
> edition, p. 120)

The inner world, where Nature truly expresses itself, is represented
by Schiller and the other Romantics as a source of creative energy
that is both calming and as the primary reference point for finding
truth and stability in a changing world—that is now seen as un-
natural, artificially technological, and dehumanizing.

It was also during this period that the notion of the "unconscious" became an additional characteristic of the inner world of the
individual. For artists and, later, educators, the unconscious represented the well-spring of creative energy. This metaphorical image of
the person having an interior and natural center, rather than living in
a part/whole relationship within the interconnected webs of cultural
traditions, was further reinforced by technological and economic
changes that gave momentum to the Industrial Revolution. The new
emphasis on inner experience, particularly in understanding it as
having aesthetic qualities, led to a series of changes that radically
separated the "products" and acts of creativity in the modern sense
from the role that art played in the daily life of oral (traditional)
cultures. Ellen Dissanayake summarizes the emergence of the modern temperament and way of understanding in the following way:

'Disinterest' implied that one could transcend the limitations of time, place, and temperament and react to the artwork of areas far removed from one's own—whether or not one understood the meaning they had for their makers and users. In this sense, art was 'universal.' Another corollary was that works of art were vehicles for a special kind of knowledge—a knowledge that, with the waning of religious belief, often took on the spiritual authority once restricted to the church. Still another was the idea of art for art's sake (or life for art's sake), suggesting that art had no purpose but to 'be' and to provide opportunities for enjoying an aesthetic experience that was its own reward, and that one could have no higher calling than to open oneself to these heightened moments. (1990, p. 575)

Thinking of the products of creative expression as combining the opportunity for inner self-expression and the fulfillment of a heightened aesthetic experience, as well as a commodity to be interpreted and evaluated by an art expert (and sold), is a powerful metaphorical image that is also basic to the contemporary educator's way of viewing creativity. Today's educators also view creativity as a universal—that is a special way of knowing and expression that emerges from within all individuals. They also share the modern artist's belief that creativity need not contribute to the well-being of society. Indeed, that creativity contributes to the vitality of the student's subjective experience is considered as sufficient justification.

But the artists who gave expression to the Romantic's essentialist view of human nature were not immune to the rapid spread of modern technology. Even though technology led to standardization, mechanization, and a growing obsession with using purposive rationality to increase efficiency and control—all aspects of modernity disdained by artists and intellectuals who shared Eugene Delacroix's observation that "the subject is yourself . . . your emotions before nature"—technology also provided, as Jacques Ellul points out, the means for expressing the artist's natural sense of spontaneity and freedom. The development of modern technology made available new materials that became both part of the artwork as well as the means of its execution. But more importantly, modern technological developments helped to give substance to other metaphorical images that became essential elements of modern consciousness. Without these corollary ways of understanding, the metaphorical connections between creativity, subjectivity, and individualism might have appeared as aberrant and out of touch with the times. In effect, technology provided the mundane and material analogs for linking creativity with change—which modern consciousness translated to mean social progress.

As Ellul put it:

> the artist receives from technology the means which allow him to completely impose his will . . . But at the same time, technology brings him another dimension of possibilities: the artist discovers a universe of motion. This is not only the banal truth that everything passes away, for indeed the work of art as an affirmation of eternal values could largely be a protest against this trend toward destruction. Under the influence of modern technology, it has emerged that everything in the external world consists of movement, that material is in itself energy and speed, that the very essence of life is change, and all this plays a part in familiar objects which are all characterized by speed. The artist is therefore thrust into a world which he can now see only as movement and in which he must participate by integrating speed into his work. (1966, p. 36)

Speed and movement are synonymous with change. As the awareness of the connection between modern technology and change (social progress) became part of the natural attitude toward everyday life, anything that endured over time became viewed as contrary to the fundamental nature of existence itself. Indeed, anything suspected of enduring over time became perceived in terms of modern consciousness as a tradition that threatened to oppress the creativity of future generations. Greene expresses this modern view of tradition in her comment about "ordinary petrified reality." The irony is that the technological advances that created the materialistic culture that threatened the "authentic, subjective way" to self expression and creation also provided an evocative image of change as being inherently progressive in nature. This image, in turn, made it unnecessary to consider whether creativity might lead to destructive, even retrogressive changes. With the exception of a few marginalized voices in the art education community, such as Karen Hanblen's (1988) argument that art education should provide students with the conceptual basis necessary for thinking critically about the cultural assumptions encoded in artworks as well in how they are used, and Harry Broudy's (1972) views on the need to balance tradition, criticism, and creativity (a synthesis he describes as "enlightened cherishing"), the majority of educators have seen no reason to reflect on the connection between creativity and social progress. Even the more cautious views of psychologists such as Feldman and Gruber did not bring into question the modern cultural assumptions encoded in the current image of creativity. Rather, they viewed creativity as an exceptional event in the lives of exceptional people and centered more in the development of the rational process.

There is another critically important cultural assumption encoded in the creativity metaphor that legitimates the creativity-progress connection. As Lynn White Jr., Herbert Schneidau, Max Oelschlaeger, and others have pointed out, the Judeo-Christian tradition is based on meta-narratives that represent humans as essentially separate from the natural world. In the most optimistic version of these meta-narratives, humans are to view themselves as "stewards" of the natural world. Although God has a special role in these meta-narratives, the human/nature relationship was framed in an anthropocentric language. Friedrich Nietzsche's observation that "God is dead" (that is, that God is no longer a reality—part of the natural attitude—in modern consciousness) highlights another background assumption that enabled those who adopted the Romantic view of creativity to frame the question of accountability in terms of the subjective judgment of the individual. The Judeo-Christian form of anthropocentrism often involved representing nature as God's instrument for punishing human sinfulness. Without God in the picture, a more extreme form of anthropocentrism became part of the natural attitude of the modern individual. Indeed, nature became metaphorically diminished to the point where the Romantic and now modern artist (and educator) turned it into an adjective for describing (and legitimating) the necessity of giving expression to inner subjective forces. Witness the lack of a person/environment relationship in Bruce M. Holly's account of how he experiences this inner nature:

> It is the energy that arises from the desire to create change in the present. Before the present ends, forever. But there is another facet to creative motivation, a necessary presence, that actually makes a particular creative act 'impossible' to postpone: it is the imperative that really releases the energy into action. I mean: what must be done, will be done . . . If it is in you to produce, you produce. You cannot do otherwise. (1992, p. 9)

As pointed out in the earlier discussion of moral education, language encodes the cultural group's way of understanding and communicating about relationships. Holly's use of language is no exception. But the fundamental relationship that defines the person is framed by the inner (natural) forces that Holly represents as bursting forth in the creative act. That is, Holly's metaphorical image of the creative self not only lacks a cultural and historical context, it is also disconnected from any sensory (not to mention moral) relationship with the natural environment. In effect, the creative individual is represented as an autonomous being who is accountable only to her/himself, and the moral imperative that guides this self-accountability is to avoid repressing "what *must* be done."

Educators, of course, often frame their discussions of the need for nurturing the student's inner creative powers by making references to how creativity contributes to a more democratic society, and to social progress in general. But even this more connected view of creativity retains the anthropocentrism that was incorporated into the earlier Romantic's identification of creativity with the subjectivity of the individual, and the reduction of nature to the inner domain of the self.

CREATIVITY IN AN ECOLOGICALLY-CENTERED CULTURE

The way of understanding relationships encoded in the educator's discussion of creativity should now be viewed both culturally and historically as being out of touch with current changes in consciousness. In effect, the continued focus on students learning to develop *their own* ideas, values, and forms of expression can be understood as a hold over of the modern era which represented the development of the individual's inner "resources" as the basis of a more authentic and fully realized personal life and, by extension, social life. But as we now know, this modern vision (particularly the more material aspects) could be realized only through a worldwide expansion of the technological/economic system that reduced local ecosystems to "natural resources" to be exploited for the benefit of distant (and indifferent) consumers. The juxtaposition of the following statement by Rob Barnes, who teaches art education at the University of East Anglia, with the now daily warnings of scientists who are studying the rapid degradation of natural systems, helps to put the educator's penchant for disconnected (actually, ideologically driven) thinking in a wider perspective. Writes Barnes:

> Art lessons give children the chance to allow their individuality to be expressed through tangible form. Those qualities which

make art individual are the ones which demonstrate to others that there is more than one way to interpret things. In a field where there is no 'right' answer, individuals learn that art can be a celebration of diversity, a celebration of individuality for its own sake. (1987, p. 16)

The message of the art educator (indeed, Barnes is representative of how most educators understand the creativity/individualism connection) is that everything is relative and that the only real continuities are those constructed and maintained through individual judgment. This form of tunnel thinking is strengthened by leading educational theorists such as Paulo Freire, Maxine Greene, and Henry Giroux who, in essence, argue that the purpose of education is to empower individuals to become critically reflective agents of social change. This relativistic stance, which is dependent upon a deep romantic faith in both the inherent goodness of individuals and the progressive nature of change, is further reinforced by Richard Rorty, a leading American philosopher, who writes:

The social glue holding together the ideal liberal society . . . consists in little more than a consensus that the point of social organization is to let everybody have a chance at self-creation to the best of his or her abilities, and that that goal requires, besides peace and wealth, the standard bourgeois freedoms. (1989, p. 84)

Ironically, this individually-centered view of creativity, with its assumptions about alleviating the human condition, has been criticized by postmodern artists and intellectuals for a number of years. The term "postmodern" first appeared in the area of literature in the 1960s. It's new vocabulary and accompanying shift in ways of understanding (and seeing) spread by the 1970s into other fields, including architecture, dance, theater, and the visual arts—and across a number of academic boundaries. Although the term "postmodernism" encompasses a wide and often contradictory array of points of view and theoretical emphases, with some critics even arguing that postmodernism represents only the most recent reincarnation of the creative/critical ethos of modernism, there are several common elements widely shared within this antimodern movement. It should also be added that this widely based, though socially thin, rethinking of the foundations of modernism has gone unnoticed by both the mainstream of educators and by radical educational theorists who want to push the cultural trajectory of modernism to its nihilistic end. The elements that hold together postmodern thinkers are best summarized by Andreas Huyssen:

> My main point about contemporary postmodernism is that it operates in a field of tension between tradition and innovation, conservation and renewal, mass culture and high art, in which the second terms are no longer automatically privileged over the first; a field of tension which can no longer be grasped in categories such as progress vs. reaction, left vs. right, present vs. past, modernism vs. realism, abstraction vs. representation, avantgarde vs. Kitsch. (1986, p. 217)

Another example of binary thinking he could have mentioned is the modern educator's way of viewing creativity as being in opposition to conformity (and tradition). Huyssen makes a further observation about modernism that is supportive of my argument that the educator's way of understanding creativity is part of the mind-set upon which the Industrial Revolution was based, and now provides the conceptual legitimation for the emerging Age of Information. As Huyssen puts it:

> Despite all its noble aspirations and achievements, we have come to recognize that the culture of enlightened modernity has also always (though by no means exclusively) been a culture of inner and outer imperialism, a reading already offered by Adorno and Horkheimer in the 1940s, and an insight not unfamiliar to those of our ancestors involved in the multitude of struggles against rampant modernization. (p. 219)

The ecological crisis, as I have argued elsewhere (1993), brings into question whether all of the modern assumptions upon which our taken for granted world is predicated are only exhausted, or represent a profoundly misguided pathway of cultural development. The sense in which the ecologically-minded critic uses the word "exhaustion" to describe the culture of modernism is meant in a fundamentally different way than how the word is used in postmodern literature. Within an ecological context, exhaustion refers more to the decline of natural systems (the exhaustion of salmon runs in the Northwest, old growth forests, top soil, aquifers, etc.). For postmodern thinkers like Foucault, Lyotard, Lacan, and Barthes, exhaustion is the metaphor used to designate the condition of the modern ethos, with its emphasis on the subjective expression and thought process of the autonomous individual. Although I find certain aspects of postmodern thought supportive of the cultural/language/thought connection that has been highly visible in the recent writings of anthropologists and social linguists (which can be traced back to the work of Edward Sapir and others in the 1920s and 1930s), I have introduced postmodernism into the discussion primarily for the purpose of demonstrating that the view of creativity advocated by educators has been insulated both from anthropological studies and from major intellectual developments that have occurred over the last two decades. While postmodern thinkers like Foucault and Lacan were representing the human subject as the "effect" of the episteme encoded in a language system (a discursive formation for Foucault), educators continued to represent creativity as the expression of the individual's inner self. The sense of being on the cutting edge of modernity and progress, which is so visible in the educational writings on creativity, turns out to be the banal litany of a mutual quoting circle now inhabiting an intellectual island.

But in fairness, it must also be kept in mind that postmodern thinkers, for all their varied decenterings of modern themes, also remain isolated from the growing awareness of how the world's ecosystems are being devastated by the demands of different cultural groups. Postmodern thinkers and artists have indeed added to our body of theory and altered the visual languages we feel comfortable with, but they have not engaged the fundamental question of how to live in a sustainable relationship with other life forms we now understand as interdependent. To put this another way, the postmodern thinkers have not decentered the central element of modernism—namely, the anthropocentric way of understanding relationships. They have simply shifted the locus of power from the individual as the primary social entity to the dominant language systems and, in some cases (such as in Rorty's thinking), have used the symbolic openness that characterizes the metaphorical nature of language to argue for an even more extreme form of individually-centered relativism. Thus, while certain aspects of postmodern thinking help illuminate how the modern notion of creativity can be reconstituted as the expression of the language system of a cultural group, we shall have to turn elsewhere for guidance in how to understand the nature of a more ecologically responsible form of creativity.

Two books that challenge the reader to rethink the modern assumptions about art serve as a good point of departure for addressing both the nature of a nonsubjectivist form of creativity and the role it might play in contributing to the aesthetic and symbolic richness of everyday life. The two books, Suzi Gablik's *The Reenchantment of Art* (1991) and Ellen Dissanayake's *What is Art For?* (1988), provide two different ways of reinterpreting the nature and role of creativity. Gablik's book provides a particularly powerful indictment of representing creativity in terms of the subjective interests of the individual (which often is expressed by artists in metaphorical constructions that are oppositional rather than affirmative). In assessing the state of the visual arts, she observes that:

> What we clearly do not have, at this point, is any working framework for a socially or ecologically grounded art—an art that is accountable to the larger whole, in the sense of being contextually rooted in a living connection with a containing organic field. And I would submit that we *can't* have such a concept as long as we remain hooked on the myth of pure creativity and the inherent purposelessness of art for art's sake—which acquiesces willingly in the value vacuum that keeps art separate from any social, moral, or practical use. We can't have such a concept as long as our idea of what constitutes 'good art' follows the patriarchal ideal of an autonomous aesthetic culture that translates, finally, into the refusal to take on social tasks. (1991, p. 139)

What Gablik argues for is the recovery of a communal/ecologically-centered approach to creativity. This is to be achieved by abandoning the Cartesian dualisms that helped to sustain the modern idea of individual autonomy, the expression of mastery in the creative arts, and the spectator relationship to art objects. The shift in cultural paradigms that will lead to corresponding changes in how creativity is expressed is summed up in a statement by Gablik that is highly reminiscent of Bateson's argument that relationships are interactive rather than atomistic and detached:

> It seems clear that art oriented toward dynamic participation rather than toward passive, anonymous spectatorship will have to deal with living contexts; and that once an awareness of the ground, or setting, is actively cultivated, the audience is no longer separate. Then meaning is no longer in the observer, nor in the observed, but in the relationship between the two. Interaction is the key that moves art beyond the aesthetic mode: letting the audience intersect with, and even form part of, the

process, recognizing that when observer and observed merge, the vision of static autonomy is undermined. (p. 151)

Gablik also documents a growing sensitivity to the ecological crisis among members of various art communities. The use of creativity as part of an alternative meta-narrative, an alternative "cultural coding" to that of modernism, as Gablik puts it, can be seen in Beth Ames Swartz's creation of a public meditational environment (called a "Moving Point of Balance"), Bene Fonteles performance work in the central plaza of a Brazilian city where he reassembled for the citizens the litter left spread across the countryside during their weekend retreats, and Othello Anderson's painting, "Acid Rain 1990." The shift from an individual to an ecologically-centered approach to creativity involves, according to Gablik, recovering a much older (and discredited in terms of modern thinking) way of viewing creativity as helping to renew and sustain a moral universe. That is, creativity should be expressed in ways that help connect the person to a larger sense of community that is morally coherent. It may take the form of social criticism, such as David T. Hanson's aerial photographs of hazardous waste sites; it may also affirm values and behaviors that contribute to a sense of connectedness with the larger biotic and social community. To put this another way, creativity should be used to reinforce the cultural code of a part/whole relationship, rather than the modern coding of one/many relationship where authority is centered in the subjectivity of individuals who may (or may not) feel a sense of connectedness to something beyond themselves.

Yet Gablik's arguments for adopting a new conceptual framework, and thus ways of understanding and appreciating the creative process, lack a sensitivity to an aspect of human experience that must also be taken into account when seeking viable answers to the question of how creativity can be reconciled with the ecological imperative that face all cultural groups. For readers who take for granted the premises of modernism, the following statement by Gablik may seem like a declaration of interdependence that will replace the worst aspects of modernism (the emphasis on atomistic subjectivity) while, at the same time, preserving the modernist's way of viewing tradition as a source of authoritarian imposition. If we start, as Gablik suggests, with a new set of premises about the basic nature of reality we can then change cultural practices accordingly—including our approach to creativity. As she puts it:

certainly the new world view, ushered in by twentieth century physics, ecology and general systems theory, with its call for integrative and holistic thinking, is no longer based on discrete objects; rather it represents a continuous flux of process and the dynamics of interpenetrating energy fields. (p. 163)

With the basic stuff of reality now understood in terms of process, energy, and pertubations that trigger structural changes in autopoietic unities, it is now possible, as I read her, to replace the old (modern) cultural patterns with "something better." The something better includes:

closeness, instead of distancing; the cultivation of ecocentric values; whole-systems thinking; a developed discipline of caring; an individualism that is not purely individual but is grounded in social relationships and also promotes community and the welfare of the whole; an expanded vision of art as a social practice and not just a disembodied eye. I have tried to show that none of these intentions is irrelevant to a value-based art, and that all of them are crucial to its reenchantment. The sacredness of both life and art does not have to mean something cosmic or otherworldly—it emerges quite naturally when we cultivate compassionate, responsive modes of relating to the world and to each other. (p. 181)

Indeed, there is much I find attractive about this list of priorities for reorienting relationships. But like her reading of the new physics, Gablik's list of goals omits a fundamental aspect of culture and, as articulated in the writings of Humberto R. Maturana and Francisco J. Varela, biological coding.

Like all metaphorical frameworks of understanding, the language of process, change, and information and energy fields illuminates and hides at the same time—as William E. Doll Jr.'s analysis of the differences between modernism and postmodernism so clearly demonstrates (1993). The illumination of aspects of reality that cannot be comprehended by the Cartesian mind-set is important for a number of reasons, including the need to align cultural patterns with patterns that characterize natural systems. What is hidden by the new metaphorical framework of physics that Gablik wants to extend into the area of human culture is also vital. The modernist's interpretation of the "process" paradigm, which is reflected in Gablik's own thinking, hides the element of conservation; that is, how entities conserve themselves over time—even as they undergo transformations in response to changes in the larger ecosystem of which they are an interactive part. To ensure that readers do not see this statement as an expression of my own ideological/cultural orientation, I shall quote how Maturana and Varela account for the interactive nature of continuity and change. In *The Tree of Knowledge* (1987), they explain this interactive process in the following way:

> Structural coupling between organism and environment takes place between operationally independent systems . . . We say it again: conservation of autopoiesis and conservation of adaptation are necessary conditions for the existence of living beings; the ontogenic structural change of a living being in an environment always occurs as a structural drift congruent with the structural drift of the environment. This drift will appear to an observer as having been 'selected' by the environment throughout the history of interactions of the living being, as long as it is alive. (p. 103)

This statement by the two Chilean biologists also applies to the interactive process of continuity and change in cultures. But it must also be kept in mind that the symbolic nature of coding systems essential to the conservation of the identities of cultural patterns and practices may become rigid (reified) and thus unresponsive to changes taking place in the larger ecosystems that provide the basis of life for members of the culture.

Gablik's list of desired values and forms of relationship can easily be interpreted to mean that process is all there is, and that the conserving of existing practices, beliefs, institutions, and the aspects of material/symbolic culture obstructs the free expression of process. This is where Ellen Dissanayake's book, *What is Art For?* introduces an important corrective to the modernist tendency to emphasize the process aspect of post-Newtonian physics and the ecological/systems way of thinking, which is often expressed by modernists in ways that lose sight of the fundamental truth that without conservation change would be chaotic and formless. Conservation and change go together, even though the tension between them is not always worked out in ways that contribute to long-term survival—which Bateson understood as "a flexible organism (or culture) in-its-environment" (1972, p. 451). That is, cultures in which the conserving processes become rigid and unresponsive to changes in the larger environment die out, as they undermine the sources of their food, water, and other forms of energy. Having acknowledged the possibility of a pathological expression of the conserving/change dialectic (with the word "dialectic" being used here in a non-teleological sense), we can now consider Dissanayake's contribution to a post-subjectivist understanding of creativity.

Her contribution to reframing our understanding of creativity, and thus the form creativity should take in educational settings, is threefold. First, by seeking answers to the question "What is Art For?" in such diverse fields as ethology and cultural anthropology, she is able to avoid modern formulaic thinking that has oscillated between viewing creativity in ways that made the relativizing of individual perspectives the expression of a cultural ideal and high art as the outcome of creative acts that must be explained to the public by art critics and theorists. For Dissanayake, creativity (in terms of its aesthetic dimensions) is an integral aspect of the behavior which she refers to as "making special"; and thus is as much a necessity of humankind's biological make-up as the ability to use language and to hear a certain range of sounds. By grounding creativity in human biology, rather that in the Romantic's notion of an inner essence (freedom, inner truth, natural and authentic expression, etc.), Dissanayake makes a powerful argument that making special is essential to human adaptation to environmental contingencies—and thus to human survival itself. As she explains it:

> Making special implies intent or deliberateness. When *shaping* or giving artistic expression to an idea, or *embellishing* an object, or recognizing that an idea or object is artistic, one gives (or acknowledges) a specialness that without one's activity or regard would not exist. Moreover, one intends by making special to *place the activity artifact in a 'realm' different from the everyday.* In most art of the past, it would seem, the special realm to be contrasted with the everyday was a magical or supernatural world, not—as today in the advanced West—a purely aesthetic realm. In both, however, there is a sort of saltation or quantum leap from the everyday humdrum reality in which life's vital needs and activities—eating, sleeping, preparing or obtaining food—occur to a different order which has a different motivation and a special attitude and response. In both functional and nonfunctional art an alternative reality is recognized and entered; the making special acknowledges, reveals, and embodies this reality. (p. 92)

The recognition of this human need to make special—to transform the ordinary and mundane into communal ritual, metaphorical playfulness, sensory pleasure, memorableness, expressions of special skillfulness, and so forth—is the second contribution she makes to reconstituting how the nature and function of creativity are understood. The creative aspect of making special is not limited to the narrow range of expressive behavior that modern thinkers often associate with art. Nor is it framed in the equally limited sense of an intensely personal relationship between artist and the "product" of creative expression which seems to be elevated by the spectator relationship the rest of society has with the artwork. Rather, Dissanayake's reading of the anthropological record of humankind, especially how making special has been found to be integral to nearly every aspect of daily life of many so called "primitive cultures," leads her to conclude that making special is not unique to a few gifted individuals. What aspects of daily routines and behaviors are elevated and transformed by special treatment varies from culture to culture, just as the way creativity is expressed varies widely.

A third observation Dissanayake makes about the role of making special, particularly in traditional oral-based cultures, that is relevant to our task of articulating a more ecologically oriented interpretation of creativity is that throughout human history making special has been an important aspect of communication. If we keep in mind that creative expression might be used to embellish (make special) such diverse aspects of communal life as the digging stick, eating utensils, a narrative of past events, and even the physical appearance of the body, we can see more clearly the importance of Anthony Forge's observation—which supports Dissanayake's insights about making special serving an integrative and cultural reproductive function. In commenting on art as a symbolic system, Forge observes that "In primitive art, art objects are rarely representative *of* anything, rather they seem to be about relationships" (1973, p. xviii). Clifford Geertz makes a similar observation about creative expression (meaning here a more inclusive premodern view of art) being an integral aspect of cultural communication. In a chapter titled "Art as a Cultural System," he states:

> If we are to have a semiotics of art (or for that matter, of any sign system not axiomatically self-contained), we are going to have to engage in a kind of natural history of sign and symbols, an ethnography of the vehicles of meaning. Such signs and sym-

bols, such vehicles of meaning, play a role in the life of a society, or some part of a society, and it is that which in fact gives them their life. (1983, p. 118)

Communication made special through the use of imaginative/ metaphorical expression involves, as Bateson notes, a recoding of psychic/cultural information (1973, p. 239). But the recoding of creative expression involves both storage of past meanings and their reinterpretation in ways that make them viable in terms of the present and future. To put this more simply (hopefully without oversimplifying), creative expression is part of a culture's way of re-encoding and revitalizing its storehouse of life-sustaining knowledge and values. In effect, cultural continuities and transformations are integral aspects of creative expression—even in modern forms of creativity where the dominant cultural themes are change, experimentation, and relativism.

The part/whole orientation of many traditional cultures differs radically from the one/many orientations that characterize Western individually-centered cultures. The part/whole orientation, which seems to be an essential feature of ecologically-centered aboriginal cultures in North and South America, as well as in Australia, leads to experiencing oneself as an integral part of the whole—where the whole is experienced as extending into the past and future, and as encompassing all forms of life within the larger biosphere. The one/ many orientation that characterizes the modern mind-set leads to experiencing the self as a separate social entity who is often in the role of observer, who must often express personal interests in a competitive manner, and who views the natural world either in functional or utilitarian terms (in those infrequent moments when self-engrossment allows for an awareness of the natural world). One of the ironies that emerges from considering how creativity is expressed in part/whole oriented cultures is that the emphasis on freedom of the individual in modern cultures may have led to more restrictive and trivialized forms of creative expression. The depth of meaning, aesthetic appreciation, and contribution to the semiotic processes of cultural reproduction and renewal are restricted to the interpretation and mood of individuals, and to art critics who grind their axes in the name of the public good. Creativity in traditional societies where the one/many orientation (an individual within a large aggregate of equally autonomous beings) does not exist allows for a profoundly different way of experiencing the creative/ metaphorical process. Indeed, creativity as making special is often focused on genuinely significant matters, such as the revitalization of the symbolic frameworks that encode the sense of connectedness essential to ecologically sustainable relationships. This difference in orientation may lead us to ask the fundamental question of whether innovation and individual self-expression really lead to a more important form of creativity than the making special of the daily activities and ritual celebrations that are attuned to the dangers of disrupting the fragile balance of humans and the natural systems they depend upon.

The use of creativity to express connectedness and interdependency rather than the individual's subjective sense of meaning and critical judgments can be seen in Jeannette Armstrong's explanation of creativity within the context of her Okanagan Indian culture:

> In order to move outside of custom in a harmonious sense, many native peoples have created pathways to allow for nondestructive change. The custom of training keepers of our customs through societies require a rigorous discipline to ensure continued balancing of the individual within the four main activities, with the health and life of others and all else being priority. Full creativity in any given area thus requires the fullest knowledge available about that area and its impact on others. (1991, p. 75)

The radical difference that separates how members of some traditional cultures view creativity as giving expression to a transformative language that elevates and deepens the experience of participating in the fundamental relationships that bind together the human and natural community from the modern view of creativity can be seen even more clearly in the following interviews. The first interview was between Jan Steinbright of the Sealaska Heritage Foundation and Ross Sheakley (a Tlingit artist), and the second interview was between a representative of *Flash Art* and Christo, the artist who gained national media attention through his mammoth environmental projects such as *Running Fence* in California.

> JS: The stories are so important to Tlingit culture in that they carry the history and they carry lessons for how people are supposed to behave toward each other and toward all things in nature. How are these stories integrated into the artwork?
> RS: A lot of the totem poles that we have, say Raven who brought the world daylight, is done in a way that can't mistake

it for anything else. Those poles are done so I can remember, so my grandchildren can remember the stories. There's another one about Dukt'ootl, about the strongman who tore a sea lion in half. A lot of people used to laugh at him because his skin was a little bit darker than most people. But it wasn't because he was darker, he slept real close to the fire and a lot of smoke would get on his skin. He wasn't really mistreated but he wasn't treated really correctly and they didn't understand him. He did bring a lot of good things to the people. That the story teaches you how to treat other people correctly because you don't know the goodness that will come from them in the long run. I always look at the Dukt'ootl story and feel good about it because that man was ridiculed, was laughed at, and then it turns out that he really helped his village when he tore the sea lion in half. That was the main part of the story. That's how they picture him on totem poles. He's usually holding the sea lion upside down with his hands on the hind flippers. (1992, p. 8)

The *Flash Art* interview quotes Christo as saying:

The work is irrational and perhaps irresponsible. Nobody needs it. The work is a huge individualistic gesture that is entirely decided by me . . . One of the greatest contributions of modern art is the notion of individualism . . . I think that the artist can do anything he wants to do. This is why I would never accept a commission. Independence is most important to me. The work of art is a scream of freedom. (Gablik, 1991, p. 169)

The cultural orientation that Christo restates in formulaic fashion also needs to be compared with Jamake Highwater's argument that in aboriginal cultures creativity can have a moral and spiritual dimension generally lacking in the modern view of creativity. As Highwater puts it:

Art is a way of seeing, and what we see in art helps to define what we understand by the word 'reality.' We do not all see the same things. Though the dominant societies usually presume that their vision represents the sole truth about the world, each society (and often individuals within the same society) see reality uniquely. The complex process by which the artist transforms the act of seeing into a vision of the world is one of the consummate mysteries of the arts—one of the reasons that art is inseparable from religion and philosophy for most tribal peoples. This act of envisioning and then engendering a work of art represents an important and powerful ritual. Making images is one of the central ways by which humankind ritualizes experience and gains personal and tribal access to the ineffable . . . the unspeakable and ultimate substance of reality. (1981, p. 58)

This view of creativity as both transformative and sacred is different even from our approaches to creativity where evoking a religious state of awareness is the primary purpose, such as in Chagall's exquisite painting of Biblical themes now hanging in the Musée National Message Biblique in Nice, France. His religious art still involves a spectator relationship. And even the participation in a large choir singing a requiem mass of one of the West's great composers, while possibly providing what many would call a spiritual experience, is framed by a theology that is human/God centered and not by a sense of the sacred that includes all forms of life.

The use of creative expression in traditional cultures as a means of renewing the spiritual ecology which, in turn, serves as the basis of a cultural group's sense of moral order that defines the human's responsibility to plants, animals, and other sources of life, raises the question of whether our modern views of creativity must be fundamentally altered in ways that take account of the moral and spiritual dimensions of the ecological crisis. Although it is easy (and mistaken) to romanticize the ecologically oriented forms of spirituality evolved by many indigenous cultural groups, it is nevertheless useful to keep in mind the public statement signed by a group of eminent scientists that included Carl Sagan, Freeman Dyson, Hans Bethe, Stephen Schneider, and Stephen Jay Gould. The passage most relevant to the question of whether modern approaches to creativity should express a moral and spiritual purpose states:

As scientists, many of us have had profound experiences of awe and reverence for the universe. We understand that what is regarded as sacred is more likely to be treated with care and respect. Out planetary home should be so regarded. Efforts to safeguard and cherish the environment need to be infused with a vision of the sacred. (quoted in Suzuki and Knudtson, 1992, p. 227)

The key insight here is that what is regarded (experienced) as sacred is more likely to be treated with care and respect.

Culture represents the ways in which humans code and make sense of the information exchanges that result from their interactions within natural/cultural systems. The coding process, as Bateson notes, is done in the metaphorical languages of stories, technology, architecture, political and economic discourse, art, music, dance, and so forth. And because it is metaphorical, the interplay between imagination and memory is an inherent aspect of how the members of a culture store and reproduce for the next generation knowledge of essential relationships. These are all aspects of creativity. As suggested earlier, creativity and metaphorical thinking are dimensions of the same process. Thus when creativity is grounded in an ecological epistemology it will be expressed in ways that are contextual and expressive of the interdependence that characterizes the larger system.

What are the classroom implications of this radically different view of creativity? While the many implications deserve book length treatment, the following seem especially important to putting our understanding of creativity on a more ecologically responsible footing. First, educators at all levels of the formal educational process need to recognize that the modern way of representing the individual is part of a complex cultural myth that is contributing to the continued breakdown of human community and to imperiling the viability of natural systems. Hopefully, this understanding of the larger cultural and ecological context will lead to re-metaphorizing the way in which we think and talk about creativity in the classroom. The use of a metaphorical language that represents creativity more in terms of connected and participatory relationships, rather than in terms of individual inner self-expression and a spectator relationship to the products of the creative act (both of which represent the form of consciousness associated with the Industrial Revolution), would seem more consistent with the more ecologically oriented meta-narratives now challenging the foundations of modern consciousness.

Second, in classrooms where creativity is usually foregrounded as the central aspect of the learning process (i.e., art, music, dance, creative writing, and in elementary classes where some teachers see creativity as immanent in every thought and behavior of students) there should be more attention given to developing a critical understanding of the web of ideologies (meta-narratives) that have influenced the evolution of the modern idea of creativity (as well as the evolution of modern art), and to developing a critical understanding of the nature and role of creativity in more traditional/ecologically-centered cultures. Without the historical and comparative cultural understanding of creativity, students will lack a basis for questioning how their own assumptions about the nature of creativity relate to the deepening challenges we now face.

Third, educators need to expand the areas of educational/ cultural experience in which making special is now emphasized. The transformative potential of creativity often is associated by educators and the public with classes in the fine arts. The aesthetic/ symbolic/participatory (even ritualistic) aspects of other human relationships and activities also need to be made an explicit part of other areas of the curriculum: interpersonal communication, use of technology, social construction of spaces, design of buildings, and so on. For example, students should be urged to consider how various forms of modern technology influence the experience of making special in a variety of contexts.

Fourth, students need to experience creativity within the various contexts involving trans-generational communication (the nature and importance of trans-generational communication will be discussed in a later chapter). Artists (especially in the areas of music and dance) readily acknowledge that their own creativity is built on the work of earlier artists. Teachers need to help students recognize that the achievements of the past are embedded in current practices, and that knowledge of these traditions may expand their own sense of meaning and depth of creative expression. Student participation in the creative aspects of trans-generational communication is dependent upon being exposed to art forms that encode earlier ways of understanding relationships. This may require that students and teachers, following the model of the Foxfire approach to curriculum, begin the task of identifying the folk traditions in song, dance, crafts, and forms of play that encode ways of understanding and experiencing that are not destructive of human and human/nature relationships. The challenge here is in being able to recover the special wisdom of elders in ways that make it a vital and meaningful aspect of experience for the present generation. The entertainment industry and the elitist categories that reflect the special interests of certain sectors of the academic community make this task especially daunting. That many of our elders have become disconnected from the accumulated wisdom of how to live in meaningful and sustainable relationships, and have now only confusing and even destructive knowledge to pass on, makes the problem even more difficult.

The modern view of creativity that leads educators to see the possibility of creativity in every aspect of students' experience will continue, as long as it is understood as individually centered, to be both experientially and symbolically limiting. Indeed, this is one of the ironies of modernity. It is also contributing to a form of culture that is ignoring a basic fact of existence: that our lives are connected and interdependent—both with past and future generations and with the larger biotic community.

FOUR

EDUCATIONAL COMPUTING AND THE
ECOLOGICAL CRISIS:
SOME CRITICAL CONCERNS

The liberal image of the individual held by most educators has made it difficult to recognize the formative influence of culture on human development. But with the growing awareness of cultural differences among people in American society the modern individual is beginning to be understood in a new light. Instead of the image of an individual who achieves greater freedom and self-direction through the development of autonomous judgment, which meant learning to think and value independently of traditional norms, we are now beginning to recognize that all language systems that the "individual" uses (spoken and written discourse, body language, use of dress as a message system, art, architecture, and so forth) are culturally based. Even the natural attitude toward such sensory experiences as taste, touch, and sound are based on culturally shared norms and patterns. In effect, the individual is a cultural being and, depending upon the cultural group's schemata for organizing "reality," gives varying degrees of individualized expression to its symbolic world.

How children experience meaning and choices, interpret the nature of relationships, and make moral judgments reflect the deep and generally unconscious influence of culture. Cross cultural studies of child rearing practices provide overwhelming evidence of the reality constituting nature of culture. I would like to suggest, however, that this cultural perspective on childhood formal education is itself limited by the Western categories of thought that influenced how anthropologists have understood the nature of culture. Although there are important differences among anthropologists about the nature of culture, the following definitions by Ward H. Goodenough and Clifford Geertz represent a fundamental level of understanding widely accepted within the field. According to Goodenough, "culture . . . consists of standards for deciding what is, standards for deciding what can be, standards for deciding how one feels about it, standards for deciding what to do about it, and standards for deciding how to go about doing it" (1981, p. 62). Geertz's definition also emphasizes the role of culture as a symbolic system that unconsciously guides thought and behavior in the everyday world. As he puts it, "culture patterns—religious, philosophical, aesthetic, scientific, ideological—are 'programs'; they provide a template or blueprint for the organization of social and psychological processes, much as genetic systems provide a blueprint for the organization of organic processes" (1973, p.216). The achievement of these two definitions, and I think they are significant though fundamentally flawed, is to establish the primacy of the symbolic world the child is born into. But this view of culture, which helps illuminate how the present patterns of consciousness and behavior involve the reenactment (often with modifications) of traditions deeply rooted in the past, continues to reinforce the anthropocentric meta-narratives that are essential characteristics of Western thought. Following the lead of cultural anthropologists, educators may begin to focus on the formative influence of culture, and even begin addressing problematic aspects of modern culture. But if they do not recognize the problems associated with basing both their analysis and prescriptions for classroom practice on anthropocentric categories their well intended efforts may contribute to further deepening the real crisis we face— which is the degradation of the natural systems upon which all cultures depend.

In addressing the problematic aspects of modern culture that influence the kind of cultural beings that youth will become as adults, I want to use a metaphor that overcomes the silences fostered by the anthropocentrism of understanding humans primarily as cultural beings. Gregory Bateson's metaphor of a mental ecology is useful here because it accounts for both the conceptual/psychological/ behavioral mapping processes that cultural anthropologists are concerned with and the way in which the individual interacts with the natural systems increasingly being put at risk. For Bateson, the basic unit of information or idea is a "difference which makes a difference," and an ecology is the totality of interactions (difference which makes a difference in response to changes in other organisms or elements) that make up a natural system. Changes (difference) in sunlight causes changes (difference) in the chemical processes within a plant; the changes in the plant (which represent complex information exchange processes) will lead down the road to changes in human action (perhaps there was not adequate sunlight for the plant to achieve full maturity and thus become edible). What Bateson is helping us understand is that humans are participants in a larger and vastly more complex system of information exchange. As he puts it, "the total self-corrective unit which processes information, or as I say, 'thinks' and 'acts' and 'decides' is a *system* whose boundaries do not at all coincide with the boundaries either of the body or what is popularly called the 'self' or 'consciousness' . . ." (1972, p.319). This brings us to Bateson's "the map is not the territory" metaphor, which he uses to explain why a cultural group may be less or more aware of what is happening within the larger mental ecology of which they are an interactive part. An ecology, with its continual flow of information, is the "territory"; the "map" (the cultural way of knowing) as we know from the experience of using a map as a guide does not always represent all the features of the territory—or even the more important ones. That is, a cultural way of knowing may put out of focus (awareness) many of the information exchanges critical to the long term survival of the system. To summarize the key points that help to correct the limitations of understanding humans only in terms of culture: (1) the person is always an interactive member of a natural environment (mental ecology); (2) which information exchanges the person responds to depends largely upon the interpretative framework of the cultural group; and (3) humans (cultural groups) cannot sustain unilateral control over the ecosystems upon which they are dependent, or ignore the patterns of human activity that are degrading the system, and survive over the long term. Put more simply, recognizing the primacy of culture in the educational process is important not only in terms of the kind of individual it helps to constitute but also in terms of whether the human/natural environment relationship is sustainable over the long term.

As American society encompasses many distinct cultural groups, and allows for having multiple cultural identities, it is important to specify that the analysis here will focus on the dominant middle-class culture that has its roots in the Western traditions of thought. Not only does it set the standards against which other cultural groups are judged, it has also created a modern life style that threatens to overwhelm the viability of the Earth's ecological systems. The influence of the dominant culture on the development of childhood is already well understood, although a strong case can be made that the cultural ideals children are supposed to internalize as part of their natural attitude are ecologically problematic. Greater self-autonomy, a consumer-oriented way of understanding success, continual preparation for change (viewed as progressive), and the reliance on data as the basis of individual empowerment are the standards by which many classroom teachers still judge the character and potential of children. As we begin to understand the connection between these cultural orientations and the Industrial Revolution that put us on our current environmentally destructive pathway, as well as the characteristics of ecologically sustainable cultures, we may begin to recognize the limitations of these cultural ideals. What is less well understood about the dominant culture is the influence of technology on the formation of consciousness (both in terms of explicit and taken for granted patterns of understanding) and self-image.

Although both mechanical and social forms of technology permeate nearly every aspect of everyday life, technology is perhaps one of the least understood aspects of mainstream culture. Evidence to support this generalization can be found in the way university liberal arts and social science curricula marginalize technology as an area of study. Teacher education programs, ironically, make "training" in social and mechanical technologies the central core of professional knowledge and competency, but few teachers understand how technology influences thought and social relationships, or affects the forms of knowledge communicated from one generation to the next. Unknown to them will be Peter Berger and Thomas Luckmann's analysis of how technology has influenced taken for granted patterns of thought, and Jacques Ellul's arguments about the differences between technology in traditional cultures and modern cultures (as well as his technological determinism thesis). Nor are Lewis Mumford, Joseph Weizenbaum, Theodore Roszak, Harry Braverman, and Michel Foucault likely to be names teachers recognize, even though they have written seminal books on aspects of technology most utilized in the classroom. In not possessing a deep knowledge of the cultural/existential mediating characteristics of technology, most teachers are limited to socializing students to the uses of technology and to an uncritical acceptance of the legitimating ideology that is now part of one of the most powerful mythic narratives within the dominant culture.

Ignorance of how technology influences the most fundamental aspects of experience do not, however, lessen its impact. Our task here will be to clarify how technology can be understood as something more complex than a tool people use for achieving their own purposes, and how such specific forms of technology as computers are becoming the most formative aspect of our culture (that is, how computers are helping to constitute a particular form of subjectivity). Lastly, we want to return to the question of whether a computer-centered culture (more commonly known as the "Information Age") is ecologically sustainable.

Don Ihde gives us a basic vocabulary for understanding the human/technology relationship at all levels of socialization—from childhood through adulthood. This vocabulary helps to illuminate fundamental relationships that occur in the use of any technology, including such varied technologies as "mastery learning" and the use of a computer. First, Ihde expands upon Martin Heidegger's insight that technology mediates how a person will experience the world by pointing out that the nature of a technology influences human experience by selecting certain ways of knowing (experiencing) for amplification, and reducing others. That is, *a technology mediates human experience through its selection/amplification and reduction characteristics.* Ihde uses the example of a person who manipulates a stick in order to reach fruit located in the top branches. The technology extends (amplifies) the reach of the person but reduces those aspects of experience relating to touch and smell— which may be important to determining whether the fruit is ripe (1979, p. 53). To use a second example of technology, the telephone amplifies the ability to project voice over great distances, but reduces the use of the other senses that come into play in nontechnologically mediated (fact to face) communication. The amplification characteristics of computers are even more complex in that they alter our ways of knowing as well as communicating.

Second, Ihde identifies three different types or categories of existential/technological relationships. The first involves experiencing something *through* the technology, like the person who experiences the fruit through the use of the stick or the experience with another person through the telephone. The second type of existential/technological relationship is what Ihde refers to as an "experience *with* a technological artifact" (p. 54). In this relationship the technology is the focal point of the experience, like following the voice directions when reaching an automated answering system or synchronizing mind and body with the automated signals that regulate food preparation at a McDonald's fast food restaurant. The third type is what Ihde calls a background relationship. That is, most of modern life is lived within contexts that involve the presence of multiple technologies—the lighting, heating, acoustical systems, running motors, flashing signs, voices and images on a television, and so forth, that provide the background for the more focal experiences we have. The background of technological activity (now often unnoticed because it has become so much a part of our taken for granted reality) not only influences the ambience of daily experience but also reinforces the acceptance of the artificial world of technology as more real and vital than the "natural environment—which is often treated as a pleasant escape from reality. In examining the amplification and reduction characteristics of computer technology, particularly in educational settings, it will be important to keep in mind Ihde's categories of experiencing through technology, with technology, and as technological background.

Whereas the Heidegger/Ihde focus is on the person's relationship with technology, the selection/amplification/reduction characteristics of technology also relate to culture. That is, a technology selects for amplification certain cultural patterns, and reduces the presence of others in people's lives. As the mediating characteristics of a technology changes the cultural patterns (in language processes, ways of knowing, sense of time and space, etc.), it may have a secondary effect on the person's psychological development and sense of taken-for-granted reality that is far more influential than what is experienced *through* and *with* a technology. The cultural mediating characteristics of technology can be seen in the introduction of the phonetic alphabet, printing press, television, and computers. As the computer incorporates elements of these earlier technologies, and is becoming the dominant symbol of power in the Information Age we are supposedly entering, I will limit the following discussion to the influence of computers on the cultural patterns that serve as the primary reference point in the cognitive, linguistic, and identity formation of the child.

The argument that computers amplify certain cultural patterns and reduce others goes counter to the way of thinking of most spokespersons within the field of educational computing. As they view their task as that of expanding the educational uses of this technology, it is important to establish how they understand the connection between computers and culture, and how computers contribute to the student's ability to think. As I have written elsewhere on how the field of educational computing remains grounded in the seventeenth century epistemology of John Locke and Rene Descartes, I will cite several of the most articulate leaders in the field (1988, 1993). As editor of a special issue devoted to "Computing and Education: The Second Frontier," by the *Teachers College Record,* Robert McClintock writes: "To state it directly, the irreversible cultural action that we have initiated has two related components. The first consists in substituting a new form of coding—binary code—as the basis for storing and retrieving all the contents of our culture. The second consists in adding to the ancient cultural discovery of how to externalize memory outside the human mind, a very modern, portentous ability to externalize intelligence also outside the human mind" (1988, p. 349). "All culture," he continues, "can be coded so that it can be operated on with a digital computer" (p. 351). An extension of his argument would be that all cultures (Japanese, Hopi, Balinese, etc.) can be digitally coded and stored in a data base without changing the culture. In effect, he is arguing that the technology is culturally neutral, and that computers simply represent an advance in data storage and retrieval .

The assumption that people use a computer as a tool (that is, they determine its purposes) can be seen in how he frames the educational challenge of computer technology: "the pedagogical problem encountered in shifting from a culture of memory to one of intelligence will consist of developing educational strategies through which people will learn how to control and direct the intelligent tools that will increasingly be available to them" (McClintock, 1988, p. 351). Writing in *Scientific American* Alan C. Kay also restates the Lockean/Cartesian view that human intelligence, when based on "objective" data, is freed from the impositions of cultural traditions (i.e., memory), or as he puts it, "the barbarisms of the deep past" (1991, p. 140). And like McClintock, he views educational computing as facilitating the thought process of a culturally autonomous individual. "Each of us," he writes, "has to construct our own version of reality by main force. Literally, to make ourselves. And we are quite capable of devising new mental bricks, new ways of thinking, that can enormously expand the understanding we attain" (p. 140). To summarize the assumption which underlies Kay's way of understanding the relationship of computers and human intelligence: culture has no connection to language or thought processes; language (French, English, Japanese, etc.) is a neutral conduit for the communication of objective information and data; computers are a culturally neutral technology that empower individual intelligence and self-direction.

The epistemological/ideological orientation embedded in the thinking of McClintock and Kay is also present in the literature of educational computing, but is seldom explicitly articulated. Computer education textbooks and journals, such as *The Computing Teacher*, are used to explain the educational uses of the technology. The ambience of the literature is that of proselytizing rather than that of careful reflection on when computer mediated learning is appropriate. While those in the field of educational computing can be faulted for their failure to recognize that computers involve the use of culturally specific languages and ways of knowing, and that these processes express the reality constituting orientation of a cultural group's meta-narratives, the real source of the problem can be traced back to the parent field of computer science. For example, in accepting the prestigious Turing Award in 1987, John E. Hopcroft's speech reiterated the Lockean/Cartesian tradition of excluding culture from how intelligence is to be understood in the modern world. According to Hopcroft:

> The potential of computer science, if fully explored and developed, will take us to a higher plane of knowledge about the world. Computer science will assist us in gaining a greater understanding of intellectual processes. It will enhance our knowledge of the learning process, the thinking process, and the reasoning process. Computer science will provide models and conceptual tools for the cognitive sciences. Just as the physical sciences have dominated man's intellectual endeavors during this century as researches explored the nature of matter and the beginning of the universe, today we are beginning the exploration of the intellectual universe of ideas, knowledge structures, and language." (1987, p. 201)

His last statement about computer science helping to advance our understanding of the "intellectual universe of ideas, knowledge structures, and language" brings us back to the main theme of this discussion: namely, how technology amplifies certain cultural patterns over others, and the implications of these changes for educating future generations to live in greater ecological balance.

The patterns of a culture are, in part, stored in the stories told in response to the child's questions: "What is that?" "What am I to do?"

"What do others want?" As Alasdair MacIntyre observes, "I can only answer the question 'What am I to do?' if I can answer the prior question 'Of what story or stories do I find myself a part?' . . . I am part of their story, as they are part of mine. The narrative of any one life is part of an interlocking set of narratives" (1984 edition, p. 216). In some cultures the stories that both frame the questions and provide the group's answers that influence the child's development include experiences drawn from both the human and animal world. Among American Indian cultures these stories (tales of coyote, the women who married a bear, the wife of Swanset, he who hunted birds in his father's village, etc.) established for the child the forms of life that were to be included in the moral ecology, and how adherence to the reciprocal obligations dictated by the moral ecology was necessary to insure the future survival of an interdependent world. Other cultures, such as ours, are based on more anthropocentric centered stories which result in children acquiring the conceptual maps that make visible and real only historically selected aspects of the territory (e.g., the environment as a natural resource, as a wilderness to be conquered, as an empty wasteland). The key point here is that the form of child subjectivity, including ways of understanding relationships, is dependent to a significant degree upon the "world" constituted in the language processes of the cultural group.

Given this common sense observation, the critical question becomes: *What stories, languages, and ways of knowing do the technologists want to make the dominant feature of mainstream culture and what is the nature of subjectivity their form of culture will help constitute as the natural attitude toward everyday life?* As computers are increasingly used to integrate social and mechanical techniques, the cultural amplification and reduction characteristics of this technology become crucial to answering this question.

As our own culture is so much a part of our taken for granted world it is difficult to recognize fully the changes that are occurring; but certain changes are now becoming more visible. While the following discussion will focus on the cultural mediating characteristics of computers, it should be kept in mind that computers incorporate other traditions that have long exerted a profound influence on the development of Western consciousness. People are receptive to using this technology (even to thinking of it as a model for understanding the "intellectual universe of ideas"—to recall Hopcroft's scientific vision) because of past narratives and experiences that have equated certain forms of knowledge and individualism with social progress. For example, computers embody a print based form of consciousness, an epistemology that translates gestalts into discrete bits of data, the liberal/scientific antitradition tradition of thought, and an anthropocentric attitude toward knowing nature in order to better control it. *Computers are, in effect, simply the amplifiers of Western traditions that we currently associate with modernization.*

Keeping these important qualifications in mind, I would like to use three different categories to frame the analysis of the form of subjectivity reenforced by those areas of cultural experience where computers have become dominant. The categories are: cognitive and linguistic cultural patterns, political and moral world of play and work, and the ideology/ecological crisis connection.

AMPLIFICATION OF COGNITIVE AND LINGUISTIC CULTURAL PATTERNS

Computers both embody and facilitate mental processes, and they involve culturally specific ways of knowing: the design, engineering, and development of the machine's logic system and software programs; computing and word processing as part of a larger process of problem solving; and the use of a metaphorical language that encodes the analogue thought processes and experiences of people who had a specific historical/cultural identity. But the amplification characteristics of computers are very limited in the forms of knowledge that can be represented. Whether we are talking about a student using a data base or a simulation program, or an engineer dealing with a set of mathematical relationships, there is a commonality in the form of knowledge that is the basis of the person/machine relationship. McClintock identified this form of knowledge when he claimed that "all culture can be coded so that it can be operated on with digital computers." That is, computers amplify the *explicit* knowledge of a cultural group and represent this knowledge as bits of information that is, according to the conventional wisdom within the field, used as the basis for thinking, forming ideas, and so forth. What gets reduced (lost) as legitimate knowledge are the *tacit, contextual,* and *analogue* forms of knowledge—which are learned at a pre-reflective level as the person unconsciously uses the patterns and practices of others as examples (models, templates) to be re-enacted in similar existential/cultural situations. Furthermore, the explicit forms of knowledge amplified by computers are represented as "discovered" (observed) by an objective (disinterested, value-neutral) observer. This knower/known dichotomy, which Descartes further strengthened, also reinforces the mind/body and "man"/ nature dichotomies so central to Western consciousness. The implications of this cultural orientation are immense, and I shall only mention three: (1) local knowledge that cannot be made explicit in order to fit the language processing characteristics of computers is delegitimated; (2) narrativized forms of knowledge (including the culture's moral codes) cannot be communicated through this technology except in a sterile and distorted form that undermines the traditional sources of authority; (3) people who possess the ability to use the restricted language process associated with computer mediated knowledge will take on more status and power relative to other groups who rely upon other ways of knowing.

A second area of cultural amplification is expressed in how computers reinforce a conduit view of communication and a representational view of language that are still deeply rooted in all levels of public education, from elementary through graduate level classes. According to this tradition, words stand for or represent real things and events. As Alvin Gouldner put it in his criticism of the new class as a speech community: " 'one word, one meaning' for everyone and forever" (1979, p. 28). Ironically, this representational view of language allows the computer mediated culture to represent both the rational process and the individual as free of cultural influence. As the computer amplifies a culture-free view of language and communication, it reduces the awareness of several essential characteristics of the culture/language/thought connection. As I have discussed this more fully in *The Cultural Dimensions of Educational Computing* (1988), and in *Critical Essays on Education, Modernity and the Recovery of the Ecological Imperative* (1993), I shall only touch on several implications of hiding the metaphorical nature of the language/thought connection. As a number of observers have pointed out in recent years, cultures are not built up on the basis of data. Rather, they are based on meta-narratives, and these explanations of beginnings, relationships, and future possibilities (if everybody subscribes to the shared moral norms) are used to make sense of daily experience—including data (Roszak, 1986, pp. 87–107). Language both stores and reproduces these meta-narratives in the daily processes of analogic thinking where the "new" is understood in terms of the familiar and proven. Just as the root metaphors or meta-narratives of a culture influence the analogues that can be imagined, the iconic metaphors encode earlier processes of analogic thinking. The current use of such iconic metaphors as "memory," "access," and "intelligence"—to cite examples where the image or schema of understanding has been changed in ways that reflect the current practice of thinking of human attributes and processes in terms of computer characteristics (the latter were originally understood in terms of metaphors that reflected human qualities) are a significant aspect of the language/communication process. To put the problem more simply, computer mediated language processes hide the metaphorical nature of language, and how the metaphorical constructions of reality are located in the history of a cultural group.

The way in which the processes of language (status given to spoken and printed based discourse, signifier/signified relationships, what is perceived as the power, authority and function of language, etc.) influence the child's experiences of primary socialization is critical both to the way fundamental relationships will be understood and to the process of identity formation (Bowers, 1984, pp. 31–48). By amplifying both the view of language as representing real events and things, and the accompanying "world conceived and grasped as a picture," to recall Heidegger's phrase, computers help to hide the way in which the linguistically encoded schemata representing prior understandings influence the thought process of the student. To make this point more succinctly, computers help to obscure the way in which language thinks us as we think within the language—to paraphrase a key Heideggerian insight into the nature of language. The metaphors of "pioneer," "wilderness," "nature," "Indians," and so forth, are examples of an encoding process where earlier analogic thought processes provided a schema or image that frames how current situations are understood. To put this another way, while the computer reinforces our specific cultural way of understanding thinking as an autonomous/data based process, the person using the computer is actually participating in a thought process deeply influenced by earlier people who were trying to solve problems and make sense of their lives within very different historical and cultural circumstances. The mind-set of the British Empire, for example, is still present in the metaphorical language that divides part of the world into Near East, Far East and "down under." Similarly, the schema of understanding that until recently framed how we understand intelligence, as well as such other currently used metaphors as "natural resource" and "individualism," are examples of how the mental/ experiential processes of the past continue to influence the present. If future generations are going to understand the current condition of the "territory" (the natural systems we interact with and are absolutely dependent upon), they will need a profoundly different view of the culture/language/thought connection than the distorted understanding that computers help to foster. As it becomes clearer about how thought is part of a larger symbolic ecology, perhaps it will be easier to recognize the interactive relationships that characterize our place in the larger information exchange system that Bateson calls a "mental ecology." But this will involve radical changes in the schemata of understanding based on the metaphorical image of the autonomous individual now reinforced by computers.

OTHER FORMS OF CULTURAL AMPLIFICATION AND WORK SETTINGS

The child's development is now being influenced by a variety of other cultural message systems that reflect the amplification/ reduction characteristics of computers. I shall simply identify several of the more problematic ones in order to save space for a brief discussion of the critically important issue of how computers relate to the ecological crisis—a topic that deserves book length treatment.

The impact of computer technology on children's play has been as profound as it is disturbing. According to the findings of Eugene Provenzo Jr., twenty-five of the thirty top selling toys in 1989 were video games or video game related. The simulation games that supposedly challenge the person's reaction time in making quick judgments also reinforce the cultural messages that connect violence, revenge, death and destruction, and competition with the excitement of the fast moving and manipulatable images on the screen. As Provenzo notes, most of the games teach another message: winning requires following the rules exactly as defined (1991, pp. 13, 95). In fact, part of the challenge is figuring out the decision-making process that the game embodies. If the child's taken-for-granted reality is, in large part, constituted by the language patterns (including stories) that make up her/his symbolic environment, and there is overwhelming evidence to support that this is the case, the impact of these games and similarly value oriented television programs can only have a pathological and thus destructive effect.

Just as students spend more time watching television programs that rely upon video game plots and heroes, they are encountering more areas of the curriculum that have been adapted for computer use. The values used to justify the more widespread use of computers are often associated with economic need, the necessity of computer literacy for full participation as citizens in the Information Age, and the need to learn problem solving, decision making and "higher order" thinking skills. These values provide an important clue about the conception of the good person ("Of what story or stories do I find myself a part?"—to recall MacIntyre's question) reinforced through educational computing. Douglas D. Noble's observation, as I see it, addresses the deeper levels of the technological/cultural amplification process hidden by the rhetoric that connects computers with individual empowerment and international competitiveness. Writes Noble: "educators have unwittingly adopted the framework of a larger military/scientific enterprise that only appears to be an agenda for public education because the language—intelligence, learning, thinking and problem solving—is the same . . . This is the enterprise to harness intelligence, both human and machine, for use within complex military and corporate technological systems." But the ultimate goal, he concludes, is to increase the effective use of technology (1991, p. 171).

The integration of techniques now made possible by computers is changing the culture in ways that will have important implications for educators who want to foster a form of subjectivity that complements rather than subverts the potentialities of computers. However, educators who view the full potentiality of computers, particularly in the area of surveillance, as a threat to democratic values and traditional civil liberties, will face a different set of challenges—particularly since *all technological experiments with the culture are viewed as inherently progressive in nature and thus not requiring any sort of questioning attitude.* Basically, the capacity of computers to collect, store, and retrieve massive amounts of data is turning American society into a Panopticon culture where work performance, consumer habits, personal communications and travel, and economic circumstances are recorded and stored in data bases. The data bases of governmental agencies relating to various aspects of people's lives are now interconnected with data bases in the corporate world—and soon will be connected with the data bases of the medical establishment (Roszak, pp. 156–176). The translation of individual lives into digital code that allows economic and political decisions to be made on the basis of "objective data" by impersonal authorities will require a new form of subjectivity—one that accepts as normal the limited human characteristics that can be encoded and communicated through computers. The Panopticon culture, where the invisible data collectors keep everybody under constant surveillance in order to make decisions more rational and efficient, will lead to a new genre of stories—of lives ruined by personal behavior, character traits, and beliefs that do not conform to computer established norms, and of successful lives attuned to the moral/political requirements of the Information Age. It will be very much as Kafka envisioned it in his book *The Trial* where everything is known by decision makers who are themselves unknown—but objective, efficient, and networked together. How far we have already progressed in this direction in the work setting is described in Barbara Garson's *The Electronic Sweatshop* (1989). New stories reflecting people's experiences with the early stages of development of a Panopticon culture are already being told and will have an impact on the process of growing up in America.

COMPUTERS AND THE ECOLOGICAL CRISIS

Computers are the epistemological machines of the scientific/technologically oriented middle class culture. Computers can also be understood as embodying the liberal ideology of this cultural group, which is now influencing the form of modernization being embraced by countries around the world. The chief elements of this liberal ideology include a view of the individual as the basic social unit, knowledge as derived from objective data and formulated by individuals who are in control of their own thought processes, change and technological innovation as manifestations of humankind's progressive mastery of nature, and a man-centered universe that now requires that science and technology be utilized to insure the successful "stewardship" of natural resources that are the inheritance of future generations. It is also important to recall that this epistemology/ideology has had a long history of using a metaphorical language derived from machines for understanding both humans and the rest of natural phenomena.

The problem of a computer centered culture is that it leads to treating the ecological crisis as further evidence that more systematic planning and efficient technologies are needed. Ironically, the ways of knowing, technological practices, and moral analogues that characterize ecologically sustainable cultures (as well as groups living on the margins of the dominant culture) would not be considered as legitimate responses to the problem of living beyond the carrying capacities of the Earth's ecosystems. Ecologically sustainable cultures, while varying widely in their rituals, technologies and art forms, nevertheless appear to share common patterns that do not fit the mediating characteristics of computers. The identification of several of these characteristics will help to make two fundamental points: that the computer is a totally inadequate technology for addressing the deeper cultural roots of the ecological crisis, and that the education of youth needs to be framed in terms of an epistemological/ideological orientation that makes long-term sustainability, rather than economic and technological progress, the primary concern.

Ecologically sustainable cultures have evolved language systems (the process of semiosis in the broadest sense) that foreground relationships with the nonhuman world as essentially moral and reciprocal in nature. Like Bateson's mental ecology, their moral ecologies decenter humans as possessing a privileged status in relationship to other forms of life. Although all languages are about relationships, computer mediated languages frame relationships in instrumental terms. In effect, knowledge derived from computer models, simulations, and data become the basis for human action. This instrumental language also contributes to eroding the authority of the meta-narratives that are the basis of a culture's moral norms. A second characteristic of ecologically sustainable cultures is that knowledge (including technologies) must meet the test of long term sustainability. That is, ideas, values, and technologies are not embraced just because they are new. The conservatism of these cultures is grounded in a reluctance, borne of past collective experiences, to experiment by making new demands that will have unpredictable consequences for the local bioregion. Modern cultures, with their myth of progress and scientifically based view of knowledge, have made experimentation with their own patterns the ideal cultural norm—which has been sustained through the exploitation of the bioregions of other cultural groups. A third characteristic of ecologically sustainable cultures is that they appear to rely more on oral forms of communication. That is, the stories about how to be a moral person (and of immoral behavior that will bring the entire community to a tragic end), the uses of technologies, and the social patterns that sustain community life are shared through face to face forms of communication where local context, community participation, and memory play a more vital role. These aspects of the knowledge/communication process do not fit the patterns associated with the literacy encoding process utilized by computers. Computers, as mentioned earlier, amplify the representation of data as context free, as well as a visual/thought process between a student and the printed symbols appearing on the screen that have anonymous authorship.

Although this entire discussion has focused on the importance of understanding the culture/technology connection, and that a computer-centered culture is continuing the very traditions that have contributed to the ecological crisis, computers themselves are especially unsuited to the task of understanding the influence of culture on human development. Education during the formative years of childhood and adolescence is further complicated by the ecological crisis that now brings into question the most basic assumptions and ideals of the dominant culture. At least part of the answer to the question, "what are we to do?," as Noel Gough and Kathleen Kesson put it, "is to participate in the creative reconstruction of a language which foregrounds our kinship with nature. We need myths and metaphors that 'sing'," (they are referring to the Songlines of Australian Aborigines that combine their cosmology, local knowledge of life forms and geographical features, and the pathways that connect sacred sites—which is another form of cultural coding) "the earth into existence *in the conditions of urban and late industrial lifestyles.* Clues to such constructions can be found in the symbolic languages of premodern societies but we cannot, and should not, attempt to appropriate the meta-narratives of another culture to replace our own" (1992, p. 8). As the metaphorical foundations of modern thought and lifestyle become increasingly untenable, we will need to evolve a form of individuality, including an image of the creative person, that is grounded in a sense of connectedness and dependency within the larger biotic community. This will have profound implications for every aspect of the educational process, including the cultural norms educators use for making judgments about what forms of knowledge, language processes, and images of the good person that are to be part of the process of classroom socialization.

FIVE

TOWARD AN ECOLOGICAL VIEW OF INTELLIGENCE

Writing in *The Elmwood Quarterly*, Fritjof Capra observes that a property of all living systems is "their tendency to form multileveled structures of systems within systems. Each of these forms a whole with respect to its parts while at the same time being part of a larger whole. Thus, cells combine to form tissues, tissues to form organs, and organs to form organisms. These in turn exist within social systems and ecosystems. Throughout the world," he concludes, "we find living systems nesting within other living systems" (1993, p. 7). This ecological model of understanding not only explains the connectedness of cultures within the multileveled world of natural systems of plants, animals, soils, and fresh water, it also illuminates how the guiding metaphors of a culture are nested within deeper layers of metaphorical thought that encode the living and mostly taken for granted history of the cultural group. This connectedness applies equally to the cluster of metaphorical images currently used in the fields of education, cognitive psychology and cognitive science to represent the nature of intelligence. While the case can be made that educators borrow their images of intelligence from cognitive psychologists who, in turn, are increasingly influenced by the attempts of cognitive scientists to develop "intelligent" computers, the main focus here will be on the image of the individual used to frame their ways of understanding the nature of intelligence. As in the "systems within systems" model described by Capra, the metaphorical image of intelligence as an attribute of the individual (or computer, for the cognitive scientists) is dependent upon deeper taken for granted assumptions about the nature of knowledge, human agency, progress, and social responsibility.

Another way to explain the ecological model is to say that everything is connected. In the domain of culture, this means that the metaphorical constructions created in the past as a response to problematic situations continue to influence current thought, just as the developments in one domain of inquiry influence what is occurring on the cutting edge of other fields. For example, the secularizing and mechanistically-oriented cultural developments of recent centuries in the West are encoded in the approach to brain research that now leads educators to adapt their approaches to teaching and curriculum to the most recent findings. But the connections of systems within systems, especially in the symbolic world of culture, are not always readily discernable. Nor is it easy to sort out how a system or pattern of understanding that appeared to an earlier generation of thinkers as an intelligent and progressive response to the problems of their times, and which continues to live on in a vastly changed world as part of a taken for granted way of understanding, threatens to destroy the viability of other living systems. The problem of recognizing the "patterns that connect," to use Bateson's phrase, which is an essential first step to addressing whether they are deterimental to the long term survival of life sustaining ecosystems, is made even more difficult by the ability of certain groups to represent traditional patterns of thought (which I would prefer to call "orthodoxies") as progressive and modern. Today, the orthodox belief in the primacy and autonomy of the individual remains shielded from scrutiny by its taken for granted status among classroom teachers and educational theorists, and by the widespread practice of identifying it as one of the primary social expressions of progress and modernization.

Illuminating the consequences of basing educational practices on an individually-centered view of intelligence will require thinking against the grain of the most deeply held conventions of modern thought. But if we reframe the metaphor of individualism by foregrounding its genesis in the philosophical and political writings of men who did not understand the nature of culture and its influence on language and thought, and who universalized other culturally specific assumptions that were to become the hallmarks of modern consciousness, perhaps then we can approach the discussion of an individually centered view of intelligence as a profoundly problematic orthodoxy. In effect, we will be considering yet another aspect of educational and cultural practice that is still under the influence of a powerful metaphorical image that contributed significantly to equating progress with the exploitation of the environment as a natural resource. Just as an ecological model of understanding leads to a profoundly different approach to moral education, creativity, and to how we think about the educational uses of computers, an ecological view of intelligence has equally important implications for the reform of public schools and university education.

The immediate task will be to document how the view of intelligence currently used to justify what is perceived by professional educators, from the public classrooms to graduate programs in education, is perceived as the basis for legitimating the current direction of educational reforms. We shall then turn to how cognitive psychologists and cognitive scientists explain the nature of intelligence. The metaphorical constructions built upon the image of individually-centered intelligence, like an inverted pyramid, will then be examined in order to determine, as in the use of all metaphors, what is illuminated and what is hidden (or put out of focus). This will enable us to clarify the deeper metaphorical constructions the "individualism" metaphor is nested in. According to one critic of the pathway Western psychology has taken, these deeper and more formative metaphors (which might be referred to as the guiding ideas of the culture) contribute to the spread of nihilism (Evans, 1993). Although the connection between an individually-centered view of intelligence and nihilism deserves careful attention, the central concern here will be on explaining how this now dominant view of intelligence provides an inadequate basis for developing ecologically responsive approaches to education. Attention will also be given to examining how the metaphor of intelligence changes when it is nested in metaphorical constructions derived from an ecological model, as well as the educational reforms that would be consistent with the mental ecology that connects culture and the natural systems upon which it is dependent.

How Educators Understand the Nature of Intelligence

The pendulum of educational reform continues to swing away from the behaviorists who discounted all references to intelligence in favor of designing reinforcement schedules that would produce the behaviors predetermined by the educator *qua* social engineer. It is now safe to generalize that most classroom teachers and professors of education who keep themselves current with the most recent developments in learning theory subscribe to a cognitive interpretation of intelligence. Howard Gardner's theory of multiple intelligences is gaining popularity among educators, and while it identifies noncognitive forms of intelligence it is neverthless predicated on many of the key cultural assumptions necessary to the cognitivist's view of intelligence. For example, the key assumption of Gardner's theory is that the different expressions of intelligence are attributes of the individual.

The teacher education community has generated a plethora of labels to designate differences in emphasis in the classroom application of the basic tenets of the cognitivist position: "Higher-Order Cognitive Strategies," "Integrative Curriculum," "Practical Intelligence," "Individual Learning Styles," "Cooperative Learning," "Constructivist Learning," among others. Developments in cognitive psychology and cognitive science have also led educators to identify different forms of knowledge (e.g., general knowledge, domain-specific knowledge, declarative knowledge, procedural knowledge, conditional knowledge, practical knowledge, etc.). The different forms of learning, as well as the mental processes associated with each, have been similarly named, categorized, and incorporated into the lexicon of teaching strategies. Teachers are now expected to adjust their learning strategies in ways that, among others, take account of "right" and "left" brain functions, short and long-term memory, schemata, story grammar, episodic memory, procedural memory, and meta-cognition. Underlying this proliferation of variables that teachers are supposed to activate at the optimum moment in the learning process are a core set of assumptions that connect the most mechanistic interpretation of the cognitive position with Gardner's more eclectic view of multiple intelligences. These include the assumption that the student is the cognitive agent who actively participates in the construction of knowledge, that the student's direct experience is essential to the formation of ideas and to understanding, that procedures for fostering the construction of knowledge rather than the content of what is being learned is the primary concern of the educator, and, lastly, that the basic social/cultural unit that thinks, behaves, and experiences is the individual. With regard to the last assumption, it is important to note that educators now emphasize participation in groups as a way of facilitating the individual's learning potential.

These assumptions are clearly present in the following explanations of the goals and effectiveness of different cognitive approaches to education. In explaining the use of scaffolds (prompts) for teaching higher-level cognitive strategies, Barak Rosenshine and Carla Meister suggest that

> to facilitate reading comprehension, students may be taught to use cognitive strategies such as generating questions about their reading. To generate questions, students need to search the text and combine information, which in turn helps them comprehend what they read. To help students in the writing process, they may be taught how to organize their writing and how to use self-talk prompts to facilitate the revision process." (1992, p. 26)

Barbara Clark, one of the leading proponents for basing educational practices on brain research, makes the case with the following argument, and in the process tacitly reproduces a deeper set of core cultural assumptions. Writes Clark:

> One of the most obvious conclusions from the data being collected is the need for an integrative use of brain functions. It is clear that each function is intricately *inter*dependent on each other function; any methodology that focuses only a part of the brain process on the learning task is inefficient at best and, at worst, wasteful of human talent and ability. The vast resources of the brain/mind complex are best developed when opportunities are made available for that interdependence. The Integrative Education Model . . . and its organization and strategies create such opportunities. (1986, p. 6)

The integrative learning environment optimizes individual learning, including the student's intuitive process which Clark describes as "integrating all other brain functions" (p. 161), by stressing the importance of student experimentation and involvement, utilizing the "needs and interests" of the student as the base from which the curriculum develops, and by encouraging "self-directed learning, invention, and inquiry" as well as peer teaching (p. 33).

Other strategies and models of teaching and learning that go by the more generic labels of "learning styles" and "cooperative learning" are based on the same constructivist view that represents individual students as generating knowledge out of the various sources of information that come from their own direct experience. The differences in labels serve to differentiate how one strategy may take account of the student's distinctive learning style (e.g., "imaginative," "analytic," "common sense," and "dynamic learning") while another strategy may stress individual accountability, team rewards, and equal opportunities for success—which are the stated goals of one cooperative learning model.

Differences in the interpretation and means of legitimating the core set of assumptions that underlie the educator's individually-centered view of intelligence can be seen in Constance Kazuko Kamii's understanding of the constructivist approach to learning, and in John T. Breur's arguments for an approach to science education that takes account of how students' thought processes are identical to the problem solving characteristics of computers. In a publication sponsored by the National Education Association, *Early Literacy: A Constructivist Foundation for Whole Language* (1991) Kamii writes that "constructivism shows . . . that children acquire knowledge not by internalizing it from the outside but by constructing it from the inside, in interaction with the environment . . . Just as they learn to speak without a single lesson," she continues, "children construct their own knowledge of physics, astronomy, meteorology, biology, geology, and social institutions before going to school" (p. 18). In an earlier book, *Young Children Reinvent Arithmetic* (1985), she frames the view of the child as a constructor of knowledge in terms of the basic human need for autonomy:

> Autonomy means being governed by oneself. It is the opposite of heteronomy, which means being governed by someone else. Autonomy has a moral aspect and an intellectual one . . . As in the moral domain, intellectual autonomy also means being governed by oneself and making decisions for oneself. While moral autonomy involves questions of right or wrong, intellectual autonomy involves questions of true or false. Heteronomy in the intellectual realm means merely following somebody else's view. (pp. 40, 45)

Although she suggests that autonomous judgments must always take into account "relevant factors," such as the view of others, the final determination of what is relevant rests with the subjective judgment of the individual.

As a co-director of a learning research center at the University of Pittsburgh, and founder of the Cognitive Studies for Educational

Practices program, John Breur starts from the cognitive science model of Alan Newell and Herbert Simon, and arrives at essentially the same subjectivist position that Kamii states with such succinctness and certainty. Quoting Newell and Simon's 1972 statement that "the programmed computer and human problem solver are both species of the genus IPS" Breur further validates the mind-as-like-a-computer metaphor by stating that "both are species of the genus information-processing system; both are devices for processing symbols" (1993, p. 2). Thus, for both humans and machines, thinking is essentially a problem solving activity that depends upon "facts, skills, and strategies" unique to the domain within which the problem exists. The educational task of helping students progress from being novice problem solvers to becoming experts, according to Breur, requires that teachers "understand children's theories and concepts and build effective instruction on them—instruction that helps students map their informal understanding of how the world works on to the formal scientific theories they encounter in school" (p. 139). The recommendation that students' experience be the basis upon which formal instruction is mapped on to sounds inconsistent with the computer image of the student's thought process until one takes account of Breur's view that the implicit understandings that characterize most direct experience take the form, when made explicit, of data and information—and that what separates the novice from the expert problem solver is the ability to organize data and information into a problem solving procedure that can be modelled and tested.

As suggested earlier, the growing interest in Howard Gardner's theory of multiple intelligences represents, in one sense, a challenge to the prevailing orthodoxy that represents intelligence as an attribute of the autonomous individual. But his theory can also be seen as simply expanding the way educators understand the attributes of the individual. One interpreter of Gardner's theory, Thomas Armstrong, uses the current vocabulary of brain research to explain why each student has a particular form of intelligence. For example, the student who possesses a bodily-kinesthetic form of intelligence, according to Armstrong, has developed more in the cerebellum, basal ganglia, and motor cortex areas of the brain; the student with an interpersonal form of intelligence has a more developed frontal lobe, parietal lobe, and limbic system. The other five forms of intelligence are also explained in terms of specific areas of brain development (1992, p. 3).

The identification of seven forms of intelligence—linguistic, logical-mathematical, spatial, bodily-kinesthetic, musical, interpersonal, and intrapersonal—has given the educator's traditional concern with fitting teaching and curriculum to individual differences and needs both a new sense of specificity and scientific legitimation that was lacking in the past. Unfortunately, the professional tendency to turn a theory predicated on a set of culturally specific assumptions into a formulaic set of classroom strategies has not been diminished by the daunting challenge of identifying correctly each student's special form of intelligence. In one school reported on by Laura Ellison, teachers and parents meet to establish the learning expectations for how each student will develop in terms of each form of intelligence. For example, in the goal setting process for one of the students it was suggested that the learning outcomes that would serve as indicators of the student's development in the area of interpersonal intelligence should include making new friends, having fun, and being relaxed. Developments in the spatial form of intelligence would be indicated by improvements in the student's watercolor skills (1992, p. 71).

Other educational interpretations of the classroom implications of Gardner's theory place even greater responsibility on the teacher to identify and document how each student progresses in terms of the seven forms of intelligence. In addition to determining each student's strengths and weaknesses in each of the seven areas, teachers must plan a curriculum that contributes to the level of development the student has attained in each form of intelligence, as well as document each student's achievement in all seven categories of intelligence. As Thomas R. Hoerr, Director of the New City School in St Louis, puts it:

> One who understands multiple intelligences would be able to identify students learning in all seven ways. For example, a 4th grade teacher assigning book reports gives the student options corresponding to the seven intelligences. A 1st grade teacher plans a unit on shoes, designing activities that use all the intelligences; she records the students' progress in each intelligence. When 5th graders design an Egyptian burial place for the front hall, the decorations and artifacts in the tomb reflect all the intelligences. In the preschool, teachers create learning centers for each intelligence and document which centers children frequent (1992, p. 68).

In effect, Gardner's theory is being utilized in ways that strengthen the tendency within the field of public education and teacher education departments to use the attributes of the student as the basis for pedagogical and curricular decisions. Gardner himself argues that "intelligences are always conceptualized and assessed in terms of their cultural manifestation in specific domains of endeavor and with reference to particular adult 'end states'." But his attempt to clarify why the assessment of intelligence in a "culture-independent way" is "elusive and perhaps impossible to achieve" (1993, pp. 67–68) is undermined by his tendency to equate culture with the everyday social experiences that influence the student's pathway of development. For example, the following account of individual assessment is predicated on treating culture as essentially the same as what is usually meant in the use of the phrase "prior social experience." In an article on the educational implications of multiple intelligences, Gardner and his co-author, Thomas Hatch, write that "our examination of bodily-kinesthetic abilities in a movement assessment for preschoolers was confounded by the fact that some 4-year-olds had already been to ballet classes, whereas others had never been asked to move their bodies expressively or in rhythm" (p. 68). While Gardner and Hatch suggest that the form of intelligence manifested by students reflect, in part, the "culturally-valued activities" that were part of their earlier experiences, they could have made essentially the same qualification by referring to socially-valued activities. This would have helped bring into focus the connection between forms of intelligence and social class and ethnic differences—which would be a useful addition to the professional concern with teaching and assessment strategies. While Gardner acknowledges that cultures involve differences in fundamental areas of how life is understood and experienced, he tends to use the word to designate the milieu that provides for different kinds of experiences that, in turn, influence the development of certain forms of the student's intelligences and not others. He does not understand culture in the deep sense of encoding the epistemic/symbolic frameworks of past generations, and as complex processes of semiosis that constitute and sustain what will be experienced as "reality." This lack of a deep understanding of culture, which is particularly evident in his interpretation of his encounter with Chinese culture in *To Open Minds* (1989) makes it easy for educators to identify a cursory assessment of the student's past social/developmental activities as being consistent with his theory.

The writings on the nature of intelligence by cognitive psychologists and cognitive scientists, while making the nature of intelligence complicated in ways that legitimate their theoretical and research paradigms, provides an overly simplistic view that serves to reinforce the widespread orthodoxy in educational circles that represents the student as a culture-free being (the latter part of this assertion is made with full awareness of the current emphasis on multicultural education—which really is little more than a tourist industry level of understanding cultural differences). The following explanations of the nature of intelligence by cognitive scientists are particularly noteworthy for the lack of any reference to the influence of culture on language and thought processes. In the book, *The Anthropic Cosmological Principle* (1988), John D. Barrow and Frank J. Tipler use the analog of a computer program to explain the nature of human intelligence:

> As we argued in earlier chapters, an intelligent being—or more generally, any living creature—is fundamentally a type of computer, and is thus subject to the limitations imposed on computers by the laws of physics. However, the really important part of a computer is not the particular hardware, but the program; we may even say that a human being is a program designed to run a particular hardware called the human body, coding its data in very special types of data storage devices called DNA molecules and nerve cells. The essence of a human being is not the body but the program which controls the body (p. 659).

Marvin Minsky is even more direct about the mind/machine connection. "Our conscious thoughts," he writes in *The Society of Mind* (1988), "use signal-signs to steer the engines in our minds, controlling countless processes of which we'er never much aware. Not understanding how it's done," he continues, "we learn to gain our ends by sending signals to those great machines, much as the sorcerers of older times used rituals to cast their spells" (p. 56). Another prominent thinker within the field of cognitive science, Herbert A. Simon provides a somewhat less mechanistic though equally culture-free view of intelligence. The following explanation appeared in an article on the "Foundations of Cognitive Science" which he co-authored with Craig A. Kaplan:

> We say that people are behaving intelligently when they choose courses of action that are relevant to achieving their goals, when they reply coherently and appropriately to questions that

are put to them, when they solve problems of lesser or greater difficulty, or when they create or design something useful or beautiful or novel. We apply a single term, "intelligence," to this diverse set of activities because we expect that a common set of underlying processes is implicated in performing all of them (1989, p. 1).

For readers who think these definitions of intelligence are too mechanistic to be taken seriously by educators they might find the following explanation in a widely used educational psychology textbook especially provocative, if not alarming. After presenting readers (mainly students in teacher education programs) an account of the differences between how behaviorists and cognitive psychologists view the process of learning, the author, Anita E. Woolfolk, provides as a third interpretation the cognitive scientist's information processing model of learning. Without any critical commentary, the following is presented as a viable way of understanding human intelligence—including how learning occurs:

> The information processing approach relies on the computer as a model for human learning. Like the computer, the human mind takes in information, performs operations on it to change its form and content, stores the information, retrieves it when needed, and generates responses to it. Thus processing involves gathering and representing information, or *encoding;* holding information, or *storage;* and getting at the information when needed, or *retrieval.* The whole process is controlled by "programs" that determine how and when information will flow though the system (1993, p. 241).

W. K. Estes summarized a fundamental problem within the field of psychology that continues to plague how educators understand one of the most important processes they attempt to influence. "The view of intelligence as a measurable trait or aspect of the individual," he observed in a collection of essays on the nature of intelligence, "seems to have changed little in either content or breadth of acceptance from the time of Binet to the present" (1986, p. 63). Of all the psychologists who might have rescued how intelligence is understood from the deeply held cultural metaphors (freedom, rationality, progress, conscience, etc.) that make sense only within a conceptual framework that posits the individual as the primary reference point,

Robert J. Sternberg seemed by virtue of the breadth of his knowledge of his field as well as his productivity as a published scholar to hold out the greatest promise. He also has been a leader in focusing attention within the literature on the need to clarify and refine how intelligence is understood by both psychologists and educators. His book, *Metaphors of Mind: Conceptions of the Nature of Intelligence* (1990), demonstrates a keen understanding that the working definitions of intelligence used to guide research are based on metaphorical constructions, as well as an awareness of recent attempts by scholars on the periphery of the field of psychology to develop more culturally sensitive ways of understanding intelligence.

In fact, he often includes in his books of collected essays the views of psychologists who argue, in essence, that the dominant view of intelligence is culture-bound. For example, J. W. Berry's chapter on "A Cross-Cultural View of Intelligence," which appeared in the book, *What Is Intelligence?*, edited by Sternberg and Douglas K. Detterman, contains a summary of the double bind that mainstream psychologists have not yet acknowledged. Citing research he published in the early seventies, Berry reminds readers that he "argued for a position of 'radical cultural relativism' with respect to the construct of intelligence. As psychologists we should admit that we do not know in any absolute or a priori sense what intelligence is in other cultures, and until we do," he cautions, "we should not use *our* construct to describe their cognitive competencies, nor our *tests* to measure *them*" (p. 36).

Yet Sternberg himself continues to elaborate on what he has termed a triarchic theory of human intelligence. His theory not only retains the tradition of treating intelligence as an attribute of the individual but also incorporates the mechanistic language of the cognitive scientists. Again, it is important to note the areas of silence in the following explanation:

> The triarchic theory of human intelligence . . . seeks to explain in an integrative way the relationship between (1) intelligence and the internal world of the individual, or the mental mechanisms that underlie intelligent behavior; (2) intelligence and the external world of the individual, or the use of these mental mechanisms in everyday life in order to attain an intelligent fit to the environment; and (3) intelligence and experience, or the mediating role of one's passage though life between the internal and external worlds of the individual. (1990, p. 268)

Neither this view of intelligence nor his reference to intelligence as a form of mental self-government (1990 b, p. 20) are likely to influence educators to engage in any radical rethinking of their own interpretations of intelligence. Nor will Howard Gardner's proposals for "individually-centered schools" help to recast the discussion of educational reform in ways that take account of the complex connections that are part of the nesting hierarchy of individuals/culture/ ecosystems. A careful reading of Gardner's arguments for individually-centered schools, an idea strengthened by his personal frustration with what he regarded as the obsession of the Chinese with the need for control and authority structures, demonstrates again how the fixation on the individual, even when expanded to account for multiple intelligences, leads to educational reform proposals that are nearly identical to what progressive educators have been advocating for decades. The following quotation by Gardner, whom educators now regard as the principal source of scientific legitimation for their ideas about innovative classroom practices, will set the stage for examining more closely the cultural assumptions taken for granted by educators and the country's leading cognitive psychologists and scientists. Writes Gardner:

> The individual-centered school is based on two assumptions. First of all, not all individuals have the same mental abilities and profiles, any more than they are identical in appearance or in personality. Second of all, since there is much more to learn than there is time for learning, it is essential to make choices of what to learn and how to learn it. An individual-centered school takes these differences seriously and offers curricula, assessment procedures, and educational options responsive to each of the students in its charge. (1989, p. 294)

For many readers, the views of intelligence of Sternberg, Gardner and even Simon (I'm not sure how many readers would be comfortable with the extreme mechanistic formulations of Minsky, Barron and Tipler) may have seemed perfectly sound. I also suspect many readers may have felt a sense of irritation with what up until now has been my way of implying that the ideas underlying the constructivist psychology upon which the Integrative Curriculum, Cooperative Learning, and other recent educational innovations are predicated are deeply problematic. This sense of unease with the direction this analysis is heading relates directly to Capra's metaphor of systems within systems. The explanations of intelligence by psychologists and the teaching and learning strategies advocated by educators appear as issues within self-contained conceptual frameworks (discourses) only because both the theorists (Sternberg, Gardner, Kamii, Clark, etc.) and reader share at a taken for granted level a deeper symbolic framework of guiding assumptions. Indeed, if non-Westernized Chinese or Australian Aborigines were to read what the psychologists and educators quoted above had to say about the nature of intelligence, their profoundly different deep cultural assumptions would lead them to find the explanations quite baffling.

The deeper (and more unconsciously held) cultural assumptions that help constitute the taken for granted attitude toward the discussions of intelligence and classroom practices as being adequately self-contained (indeed, ideas that seem self-evident when they are made explicit) must now be addressed. These assumptions, or what might be referred to as metaphorical constructions, are sustained (and modified) over generations as the material/symbolic forms of culture built on these assumptions continue as part of everyday experience. The context-free nature of the international style of architecture in vogue until recently, the ubiquitous computer, and the shopping mall are just a few examples of material/symbolic culture that reproduce the culture's deepest held assumptions. Depending upon the person's cultural background, encounters with these expressions of culture will largely be experienced as part of a taken for granted world—or experienced as a source of initial disorientation. These examples of material/symbolic culture, it should be emphasized, both express and reinforce through their own patterns of semiosis the same cultural assumptions that the individually-centered views of intelligence and constructivist educational practices are based on. To make this point more directly, the view of intelligence as an attribute of the individual, as well as the educational practices predicated on it, reinforce the same deep cultural assumptions that lead us to view every technological innovation as the expression of progress, and to mistakenly interpret the visual sensation of the plenitude of shopping malls as validating the ideal of individual freedom rather than as a metaphor of a culture that is destroying the chances of future generations to live in balance with the Earth's ecosystems. The experience constituted by these cultural patterns, in turn, helps to make the theories of the cognitive psychologists and the classroom practices advocated by educators appear as common sense approaches to becoming an even more progressive society. To restate Capra's point, everything is connected; but it is the embedded nature of our cultural beliefs and practices within deeper symbolic constructions that makes the connections so difficult to recognize.

I have already alluded to several of the deep cultural assumptions essential to an individually-centered view of intelligence. These include representing the individual as the primary social unit, associating intelligence with processes occurring within the brain (mind) of the individual, and change as inherently progressive. The shift by cognitive psychologists and cognitive scientists from measuring intelligence in quantifiable terms to studying the process of intelligent behavior in various problem solving settings indicates the influence of other deeply held cultural assumptions. These include the assumption that mental processes, techniques, and procedures are what need to be understood, and that there is no privileged body of knowledge or values essential to the educated person. This point can be more easily recognized if we examine the above statements of psychologists and educators for references to what children should learn from the elders of the culture or from mentors who have made outstanding contributions to raising the quality of life.

Both the cultural emphasis on individualism (expressed in terms of the concern with individual differences, freedom, equality, empowerment, expertise, etc.) and problem solving techniques only make sense because of the deeper assumptions about the connections between a linear sense of time, change, and progress. Without the cultural belief that represents progress as ontologically guaranteed, the individually-centered view of intelligence would receive serious scrutiny indeed. The unthinking acceptance of the cultural meta-narratives that explain the progressive nature of nearly all forms of change (in ideas, values, technologies, etc.) allows educators to perpetuate the collective illusion that the content of the curriculum should be determined by the personal interests and preferred learning style (and mood) of the student. The examples given by Laura Ellison and Thomas Hoerr of what students learned in classrooms organized around the principle of multiple intelligences are evidence of the curricular relativism that now characterizes the current expression of progressive/constructivist thinking in education.

What Launa Ellison represents as significant learning might be better understood as an exercise of fitting everyday experiences into one of the seven categories of intelligence that the curriculum is supposed to take into account. The blurring of the difference between learning and individual experience, which has been promoted by progressive educators for decades, leaves many elementary teachers unable to recognize how they might differ—even at the first grade level. Would walking through a shopping mall be equally valuable to stimulating and developing students' spatial intelligence as improving their water color skills? Would the experience of feeling good about oneself as a member of a powerful and widely feared street gang develop the intrapersonal form of intelligence as well as learning to "feel good about school" (which Ellison identifies as a significant form of learning)? The everyday quality of what she sees as significant learning raises the question of whether the lack of real foundational knowledge, including significant mentoring relationships, would leave students stunted in their ability to develop fully whatever special potential they might have.

Knowledge relevant to one of the many forms of intelligence, disciplined practice, and testing one's own development against evolving and relevant standards in a special field of endeavor (e.g., sports, dance, poetry writing, musical performance, etc.) are essential aspects of Gardner's understanding of creativity, and of the role creativity plays in the development of the different forms of intelligence. The following statement by Gardner suggests a significant gulf between his understanding of development (which always involves some degree of creativity) and what appears increasingly as a 1940s life-adjustment type curriculum that some of his followers are now legitimating in the name of his theory. According to Gardner:

> it makes more sense to locate creativity at the juncture of an individual mind and its talents, working on projects that exist within an intellectual or artistic domain, and being judged ultimately by a field of competent individuals. (1989, p. 116)

Gardner himself would be the first to acknowledge that not all the forms of intelligence or, for that matter, every educational experience should be judged on the basis of meeting these criteria. But whether the curricular goals cited by Ellsion would be adequate for the discovery and genuine development of latent talents possessed by students is problematic indeed.

Thomas Hoerr's examples of learning about shoes and Egyptian burial practices, as well as Kamii's argument that "learners do not acquire knowledge that is transmitted to them; rather they construct knowledge through their intellectual activity and make it their own" (p. 11), leads to other questions about the deep cultural assumptions that now make these examples of curricular relativism appear as a new and more progressive development within the field of education. The most obvious question raised by Hoerr's examples of multi-intelligences curricula is whether they can be justified as more important than other topics teachers can imagine. Why is learning about shoes important (especially when most people grow into successful adults without having been exposed to a lesson on shoes)? Would a lesson on eyeglasses or hats be any less educationally significant? And why the need to learn about Egyptian burial practices in ways that will develop students' potential in seven areas of intelligence? Wouldn't learning about the forms of shelters built by the aboriginal peoples of Patagonia be as educationally significant? But I suspect that the larger questions about why one form of knowledge or learning experience is more important than others seem totally irrelevant to most teachers who are now faced with the daunting challenge of developing curriculum that nurtures each student's unique learning style and form of intelligence, and who must take on the additional burden of documenting each student's development. Excusing teachers now marching to the drum beat of Gardner and his many interpreters as being too overly burdened to give serious thought to their curriculum decisions would, in part, divert responsibility from the more fundamental cultural values contributing to the problem of relativism.

The constructivist theory of learning articulated by Kamii, as well as the goal of the critical thinking movement which Richard W. Paul of the Center for Critical Thinking and Moral Critique at Sonoma State University summed up in the statement that eduation "is a process of *autonomously* deciding what is and what is not true or false" (1987, p. 143, italics added) have been germinating in the seedbed of Western cultural assumptions long before Dewey, Piaget, Papert, and Gardner, among others, explained how we should think about the connections between knowledge and the direct experience of the student. Today, if the dominant cultural way of understanding tradition was the same as in the time of the Roman Empire, the arguments that "children progress from heteronomous dependence upon adults to increasing independence and autonomy," and that "each of us has to construct our own version of reality," to recall Alan C. Kay's statement, would be viewed as totally absurd. The constructivist position is predicated on a different view of tradition: namely, the Enlightenment interpretation that represented tradition as the outmoded knowledge and patterns of the past that now stand in the way of progress. To Enlightenment thinkers, as well as modern educators who are still rooted in what Edward Shils refers to as this "anti-tradition tradition," tradition threatens the emancipatory potential of both critically and instrumentally rational thought, and is thus the enemy of progress. The cultural shift from locating authority in proven (and often problematic) traditions to locating it in the direct experience, reflective processes, and later, the emotive state of the individual preceded the emergence of the constuctivist theory of learning (in all its varied modes of expression) now being embraced by educators as a new and especially insightful way of understanding how children learn. In effect, the changes in the deep cultural assumption that were part of the transition from a premodern to modern form consciousness were encoded in the multilayered metaphorical language of learning theorists and educational audiences, leading them to interpret the constructivist prescriptions as the inevitable next step in evolving an even more progressive way of understanding. More important to our discussion is that the deep cultural orientation of locating authority in the mental/experiential processes occurring within the individual is a fundamental cause of the spread of the relativism (nihilism?) that makes whatever teachers put into the curriculum equally important. The constructivist theorists and classroom teachers are simply utilizing (or are they being conditioned by it?) another deep cultural orientation to legitimate the idea that students construct their own ideas and that they learn more effectively when the curriculum corresponds to their own subjective interests and sense of relevant experience. Given this bedrock cultural premise, there is no rationally, morally, or politically correct alternative to the relativist position of educators.

As the more important task here is to clarify the deep cultural patterns of thought and behavior that are ecologically sustainable, and the form of education that will help constitute these cultural patterns as part of the student's taken-for-granted sense of reality, it is essential that one other characteristic of the individually-centered view of intelligence be addressed. The differences between Gardner's theory of multiple intelligences and Simon and Sternberg's slight variations on the mechanistic nature of mental processes are inconsequential when it is recognized that all three theorists take for granted the dominant culture's anthropocentric way of understanding human relationships with the natural environment. To make this point more simply, the mainstream psychological theories of learning, and the educational practices predicated upon them, exist in a circular relationship with an anthropocentric view of the world: the cultural meta-narratives that originally constituted and continue to sustain the privileging of humans as separate form the rest of the biosphere (and as existing in an instrumental relationship with it) provides the conceptual framework and language that continues to foreground the primacy of the individual. The psychological theories and educational practices, in turn, reinforce the more contemporary reformulations of the meta-narratives—even as the evidence mounts that science and technology cannot provide substitutes for natural systems poisoned by toxic wastes and exploited beyond sustainable limits. The deep assumptions about the progressive nature of change and the authority of individual experience and intelligence are both dependent upon the myth of the anthropocentric universe and, in turn, serve to sustain it. These connections can best be described in terms of the metaphor suggested by Bateson:

> there is an ecology of bad ideas, just as there is an ecology of weeds, and it is characteristic of the system that basic error propagates itself. It branches out like a rooted parasite through the tissues of life, and everything gets in a rather peculiar mess. When you narrow down your epistemology and act on the premise 'What interests me is me, my organization, or my species,' you chop off consideration of other loops of the loop structure. You decide that you want to get rid of the by-products of human life and that Lake Erie will be a good place to put them. You forget that the eco-mental system called Lake Erie is part of *your* wider eco-mental system—and that if Lake Erie is driven insane, its insanity is incorporated in the larger system of *your* thought and experience. 1972, p. 484

This is a good place, given Bateson's warning about an ecology of bad ideas, to change the focus of discussion from what is an intellectually and ecologically problematic view of intelligence to one that takes account of the culture/language/thought connection and, at the same time, is more ecologically viable in the sense of a cultural system nesting in a more sustainable relationship with natural systems.

AN ECOLOGICAL/CULTURAL VIEW OF INTELLIGENCE AND ITS EDUCATIONAL IMPLICATIONS

There are several basic questions that need to be asked: What motivates psychologists to study the nature of intelligence? Are educators who utilize a theory of intelligence motivated by similar rationally stated justifications and values? When an earlier generation of psychologists were obsessed with adjusting their definitions of intelligence to what mathematical models and testing instruments were able to measure, the answer was as clear as it was politically and morally problematic. Measuring intelligence was then seen as essential to fitting people into the right work careers and social class. Today, psychologists such as Sternberg and Gardner would probably explain their motivations, aside from the usual justifications dictated by a chosen career path, in terms of helping other people achieve their fullest potential, contributing to the efficacy of other professionals who deal with educational and personal crisis management in all its modern forms, and finally, to the advancement of knowledge in ways that insure human progress. These are pretty standard motivations, particularly in the academic world. Educators like the ones quoted earlier would use a slightly different vocabulary to give similar reasons for wanting to understand the nature of intelligence; but their use of legitimating metaphors would include, in addition to words like "empowerment," "optimal learning," "self-realization," other terms like "motivate" and "control." For the person who takes seriously Michel Foucault's insight that knowledge is always connected to some form of disciplinary practice that acts on the body, mind, self-identity, and relationships with the Other, it is difficult to accept justifications framed primarily in terms of uplifting humanity and insuring the continuation of social progress. Regardless of the form the answer to the above question takes (e.g., as optimizing learning, developing the distinctive form of intelligence of the student, contributing to more efficacious "mental self-government," helping to build more powerful computers, etc.) it is always framed in terms of improving the well-being of humans.

My reasons for spending long hours reading the writings of psychologists and educators, and writing chapter after chapter, involve an entirely different set of motivations. The fundamental issue today is not the modern idea of progress, but the challenge of changing educational/cultural practices that violate the ecological Golden Rule that Durning articulated so clearly. As all the theorists and educational practitioners cited earlier (Minsky, Sternberg, Kamii, and so forth) use the metaphor of "progress" to justify a wide range of disciplinary practices, it is important to recognize that the cultural form of progress they take for granted does not make sense in terms of ecological systems. Scientific studies of ecosystems, as well as our own direct bodily experiences with the effects of toxins in the air, water, and soil, make it increasingly clear that the dominant cultural view of progress cannot be separated from the condition of the ecosystems we are dependent upon. Metaphorically constituted images of human progress and empowerment cannot protect us from the consequences of a degraded environment—as the people in the Maritime Provinces of Canada are now discovering as a result of over fishing what seemed to be an inexhaustible resource, and the people living along the lower Mississippi and the Mexican/American border are learning about the connections between the toxic by-products of other forms of progress and myriad forms of cancer and birth defects. The bottom line, as Bateson tirelessly reminded us, is "the unit of survival is not the breeding organism, or the family, or society . . . The unit of survival is a flexible organism-in-its-environment" (1972, p. 450).

A second source of motivation has to do with the archaic conceptual boundaries that lead cognitive psychologists like Sternberg and Gardner to frame the nature of intelligence in such a limited way. The areas of cultural anthropology, social linguistics, sociology of knowledge, semiotics, and political/cultural ideologies all deal with different aspects of intelligence. The list could be extended to include cultural geography, music, architecture, mathematics, and so on. While the vocabularies of each domain of inquiry are often distinct, each area is concerned with patterns of human intelligence and behavior—including solving problems, experiencing meaning, communicating and negotiating with others their individual/ cultural perspectives on reality, creating and using technologies, and so forth. All of these activities involve various forms of intelligence that are interactive with each other: the intentional intelligence of the subject or knower, the tacit (taken for granted) forms of knowing largely acquired from the person's cultural group, and forms of intelligence encoded and embodied in the material/symbolic culture of buildings, technologies, songs, narratives, and so forth. With electronic technologies now providing access to different forms of cultural intelligence around the world, as well as the vast accumulation of theoretical and research-based knowledge in these more culturally-oriented disciplines, one can only wonder why mainstream psychologists (including the subfield of cognitive science that now threatens to cannibalize its parent) and education continue to base their theories and applied techniques on the metaphorical image of a culture -free individual.

Given these two motivations, which I see as connected, I shall first address how intelligence can be more accurately represented as essentially cultural in nature. We shall then move on to consider the ecological view of intelligence articulated by Gregory Bateson, Humberto Maturana and Fancisco Varela; and then return to the challenge of articulating an educational/cultural view of intelligence that takes account of the problem of living in a sustainable relationship with the rest of the biotic community.

Intelligence as a Cultural Phenomena

The current view of intelligence that represents the mind as processing information and the raw data of direct experience, and as utilizing different bodily and mental attributes to express the other six forms of intelligence, is based on a superficial understanding of culture. When culture is referred to, it is primarily as a context that influences what forms of intelligence are valued. But the more complex sources of influence on intelligence are ignored. This is surprising because the seminal writings and field research of Edward Sapir and Benjamin Lee Whorf have been available since the nineteen twenties and thirties; and the English translation of Lev Semenovich Vygostky's book, *Thought and Language,* appeared in 1962. Using field work with a variety of cultural groups, they argued that the individual's thought process is highly influenced by the conceptual categories shared and communicated through the languages of the culture of which the individual is a member. In the essay, "The Status of Linguistics as a Science" (published in 1929), Sapir entirely decenters the autonomy of individual intelligence. "Language, " he wrote, "is a guide to social reality . . . The fact of the matter is that the 'real world' is to a large extent unconsciously built on the language habits of the group." He then went on to explain that there are multiple realities, and thus multiple forms of intelligence. As he put it: "the worlds in which different societies live are distinct worlds, not merely the same world with different labels" (1949, pp. 68–69).

Whorf was even more emphatic about the influence of culture, through its language systems, on the mental processes of the individual. He directly challenged what he saw as the misconception sustaining the individually-centered view of intelligence of his day in the following way:

> Formation of ideas is not an independent process, strictly rational in the old sense, but is part of a particular grammar, and differs, from slightly to greatly, between different grammars. We dissect nature along lines laid down by our native languages. The categories and types that we isolate form the world of phenomena we do not find there because they stare every observer in the face; on the contrary the world is presented in a

kaleidoscopic flux of impressions which have to be organized by our minds—and this means largely by the linguistic systems in our minds. We cut nature up, organize it into concepts, and ascribe significances as we do, largely because we are parties to an agreement to organize it in this way—an agreement that holds throughout our speech community and is codified in the patterns of our language. The agreement is, of course, an implicit and unstated one, *but its terms are absolutely obligatory;* we cannot talk at all except by subscribing to the organization and classification of data which the agreement decrees. (1968, pp. 324–325)

During his highly productive years with the Pedagogical Institute in Moscow (1924–34), Vygotsky's research and writings reaffirmed the basic insights of Sapir—whose influence he acknowledged. He avoided the extremes of subjectivism and behaviorism by arguing that "thought is not merely expressed in words; it comes into existence through them, every thought tends to connect something with something else, to establish a relationship between things" (1962, p. 125). That is, the language acquired as a condition of becoming a member of a speech community (culture or subculture) encodes how other members think about and experience the constantly changing web of relationships that characterize everyday life. A contemporary example of this shared encoding process can be found in how Sternberg, Gardner, and the others organize and express their thoughts in terms of the subject, verb, object pattern shared by other members of their language community. This linguistic/cultural pattern not only organizes how the subject is represented as relating to and acting on the rest of the world, it also influences the patterns of experience. "I am talking to John," "Our conscious thoughts . . . steer the engines in our mind," and "The pioneers settled and tamed the wilderness" provide information about relationships, but they are relationships where the subject is acting on what is represented as a passive and fixed world. The Japanese linguist, Yoshihiko Ikegami, provides another example of how cultural ways of knowing are reflected in the language patterns. In commenting on the differences between an English translation of the last lines ("tazu naki wataru") of a Japanese poem as "the cranes go crying," and how a Japanese would understand it, he observes that "the English translation focuses on the cranes as they undergo a change in locus; the Japanese expression concentrates on the change in the state of the whole scene, of which the cranes constitutes only a part" (1991, p. 287). As this example suggests, the linguistic/cultural differences represent different mind-sets, or forms of intelligence. And it would be incorrect to say that the cultural form of intelligence is chosen by individuals who supposedly are in control of their own mental self-government—to recall Sternberg's metaphor.

This point takes us further in understanding a problem we shall address later: namely, how a cultural form of intelligence can be based on ways of understanding cultural/environmental relationships that are not sustainable—and thus how the form of cultural intelligence encoded in the language (that thinks individuals as they think and act within the language) may contribute to being stupid. The dictionary definition of stupid includes "lacking in understanding," "in a state of stupor," "crassly foolish," "a dazed state of mind." In ecological terms being stupid means relying on patterns of thought and behavior that contribute to the destruction of natural systems upon which human life depends. Later, we shall return to consider how the curriculum of the schools and the ideology of educators are contributing to a form of intelligence that leads to stupid behavior in an ecological sense. The task now is to identify briefly other examples of the cultural nature of intelligence. The widespread examples of culturally different ways of knowing, the increased communication across disciplines that are more sensitive to the deep influence of culture, and the high priority given to multicultural education raise the question of why a more cultural approach to understanding intelligence has not become a central concern of cognitive psychologists and educators. Part of the answer may be found in the constitutive role that language plays—which we shall shortly examine. That is, the metaphorical language that sustains the subculture of academic psychology (as in the case of all metaphors that illuminate and hide at the same time) illuminates by foregrounding the individual, and hides by not naming the dimensions of experience that cannot be reconciled with the image of internal mental processes and feelings—namely, culture.

Cultural differences in forms of intelligence have been widely reported and studied. However, before identifying the more typical examples that come from the field work of anthropologists and linguists, examples of cultural differences in intelligence can be found closer to home. Minsky's use of language and way of thinking of the mind as a computational machine, for example, suggests that he is part of a distinct subculture. The members of this subculture, which would include cognitive scientists working in the area of artificial intelligence, possess a qualitatively different form of intelligence than we would find expressed in the thought processes of an anthropologist like Clifford Geertz or social linguist like Whorf. Certain relationships and patterns in life would simply not be understandable to Minsky; and Geertz and Whorf would undoubtedly have difficulty making sense of relationships that Minsky would take for granted.

By shifting the focus to more traditional examples of cultural differences, we find nearly as many forms of intelligence, and ways of expressing it, as we find cultural languages. In order to illuminate these differences in a way that helps us at the same time to recognize the characteristics of the mind-set of a very powerful subculture group in our society, it will be useful to identify what Alvin Gouldner refers to as the cultural grammar that largely dictates how intelligence is understood and expressed by Western intellectuals, theorists, and technocrats. According to Gouldner, the cultural grammar that separates the intelligent individual from the unintelligent and culturally backward is predicated on strict adherence to the following: "an historically evolved set of rules, a grammar of discourse which (1) is concerned to *justify* its assertions, but (2) whose *mode* of justification does not proceed by invoking authorities, and (3) prefers to elicit the voluntary consent of those addressed solely on the basis of the arguments presented." Gouldner goes on to observe that the culture of critical discourse is characterized by "speech that is *relatively* more situation-free, more context or field 'independent'." Furthermore, the individual exhibiting this form of intelligence puts more value on abstract definitions that can be generalized across cultural boundaries, and "devalues tacit, context-limited meanings." This cultural/thought process also involves the de-authorization of "all speech grounded in traditional societal authority" such as community elders, sacred texts, traditional beliefs and practices that have been relied on by the community for generations—even centuries (1979, pp. 28–29). This cultural grammar (guiding assumptions), which both helps to organize the thoughts of Sternberg and Gardner as well as influences their patterns of communication, is fundamentally different from that of the Micronesian navigator whose test of intelligence and mode of learning is in whether his outrigger canoe reaches a landfall. It is also different in other ways from the cosmology of the aboriginal tribal cultures of Australia mentioned in the earlier chapter on moral education. Summing up essential characteristics of how they understand the world and their place in it, Lawlor notes that:

Each Aborigine knows his country as he knows himself, through his own body and the internalized images of his dreaming places—these *are* his identity. There is no Aboriginal story that does not make reference to places, and land formations are never discussed without reference to their mythological stories . . . (in the Aboriginal way of understanding and being) there is no standard progression in species; each creature perceives a facet of the world and all together they cause the fullness of the world to come into existence. The wonders of the world are not reducible to human intelligence. For the Aborigines, the joy of life is to enter into the spiritual intelligence of all species and to share in life's diversity through the unique intelligence of each of its creatures. (1991, pp. 237, 308)

If further examples are needed to make the point that a culture's cosmology, including the meta-narratives that give rise to its distinctive categories of thought, influence both the nature and form of expression of its members' intelligence, we could go back to the Scollon/Hanson discussion of how an emphasis on the use either of count or mass nouns influences how relationships, events, and objects are understood. We could also cite Robin Horton's study of the different approaches to science in Western cultures and traditional cultures in Africa, as well as the numerous studies of the aboriginal cultures of North and South America. Indeed, the evidence of profound differences in what might be called cultural epistemologies is becoming increasingly difficult to ignore, especially now that members of previously marginalized cultural groups are publishing more articles and books. There is yet another way to clarify how culture influences the form of intelligence exhibited by the individual; namely, the role the languages of a culture play in constituting and sustaining a shared intersubjective reality that enables its members to understand and respond intelligently to each other's use of a shared symbol (i.e., metaphorical) system.

As a number of scholars have already written extensively on the metaphorical nature of the language/thought connection (Friedrich Nietzsche, Donald Schon, Michael Reddy, George Lakoff, Mark Johnson, among others), I shall summarize only those points that seem essential to clarifying how intelligence can be understood as encoded in the formative and problem-solving process of analogic thinking, and how this encoding process provides the schemata of understanding that become integral to the individual's intelligence. As Nietzsche pointed out in the latter part of the nineteenth century, "in our thought the essential feature is fitting the new material into old schemas . . . making equal what is new" (1968, p. 273). That is, in not being able to understand on its own terms what is totally new to us, we are forced to utilize past experience, and thus what is already familiar to us, as the initial basis of understanding what would otherwise remain incomprehensible. Our past experience thus provides the analog that enables us to grasp the familiar in the new experience, and to expand on our understanding. This process retains elements of the familiar analog, as well as the language used to represent it, until a more suitable metaphorical framework is found. In effect, to understand the new involves thinking of it "as if" it were like something else (the already familiar). The "New World," "Indians," "wilderness," as well as the names given to the features of the land, were expressions of analogic thinking where the old (familiar) schemata were mapped onto the new. Even developments in the supposedly culture free inquiry process we know as science were dependent upon the use of analogic thinking (e.g., understanding the nature of the atom, energy, DNA , autopoiesis, intelligence, etc.).

Having built their theories of intelligence on the metaphorical image of the individual as essentially self-directing, Sternberg, Gardner, as well as the educational interpreters of the cognitivist position, can maintain the conceptual coherence of their theories only by continuing to represent the individual as choosing the analog that will provide the model or example that serves as the initial scaffold of understanding. Indeed, there is an element of choice, but only in some instances and within a narrow range of possibilities that are largely dictated by the root metaphors of the culture—which individuals do not choose unless they are aware that the explanatory power of existing root metaphors is being eroded by events and changes in other areas of understanding. These individuals are rare, and their choice of new root metaphors, such as Taoism or the cosmology of another cultural group, often is guided by adherence to elements of the old root metaphor they are attempting to escape. Even now as we are witnessing the dominant root metaphor that represents the world as a machine being challenged by theoretical physicists, Deep Ecologists, and feminists, among others, the cognitive psychologists and educators continue to sustain this now archaic root metaphor through their explanations of how human thinking occurs. It is the shared and taken for granted nature of this root metaphor rather than coincidence that leads Seymour Papert to state that "when knowledge can be broken into 'mind-size bites,' it is more communicable, more assimilable, more simply constructable" (1980, p. 171), and Sternberg to refer to the process of thinking as "mental mechanisms." Although it may surprise liberal educators like Kamii and Paul who make individual autonomy the goal of education, their metaphorical image of the individual has its roots in the thinking of the philosophers who helped to establish the mechanistic view of the world. While they may not use metaphors that suggest machine-like characteristics, as is the proclivity of some psychologists, the notion of autonomy only makes sense in terms of the machine root metaphor where each part can be viewed as a separate entity.

Other examples of cultural root metaphors that influence the language/thought process can easily be cited: the anthropocentric view of the world that still leads to statements about "our natural resources," and "the land had no value to us"; the patriarchal/masculine-centered world where the masculine pronoun is used to designate human activity, as well as the language of social relationships and property rights that privileged male authority; the ecological model that represents everything as interconnected in the flow of energy and information, and thus leads to viewing the autonomous individual as a symbolic construction based on a fundamental misunderstanding of life processes. The key point needing to be emphasized here is that the root metaphors of the culture exist prior to the individual; indeed, they are encoded in the language in which the child learns to think and speak. Children's dependency on the use of analogs that encode the deeper schemata of the culture contributes to an encoding process that will later become part of their natural attitude as adults. Gardner's self admitted frustration with the Chinese passer-by who insisted that his son, Benjamin, should be given a model of how to insert the key into the door lock, rather than experiment on his own with how to use the key (what Gardner referred to as "exploratory behavior"), is a good example of how an adult utilizes the multiple languages of socialization to reproduce as part of the child's (Benjamin's) natural attitude the dominant root metaphors of his culture (1989, p. 4). The Chinese person made sense of the situation in terms of a different root metaphor that framed differently a whole set of relationships—including the responsibility of the adult to pass on the analog (pattern) that had been proven successful over centuries as the way to put the key into the lock. Gardner wanted Benjamin to learn the power of self-discovery; that is, he wanted to reinforce his son's take for granted attitude toward one of the root metaphors underlying a modern form of consciousness.

In terms of our modern and highly syncretistic culture, the connection between deep historically grounded root metaphors and the process of analogic thinking is more complicated. The wide range of competing root metaphors that characterize modern culture (masculine vs. feminine, anthropocentric vs. ecological models, mechanistic vs. process, God-centered vs. secular and individually-centered—to identify just a few) makes it possible, even necessary in some instances, to select which root metaphor and accompanying metaphorical language will be used to think and communicate about relevant aspects of the world. But even when there is a wider linguistic and conceptual range of choices, the encoding process necessary to the formation of a particular metaphorical language continues to influence how relationships will be understood. The following statement by Paul, a leading advocate of teaching critical thinking skills, provides an excellent example of how an advocate of individual autonomy cannot himself escape the influence of the analogs encoded in the language at an earlier time in his culture's development. "Teaching critical thinking in the strong sense," writes Paul as he is being thought by the metaphorical language he uses," is teaching it so that students explicate, understand, and critique their own deepest prejudices, biases, and misconceptions, thereby allowing students to discover and contest their own egocentric and sociocentric tendencies" (1987, p. 140). Paul's statement serves as a reminder of Vygotsky's observation that "the primary word is not a straightforward symbol for a concept but rather an image, a mental sketch of a concept, a short tale about it—indeed, a small work of art" (1962, p. 75). Indeed, Paul uses many primary words: for example "teaching," "critical," "thinking," "understand," "critique," "prejudices," "discover," and so forth. These images or mental sketches, to use Vygotsky's phrase, are strung together in a way that represents a powerful set of connections. What Vygotsky refers to as images and mental sketches can also be understood as iconic metaphors that encode the analogs that prevailed over others during an earlier period of analogic thinking.

To put this another way, the earlier expression of cultural intelligence of the people who prevailed in getting prejudices associated with the irrational and mentally backward, as opposed to its earlier meaning of a predisposition that influences how a person makes sense of the world (a meaning similar to what the "intersubjective self" means today), is encoded in Paul's use of the iconic metaphor. The other words he uses in his statement, such as thinking, critique, egocentric, at some point in the past were also associated with specific analogs, and continue to reproduce these earlier expressions of metaphorical thinking (intelligence). As languages are metaphorical in the sense that they encode earlier processes of analogic thinking, and continue to evolve because of the need to revise outmoded analogs in order to take account of other changes in our symbolic and natural world, the way in which these earlier expressions of intelligence continue to empower, haunt, and restrict the possibilities of the present need to be taken into account in any discussion of individual intelligence.

It is important to recognize that what is being referred to as "cultural intelligence" is not limited to the encoding process that reproduces the root metaphors of the culture in the patterns of analogic thinking, and then in the iconic metaphors that become a taken for granted aspect of everyday thought and communication. Intelligence is also encoded (embedded, expressed—all of these terms are only partially adequate here) in other aspects of culture: the design of buildings; the way the landscape is organized in terms of the placement of buildings, roads, open spaces; the technology of computers, cars, and children's games like Nintendo; the rules and institutions that govern a system of government; the way goods are displayed on supermarket shelves and in windows; and so forth. When the question is asked within the context of culture: "What communicates?" the answer is everything. And if the question were asked about the locus of intelligence, a similar answer would be more correct than the current practice of associating it with the mental processes occurring in the head of the individual. The answer that intelligence is being expressed everywhere would also apply to the interactions between the smallest organism and the hierarchically layered systems that make up an ecosystem. The anthropocentrism in the West, with its emphasis on intelligence as essentially a human attribute, as well as the practice of treating communication as a sender-receiver process of sharing information between individuals, has contributed to a form of conscious awareness that recognizes only a limited range of communication. Spoken and written communication are readily acknowledged, but the use of the body and certain forms of advertising are more in a gray area where people's internalized cultural patterns largely dictate their responses. What is being communicated through the visual image or printed word often is seen as representing a truth about some aspect of existence or as the representation of the reality individual behavior and expectations are to conform to. When we move beyond these forms of communication, most people simply respond mentally (used here as encompassing the total sensorium of bodily feeling, awareness, conscious thought, and intentionality) to buildings, street signs, store shelves, computer printouts, air pollution, and so forth, as the givens of every day existence. But they seldom recognize at the explicit level of awareness the placement of a door (including its size and form of material), the shape of a room, as well as a less banal example of the constant electronic collection of data in areas of personal experience that range from personal travel to the use of public services and work performance, as forms of communication that encode the individual/cultural intelligence of others.

The field of semiotics, which recently has been given greater attention, helps us recognize that everything humanly created involves the use of signs organized into culturally specific codes and texts. These sign systems, organized in accordance with the guiding assumptions of the culture, communicate messages and ultimately meaning to the people who interpret them. That is, the use of a certain material, its design and use in relation to other materials and space, serve as signifiers that communicate. What they communicate are the values, ways of thinking, level of craft skill of the individuals who designed and fashioned the materials into a building. In short this constellation of signifiers communicates the current state of accumulated (dominant) knowledge, sensitivity to the aesthetic aspects of craft ability, and awareness of relationships between human activity and the natural world. The acquired symbolic framework influences such seemingly mundane choices of whether door moldings are to be made of inexpensive material and mass produced or are to be hand crafted in a way that retains the aesthetic qualities of the wood. To stay with this example, we have all been aware of the difference between a chain budget motel and the hotel built for the traveler who can afford every expression of luxury and good design— even in the door moldings made of an exotic wood. The differences between the two types of buildings are in what is being communicated; that is, the use of materials, color of walls, choice of painting, design of furniture, and so forth.

The cultural formation of the physical environment (layout of roads and walkways, the positioning of houses on the street, the design of a book cover, the use of color in a television commercial, etc.) are all expressions of the processes of semiosis that require a constant series of interpretations as to the meaning of the encoded messages. But the level of interpretation seldom is at the level of understanding how the sign system encodes the cultural traditions that influenced the intelligence, values, and level of skill of the persons who designed or constructed the object or system. The integration of technology and human routines at a franchise fast food restaurant and airline ticket desk, for example, are texts to be "read" by the customer who wishes to interact with them for desired services. In turn, the system of signs that constitute the work setting must be read by employees if they are to adapt themselves to the efficiencies (or inefficiencies) designed into the system. Part of what is communicated encodes the cultural intelligence, which includes gender, class and other determinants of identity and interpretive framework. The participants in these cultural systems also bring a mixture of culturally constituted taken for granted behaviors and attitudes, as well as more individualized responses. As everything communicates its message about relationships the processes of semiosis make the everyday world an ecology that encompasses the whole range of archaic, hidden, tacit, and explicit mental/cultural processes.

When culture is viewed from a semiotic perspective, it is even more difficult to accept the cognitive psychologists' narrowing of intelligence to the efficacy of the individual's own thought processes and other modes of expressing specific talents. What they term individual intelligence always reflects to varying degrees the patterns shared by other members of the culture. The reality constituting power of the cultural message systems, in effect, shapes the form the individual's intelligence will take. If this commonality did not exist, communication with others, including communication with the forms of intelligence encoded in the more material expressions of culture by previous generations, would be an impossibility. Learning to be intelligent within the culture's symbolic systems of communication is, in part, what leads to taking so much of the internalized cultural knowledge for granted. How many individuals, for example, view modern and postmodern architecture in their cities in terms of shifts in fundamental guiding ideologies, and how many educators look upon computers as encoding (and thus privileging) a particular form of intelligence that strengthens the position of the social class that takes for granted the rules Gouldner identified as determining who will be allowed to participate in significant discourse? What most people take for granted is not recognized as expressing the cultural/mental processes of others; rather, they experience the "factualness" and "objectivity" of a world within which they must solve problems, meet the expectations of others, and determine meaningful loyalties.

Before turning to an even more radical way of understanding

intelligence, one that needs to be integrated with the cultural view of intelligence, I would like to suggest that "intelligence" is too general a word for illuminating both the cultural and more individualized forms of expressions. The cultural evidence derived from comparative studies appears overwhelmingly to support the argument that as individuals think within the language of their culture their language thinks them. It is because of this dialectical process that it seems necessary to account for different degrees of cultural influence and the individualization of thought and intentionally expressive behavior. In suggesting three categories that can be used to account for differences in human intelligence it should be kept in mind that they are not meant to represent sharp boundaries. Rather, they are used here to designate special characteristics on a continuum that stops short of representing intelligence as an attribute of the autonomous individual. To make this last point differently, if individuals think and communicate in a culturally derived language they are cultural beings, and not the Lockean type of individuals who choose the terms upon which they will become involved with society. The three categories are *intentional* intelligence, *tacit* intelligence, and *embodied* intelligence. Again, it needs to be emphasized that these types of intelligence are never expressed in isolation from the others; but they do represent distinct differences that may be present at different moments in the ecology of cultural signifiers, codes, and the liminal conceptual space that leads to further extensions in metaphorical thinking.

The metaphor of intentional suggests that this type of intelligence involves relatively more explicit awareness, deliberate reflection, and conscious choice about mind/body expression and behavior. It also is a way of recognizing the more individualized (sometimes even creative) expressions of intelligence. Tacit intelligence is based more on the individual's natural attitude (sense of taken for grantedness) both toward the more individualized understandings that have become routinized over time and to the cultural patterns that have been unconsciously learned. Tacit intelligence always comes into play as part of the unexamined background that serves as the context for the more intentional expressions of intelligence, like when a prominent psychologist writing on an informational approach to thinking relies upon the tacitly learned cultural convention of using the masculine pronoun when referring to the subject (Posner, 1962). To change the example, the tacit knowledge of how to use the body as a cultural message system that helps frame the other person's understanding of the relationship that is to evolve through the process of communication makes possible the individual's conscious (intentional) strategy for expressing a point of view that might be easily misunderstood. The recognition that most of our intentional expressions of intelligence involve the reenactment of tacit forms of cultural knowledge helps keep in focus the pervasive influence of culture. It also helps correct misconceptions about the power of rational intelligence to escape the influence of tacit culturally derived conventions. Paul's arguments for critical thinking, for example, reflect the traditional view of tacit knowledge as an impediment to rational self-direction. "Because students have alternative beliefs and frames of reference even in the area of scientific and mathematical concepts, they need," he writes, " to confront them or they will remain implicit, unchallenged, and unreconstructed." He further warns that "if we do not provide an environment in which children can discover their own *activated* ideas, they may become and remain invincibly ignorant when it comes to putting knowledge into action" (1987, p. 137). If Paul were to recognize his own reliance on tacit knowledge (the cultural conventions of writing from left to right, using standardized spelling, viewing education as a process of emancipation, etc.) perhaps he would have been able to acknowledge that tacit knowledge, like all traditions, either can be enabling or limiting—and sometimes both at the same time.

Embodied intelligence refers more to the cultural/individualized intelligence that constructed a certain style of building, designed a keyboard for the typewriter that is still used with computers, planned the layout of houses along a street, wrote a computer software program, and so forth. More importantly, the recognition of this form of intelligence is intended to bring into the foreground what is often ignored in discussions of individual intelligence: namely, that the material/symbolic cultural environment embodies the cultural intelligence of the past that continues to act on individuals' more intentional efforts to make intelligent choices about relationships and problem solving situations. A car, for example, embodies not only the taken for granted cultural assumptions of current design teams about how to design the car so that it will be read as a text that symbolizes wealth and high status, but also the earlier forms of cultural understanding that are still encoded in the development of the technology (i.e., the continued use of metal that requires inefficient engines, and so forth). The presence of embodied intelligence is all around us, and in Foucault's sense of the power/knowledge connection, continually acts upon our actions and thought processes in ways that we are generally not aware of.

An Ecological View of Intelligence

The nesting metaphor needs to be extended to include what is obvious to everyone who has not been totally mesmerized by the power of the prevailing symbolic systems (culture) that have elevated humans as unique rational and spiritual beings—namely, the world of natural systems, or what is more generally referred to as the environment. If we nest individuals in the symbolic systems of culture, and cultures in the natural systems that are the source of the many forms of energy humans rely upon, then we have a very different way of understanding intelligence. And the different view of intelligence, what is being referred to as ecological intelligence, has profoundly different implications for how we think about education. Whereas a more cultural view of intelligence leads to a form of education sensitive to the metaphorical constructions that underlie the processes of semiosis that sustain the individual's natural attitude toward cultural patterns, an ecological view of intelligence would lead to a more inclusive approach to education. This would include understanding the basic characteristics of individual/cultural dependency upon the patterns of living systems that make up the environment, the way the cultural metaphorical constructions of the past continue to influence how we think and behave in relation to the environment, as well as addressing the moral and spiritual implications of an expanded ecological intelligence. In effect, a more inclusive form of intelligence would lead to a fundamentally different curriculum than what is now viewed as empowering an individually-centered form of intelligence.

The problem for many steeped in the traditions of psychology that continue to represent intelligence as a function of the human brain is in being able to make the radical shift necessary to recognize that "all living systems are cognitive systems," and that "living as a process is a process of cognition," as the two Chilean biologists, Humberto R. Maturana and Francisco J. Varela, put it (1980, p. 13). The quotations of Bateson cited in earlier chapters involved a slightly different language for saying essentially the same thing. Several of his more critically important insights will be repeated here in order to frame more precisely how a seemingly radical, even absurd idea, is in fact a matter of common sense when it is realized that we are using two different metaphorical frameworks for thinking about the difference between human intelligence and "living systems as cognitive system"—such as an animal's environment of signifiers that provide information about other predators, prey, weather, shelter, and standing in the group. For the reader who is encountering for the first time Bateson's understanding of mind as the essential characteristic of human/natural systems, it might be useful to play off several key explanations of Maturana and Varela against Bateson's statements. It should also be kept in mind that their accounts of an ecology as a cognitive system are also meant to encompass the more reflective and metaphorical forms of intelligence of humans, as well as the many ways human/environment relationships involve important information that leads to changes in both human behavior and intentional thought processes.

The following observations of Maturana and Varela are especially helpful for understanding Bateson's statement that "the individual mind is immanent but not only in the body. It is immanent also in the pathways and messages outside the body" (1972, p. 461). A cognitive, that is, living system, according to Maturana and Varela, "is a system whose organization defines a domain of interactions in which it can act with relevance to the maintenance of itself." "The process of cognition," they continue, "is the actual (inductive) act or behaving in this domain" (1980, p. 13). They go on to identify the characteristics shared by all living (cognitive) systems:

1. Living systems are units of interactions; they exist in an ambience. From a purely biological point of view they cannot be understood independently of the part of the ambience with which they interact: the niche; nor can the niche be defined independently of the living system that specifies it.
2. Living systems as they exist on earth today are characterized by exergonic metabolism, growth and internal molecular replication, all organized in a closed causal circular process that allows for evolutionary change in the way the circularity is maintained, but not in the loss of circularity itself.
3. It is the circularity of its organization that makes a living system a unit of interactions, and it is this circularity that it must maintain in order to remain a living system and to retain its identity through different interactions.
4. Due to the circular nature of its organization a living system has a self-referring domain of interactions (it is itself a self-referring system), and its condition of being a unit of interactions is maintained because its organization has a functional significance only

in relation to the maintenance of its circularity and defines its domain of interactions accordingly.

5. Living systems as units of interactions specified by their condition of being living systems cannot enter into interactions that are not specified by their organization.

6. The niche is defined by the classes of interactions into which an organism can enter.

7. Every unit of interaction can participate in interactions relevant to other, more encompassing units of interactions. (1980, pp. 9–11)

It would be a mistake to interpret everything as ongoing interactions and processes. Maturana and Varela use the term "autopoiesis" to refer to the self-reproducing nature of all living beings. But the patterns of behavior and other internal systems that differentiate bees from frogs, and humans from trees, evolved in response to the patterns of other life forms they interact with—over eons of time. "The structural coupling between organism and environment," to quote again an especially important observation of Maturana and Varela, "takes place between operationally independent systems" (1992, p. 102). Perturbations in the system trigger responses that are determined by the unique characteristics of the organism being perturbed. That is, a change occurring in the organism's environment does not *cause* the organism to respond in a certain way, but it does trigger a response determined by the organism's internal systems. For example, it is the differences between the optic nerve of the frog and that of human beings (as well as other neurological and cultural differences) that causes the fly to be the perturbation that triggers the frog's muscular contractions that move the tongue out to catch it, and to trigger a different response in humans.

The structural coupling, or what Bateson refers to as the "patterns that connect," can be understood as an elementary form of communication that involves information about differences. And this interaction triggers changes throughout the system of the organisms that collectively constitute the larger ecosystem. This communication of information is what leads Maturana and Varela to state that "living as a process is a process of cognition." Bateson makes the same point by saying that "a 'bit' of information is definable as a difference which makes a difference. Such a difference, as it travels and undergoes successive transformation in a circuit, is an elementary idea" (1972, p. 315). He goes on to say:

The total self-corrective unit which processes information, or as I say, 'thinks' and 'acts' and 'decides,' is a system whose boundaries do not at all coincide with the boundaries either of the body or of what is popularly called the 'self' or 'consciousness': and it is important to notice that there are multiple differences between the thinking system and the 'self' as popularly conceived. (1972, p. 319)

Bateson is especially clear on what can become problematic in the way humans interact and make sense of the messages communicated through the network of information pathways essential to the life of ecosystems. Using a distinction made by Alfred Korzybski that "*the map is not the territory*," Bateson argues that humans process the information (that is, respond to differences) metaphorically. Over time humans collectively create conceptual maps (schemata) that influence what information they will be aware of, as well as the interpretion of what the information means—which often involves connecting it to larger cultural themes and anxieties. These cultural maps, in turn, are acquired by new members as they learn to think and communicate in the cultural languages of their group. As Bateson put it in a paper presented to the annual meeting of the Lindisfarne Fellows in 1980, metaphor is not just pretty poetry, but it is "in fact . . . the main characteristic and organizing glue of the world of mental processes" (1990, p. 241).

What concerned Bateson was the failure of the cultural maps (metaphorical frameworks) to take into account essential features of the territory: that is, the patterns of information being communicated through the ecosystems humans participate in. The failure of the cultural maps to provide an adequate guide to the characteristics of the territory might be due to their being borrowed from another time and territory, as was the case when the English, French, and other immigrant groups interpreted the New World in terms of the patterns of thinking they had acquired over centuries of cultural interaction in very different ecosystems. Indeed, it was the consequences of having reduced the sustaining capacities of their own ecosystems, as well as their racism, that led them to interpret the forests, plains, fisheries and minerals as natural resources that had only to be claimed as private property and exploited. As Frederick Turner documents with great lucidity in *Beyond Geography: The Western Spirit Against the Wilderness* (1986 edition), their cultural maps were totally inappropriate for recognizing the distinctive features of the new ecosystems they encountered as they moved across the continent, and for learning from the more ecologically-centered aboriginal cultures they largely destroyed.

The problem, as Bateson understood it, is twofold: the cultural maps influence what aspects of the ecosystem that individuals will be aware of, as well as how they will interpret the information. Rachel Carson's book, *Silent Spring* (1962), was really about the problem of how our cultural maps influence both human understanding and the actual functioning of the information pathways that sustain the autopoiesis of all the members of an ecosystem. Before Carson's book, farmers and agricultural scientists did not understand the interdependent nature of ecosystems. Their interpretive frameworks led them to view the environment as in need of being chemically controlled; and even though the information circulating through local ecosystems signalled that normal patterns were being radically disrupted, they failed (indeed, refused) to recognize the problem. What they saw were the pests and the power of insecticides to control them. Their conceptual (cultural) maps put out of focus the effects of the insecticides on other species.

A second example relates to the cultural map or schemata that currently leads us to view technology as a neutral tool until given a purpose by the person who uses it. The illuminating and hiding characteristics of a cultural map, in the case of computer technology, still causes people to ignore how computers privilege certain forms of knowledge over others—as we discussed earlier. Even though analog, tacit, metaphorical, and body knowledge are part of every person's experience, and they increasingly read about cultural differences, their taken for granted cultural maps continue to highlight the explicit digital forms of knowledge metaphorically referred to as data and information, and to ignore the other forms of knowledge. Both racist and sexist thinking can also be considered as examples of cultural maps providing a distorted reading of the territory.

The second concern of Bateson arose from his understanding that the cultural values and assumptions that guide human behavior, and are encoded in the technology of dams, freeways, air conditioners, and toxic wastes, have an impact on all the other natural systems connected through the network of information pathways. His statement (quoted earlier) that "*the mental characteristics of the system are immanent, not in some part, but in the system as a whole*" (1972, p. 316) helps illuminate how the cultural way of understanding property rights, a technological approach to sustaining progress, and an economy based primarily on the profit motive, are the dominant mental characteristics immanent in ecosystems stripped of trees and salmon. His point also applies to the increasing number of people suffering disabilities from exposure to toxins in their food, water, and work place. That is, the mental characteristics of the cultural/ecosystem are also immanent in their cells and neural systems. Food containing dangerous amounts of heavy metals, ground water contaminated by nitrogen and other toxins, and the widespread decline and extinction of species, all point to the danger of separating human/cultural intelligence from the forms of intelligence that characterize healthy ecosystems.

In a book that points the way to the most fundamental and generally ignored dimensions of liberation, *Earth Wisdom* (1978), Dolores LaChapelle poses the question that cognitive psychologists and educators have ignored in all their discussions of the nature and potential of human intelligence. While others were arguing for liberation from different forms of cultural oppression (social class, race, gender) during the seventies, La Chapelle was reflecting on the deeper implications of Bateson's statement that "if a creature destroys its environment, it destroys itself." "The question now is," as she put it, "how did we reach such a state of insanity? Can we honestly believe that the human being, the product of three billion years of evolution, came into the world totally cut off from the entire process?" (p. 60). Indeed, this question could serve as the basis for organizing a university level course of study. More immediately, it helps to frame the dominant anthropocentric view of intelligence as being basically pathological in nature, just as the suggestions by scientists that space exploration is the first step in colonizing space and insures the continuation of human life after the Earth becomes uninhabitable is pathological.

In earlier chapters we considered some of the educational implications of an ecological view of intelligence. The discussion of how languages encode the culture's moral schemata that govern relationships, the criticism of an individually-centered view of creativity, and the knowledge/cultural mediation characteristics of educational computing were all framed in terms of a more inclusive understanding of intelligence—one that must meet the test of not destroying the habitat. Other educational implications of an ecological view of intelligence will be introduced here for the purpose of providing a conceptual framework for the final chapters. Regardless of whether we approach the nature of intelligence from a biological (Maturana/Varela), cybernetic system (Bateson), or semiotic perspective, the bottom line is that everything participates in a field of relationships involving multiple sign systems ("living as a process is a process of cognition"). It is this network of relationships (humans nested in the *Umwelt* of culture, and culture nested in the *Umwelt* of natural systems) that should become the analog for educators who are addressing the challenge of organizing curricula that foster the growth of individual intelligence. This new (actually, ancient) view of intelligence would involve a basic change in the criterion for determining what constitutes intelligent behavior. Whereas the individually-centered view of intelligence uses individual autonomy as the primary reference point, an ecological view of intelligence would use long-term sustainability of the Earth's ecosystems as the primary criterion. Unintelligent behavior would then be seen as any behavior, way of thinking, and moral judgment that degrades the environment. This reframing, in turn, leads to radically different ways of understanding the connections between heteronomy and empowerment.

An ecological view of intelligence would also involve a radical shift away from the constructivist view that individuals grow in their ability to think and behave autonomously by constructing their own ideas out of the raw data and information they encounter through direct experience or from experiences organized by teachers. Rather, it would lead to patterns of thinking that understand relationships in terms of the eight principal characteristics of ecosystems that Capra suggests are also the basic principles of learning: *interdependence, sustainability, ecological cycles, energy flows, partnership, flexibility, diversity,* and *coevolution* (1993, p. 9). As these guiding principles are not yet part of the taken for granted schemata of the dominant culture, it will be necessary to recognize the tension between the culture's metaphorical frameworks that still promote ecologically destructive thought and behavioral patterns and the ecological principles that need to become part of the basis for a new cultural praxis. Because of this tension, the ecological model of understanding should retain critical reflection as an important aspect of intelligence; but critical intelligence should have as its primary goal achieving a balance between meeting the basic needs of humans and the life sustaining characteristics of the Earth's ecosystems. Unlike the constructivist's romantic view of the natural propensity of autonomous individuals to construct wholesome ideas and to choose community enhancing values, an ecological model of intelligence is rooted in the patterns exhibited by all ecosystems. In effect, these patterns are the givens of long term intelligence, and are not dependent upon the whim or insight of individuals who often express their autonomy in ways that reflect current cultural fads.

An ecological view of intelligence has equally important implications for teacher decision making in the area of curriculum. As pointed out earlier, the individually-centered view of intelligence leads to the kind of curricula that is supposed to foster the student's ability to solve problems in original ways, to construct their own knowledge, and to question the authority of any knowledge that has not been personally tested within the context of their own experience. In effect, it leads to a relativistic view of curriculum where the process of learning becomes more important than what students actually learned—which, according to the constructivist/Deweyian tradition, always views knowledge as contextual and on the verge of being made obsolete by the progressive nature of change. For teachers, this too often leads to viewing their responsibilities as being more in the area of keeping up on the latest techniques for fostering inquiry and group processes, and not for determining whether one body of knowledge is more significant than others.

Now that we are beginning to recognize the ecological consequences of cultural patterns based on a mythical understanding of the environment as a cornucopia for meeting an expanding set of human wants, the content of the curriculum can no longer be viewed in the relativistic terms of current educational thought. Teachers now face the challenge, if they are going to be part of the solution rather than part of the problem, of identifying and placing at the center of the curriculum the more ecologically problematic aspects of the dominant culture: the dominant view of technology, success, work, self-identity, progress, the environment as a natural resource, the science/progress connection, and so forth. Helping students acquire an historical understanding of cultural/ecological relationships, including the metaphorical frameworks that influenced critically important cultural developments in the past, should now be seen as an essential responsibility of teachers. Helping students understand how the dominant culture developed along the pathway of basing progress on the degradation of natural systems is only half of the teacher's curricular responsibility. The other half confronts teachers with even greater challenges because it involves the identification of practices and patterns both in the dominant and marginalized culture groups that are ecologically sustainable. As the diverse groups in society have not really addressed the question of what constitutes ecologically sustainable cultural practices and beliefs outside the sphere of environmental regulation of some areas of technological and economic activity, we do not have a clear understanding of (much less agreement on) what all should be included in a curriculum oriented toward life enhancing relationships within the larger biotic community. But this does not mean teachers should ignore their responsibility for including in the various areas of the curriculum the knowledge we can agree upon as being ecologically sustainable.

As an ecological view of intelligence places a different form of responsibility on teachers it will be necessary to examine more carefully why teachers should view themselves as part of the process of trans-generational communication that is one of the basic characteristics of ecologically-centered cultures. The current educational emphasis that encourages students to create their *own* ideas, values, and personal sense of identity, is predicated on cultural assumptions that represent the anomic individual and the lack of ecological awareness as expressions of freedom and progress. It also makes it particularly difficult within the dominant culture for elders to come forward and share their knowledge of how to live meaningful lives more in balance with the systems we are nested in. As current educational ideals are expressed in metaphors (freedom, empowerment, equality, individualism, creativity, new ideas and values, etc.) that misrepresent both the actual nature of daily experience and the basic test that all new ideas and values must meet (long-term sustainability), it will be necessary to focus on the ideology that undermines the students receptivity to the teachings of elders who possess various forms of ecologically sensitive knowledge. It will also be necessary to examine more closely how dependent we are today, in spite of all the educational rhetoric about the need for students to become autonomous thinkers, on trans-generational communication. Examples will be taken from both the dominant culture, as well as more marginalized cultural groups. By focusing on another educational orthodoxy, that students learn more effectively and acquire more reliable knowledge when they rely upon their own insights and experiences, it is hoped that we can begin deconstructing the various expressions of educational liberalism that help sustain the current double bind that causes many teachers to deny their responsibility in the process of trans generational communication. As there are many different types of self-styled conservative thinkers who also want to deconstruct the foundations of educational liberalism in order to achieve social agendas that have nothing to do with addressing the educational/cultural roots of the ecological crisis (indeed, they would add to our plight and call it "human progress"), the next chapter will also require a willingness on the reader's part to think against the grain of current educational ideals.

SIX

TOWARD THE RECOVERY OF TRANS-GENERATIONAL COMMUNICATION IN THE EDUCATIONAL PROCESS

The argument that will be developed in this chapter is that long-term cultural/ecological survival will depend, in part, on our collective ability to accumulate, communicate, and renew ecologically sustainable forms of knowledge and values. This will mean placing more emphasis on the importance of trans-generational communication, and less on the student's ever changing sense of relevance and critical judgment. Trans-generational communication, which will be represented here as an alternative to the current emphasis on student-centered learning, is a somewhat cumbersome phrase. But it is intended to foreground the complex processes of encoding, storing, and renewing a cultural group's ways of understanding and valuing the primary life sustaining relationships between humans and the rest of the biome. This shift from a youth-oriented culture to one that shares some of the characteristics of traditional and more ecologically-centered cultures means that the elders of the culture must be recognized as carriers of essential knowledge and values.

But a careful assessment of the knowledge and values of most older people in modern, mainstream culture makes it difficult to ignore a major problem that the ecological crisis is forcing us to confront. The problem is that most older people are promoting consumerism, salvation through technological development, and the core values and beliefs that are part of the myth that equates competitiveness and the pursuit of self-interest with progress. Indeed, every President since the World War II has used "growth," "change," and "progress" as the primary legitimating metaphors for sustaining our present course. Among the cultural messages youth encounter through the media, when older people are allowed to be spokespersons, is that a youth-oriented culture is the basis of personal success and happiness. Why older people have allowed themselves to be identified in a way that denies what should be their own distinctive perspective and voice, by virtue of having learned from a lifetime of experiences, is an interesting question in itself. But our pimary concern here will be to examine how modern culture, particularly as interpreted by educators, has marginalized the importance of older people taking on the responsibilities of elders. This, in turn, leads to other vital issues that now need to be addressed.

The modern assumption that change is a basic characteristic of life creates a double bind. As change is viewed by educators and others as inherently progressive, the form of learning that is interpreted as contributing to further progress is seen generally as irreconcilable with learning from the elders of the community. This double bind has led to other problems of trans-generational communication that few educators can even articulate. *How to distinguish between an older person and an elder in the traditional sense thus becomes a critically important part of any discussion of an ecologically sustainable culture.* The responsibility of the younger generation in the process of trans-generational communication is no less an important issue. As most modern individuals, both young and old alike, are likely to be uncomfortable with any discussion that does not uphold the values associated with a youth-oriented culture, part of our discussion here will focus on the role and contribution of elders in minority cultures. As suggested earlier, the scale of the current impact of modern technologies and consumerism on the environment will force us to engage in a radical re-thinking of many of our taken for granted assumptions. Whether we can continue to base cultural practices on highly experimental forms of knowledge, while denigrating or ignoring the responsibilities of elders in the process of accumulating and renewing ecologically sustainable wisdom, is perhaps one of the most critical issues we now face. As elders continue to play a vital role in the renewal process of traditional cultures, it is especially important that the following discussion of the complementary responsibilities of youth and elders not be interpreted as an appeal to copy from these cultures. Rather, it is should be interpreted as an introductory attempt to frame the issues that modern educators, as well as others, must begin to address within the context of our own Western traditions.

CHANGE, PROCESS, AND PROGRESS AS EXPRESSIONS OF A CULTURAL ROOT METAPHOR

Although a strong case can be made that the role and thus the wisdom of elders within the mainstream Western intellectual tradition was fundamentally altered by a succession of philosophers (Socrates, Plato, Locke, Descartes, etc.) who argued variously that knowledge is derived directly either through the rational process of the individual or through a combination of direct experience and procedural thinking, classroom teachers have been more directly influenced by the ideas of John Dewey. Indeed, educational theorists are now attempting to represent him as the philosopher of the postmodern age. Educational theorists are also embracing the ideas of Alfred North Whitehead as well as those of the more contemporary philosopher, Richard Rorty. In the writings of all three philosophers, change is represented as the most basic (and dominant) characteristic of reality. It should also be added that all three philosophers understand change as moving forward. According to this way of thinking, humans can more fully actualize the progressive nature of change by learning to be process thinkers—that is, by learning to continually reconstitute ideas and values in response to the perturbations that send change throughout the interconnected life systems.

The central importance that Dewey gives to change, and by extension, to a form of process thinking he calls the "method of intelligence," can be seen in his statements about the context within which human intelligence is exercised. It should also be noted in the following quotation how he sees the method of intelligence transforming the otherwise indeterminate flux and perturbations of experience into progressive possibilities. According to Dewey:

> The realm of the practical is the region of change, and change is always contingent; it has in it an element of chance that cannot be eliminated . . . The new center is indefinite interactions taking place within a course of nature which is not fixed and complete, but which is capable of direction to new and different results through the mediation of intentional operations. (1960 edition, pp. 19, 295–296)

This view of the natural world led Dewey to argue that knowing is an activity that occurs within the context of the interactive relationships he calls "experience." He also stressed over and over again that "knowledge" and values arising out of this process must always be considered as contextual, and thus as relative to the ongoing experience of the social group. That is, the changes in relationships and patterns that constitute the ground of human experience require that ideas and values, as constituted in plans of action, must be continually revised and tested in terms of their consequences. In other words, knowledge is not accumulated and handed down from generation to generation, but continually reconstituted by individuals who encounter the "new arrangement of things." As Dewey put it:

> thought, our conceptions, and ideas, are designations of operations to be performed or already performed. Consequently their value is determined by the outcome of these operations . . . 'Thought' is not a property of something termed intellect or reason apart from nature. It is a mode of directed overt action. Ideas are anticipatory plans and designs which take effect in concrete *reconstructions* of antecedent conditions of existence . . . Knowing marks the conversion of undirected changes into changes directed toward an intended conclusion. (1960, pp. 137, 166–167, 205)

Given this view of how knowledge and values are continually being outmoded by the changing relationships and patterns, Dewey argued that knowledge constituted in response to past circumstances might be relevant to understanding the nature of current problematic situations. He even acknowleged that elements of past experience (plans of action) may be incorporated into the new plan of action. But the ongoing challenge of continually reconstructing experience requires that the shared intelligence of the social group would be the final source of authority for determining which aspects of past experience would be considered useful. The only wisdom that can be legitimately passed from generation to generation would be the insight that change is the basic characteristic of existence, and that the efficacy of the scientific method of inquiry, combined with participatory decision making, are the only certainties humans can rely upon. Given this view of human life as a series of problematic situations, Dewey viewed the teacher as responsible for engaging students in the cooperative use of the method of intelligence, and for using the ongoing problems of society as the basis of the curriculum. That is, teachers were to foster the student's growth in problem solving.

Although Alfred North Whitehead's *The Aims of Education* has been read by generations of serious students of education, his more general reflections on the nature of reality and how humans can most fully participate in it have become in recent years a central interest of curriculum theorists. They see his ideas as not only complementing Dewey's more scientifically-oriented view of reality as process, but also as an additional source of validation. Whitehead is also being seen as providing a way of understanding how the insights of post-Newtonian physics can be translated both in terms of how students learn and what should be the basis of the curriculum. Like Dewey, Whitehead also reduces the symbolic world of the individual to the immediacy of ongoing experience. In a world of constantly changing patterns and relationships, individuals continually remake themselves—emotionally, aesthetically, rationally, and socially—as they interact with the dynamic world around them. Whitehead's centering of life in the immediacy of ongoing process can be seen in the following two statements.

> I (referring to himself) find myself as essentially a unity of emotions, enjoyments, hopes, fears, regrets, valuations of alternatives, decisions—all of them subjective reactions to the environment as active as my nature. My unity . . . is my process of shaping this welter of material into a consistent pattern of feelings." (1938, p. 166)

> . . . creativity is not separable from its creatures. Thus the creatures remain with the creativity. Accordingly, the creativity for a creature becomes the creativity with the creature, and thereby passes into another phase of itself. It is now the creativity for a new creature. Thus there is a transition of the creative action and this transition exhibits itself in the physical world in the guise of routes of temporal succession.

> This protean character of creativity forbids us from conceiving it as an actual entity. For its character lacks determinedness. It equally prevents us from considering the temporal world as a definite actual creature. For the temporal world is an essential incompleteness. It has not the character of definite matter-of-fact, such as attached to an event in past history viewed from a present standpoint. (1926, pp. 88–90.)

Educational theorists are also finding support for their recommendations in the areas of curriculum and learning theory in the writings of the contemporary philosopher, Richard Rorty. His book, *Contingency, Irony, and Solidarity* (1989) combines the Classical Liberal view of the individual, the modern Western myth that change is both constant and progressive in nature, and an epistemological orientation that makes nihilism the highest expression of moral and intellectual integrity. Dewey's world of ceaseless change is incorporated into Rorty's image of the new individual who does not live a life of self deception and false expectations of others. The "ironist," as he describes the person,

> spends her time worrying about the possibility that she has been initiated into the wrong tribe, taught to play the wrong language game. She worries that the process of socialization which turned her into a human being by giving her a language may have given her the wrong language, and so turned her into the wrong kind of human being. But she cannot give a criterion for wrongness. (1989, p. 75)

Rorty's vision of the ideal society, which he never recognizes as being dependent upon the continued viability of natural systems, is described in the following way: "The citizens of my liberal utopia would be people who had a sense of contingency of their language of moral deliberation, and thus of their consciences, and thus of their community" (p. 61).

Paulo Freire, who ironically is seen as an elder by a whole generation of educational theorists within the tradition of Critical Pedagogy, understands the individual's relationship to the accumulated knowledge of her/his culture as posing the continuing challenge of education. According to Freire:

> Human existence cannot be silent, nor can it be nourished by false words, but only by true words with which men can transform the world. To exist, humanly, is to *name* the world, to change it. Once named, the world in its turn reappears to the namers as a problem and requires of them a new *naming*. Men are not built in silence, but in word, in work, in action-reflection.
>
> But while to say the true word—which is work, which is praxis—is to transform the world, saying that word is not the

privilege of some few men, but the right of every man. Consequently, no one can say a true word alone—nor can he say *for* another, in a prescriptive act which robs others of their words. (1970, p. 76)

Educational theorists who are attempting to articulate an alternative vision of human possibilites to that of the school/workplace nexus advocated by more technicist-oriented thinkers and politicians are now using the ideas of Dewey, Whitehead, Freire, and Rorty as justification for centering the authority for intellectual and moral judgments within the time frame of the students' immediate experience. The accumulated knowledge of the culture, as these theorists represent it, must meet the students' immediate sense of relevance. Indeed, the following statements are representative of educational theorists who are widely seen as leading thinkers within the emancipatory tradition of education.

Peter McLaren, who was recently awarded an endowed chair in the philosophy of education at the University of California, Los Angeles, urges teachers to utilize the following as a guideline for empowering students:

> First, encourage students to develop a *pedagogical negativism*—to doubt everything, and to try to identify those forms of power and control that operate in their own social lives. Second, assist students in *making a judgment* about these forms of power and control. What can be used to promote empowerment and what must be discarded? Finally, help students affirm their judgments.
>
> I suggest, with Henry Giroux and Paulo Freire, that we must take the *experiences* and *voices* of students themselves as the starting point. We must *confirm and legitimate the knowledges and experiences through which students give meaning to their everyday lives* (1989, pp. 233, 235)

In a book on the educational implications of Whitehead's process philosophy, which he co-authored with Kathleen Gershman, Donald Oliver suggests that a postmodern approach to education be based on an understanding that:

> Process teaching . . . begins by assuming that teacher, student, curriculum, materials (books, crayons, paper, etc.) are all moving into a novel occasion. We do not begin with the special

position of nothing (before the class begins) to 'making something happen.' Teacher and students are constantly in the flow
of occasions as they move toward fulfillment, are transformed,
perish, and become part of a new occasion. The major thrust of
planning for the teacher is to imagine what circumstances
might move an occasion from potentiality into concrescence.
The teacher sees himself or herself as moving within time in
the midst of a happening, in the midst of an emerging pattern.

We assume that every act of coming to understand, feel, and
know, is novel. Each act of knowing comes out of relationships
among the various prehensions of an occasion. Student and
teacher learn by being part of an occasion that itself is novel,
one which demands that certain aspects of persons participate
and consequently change. (1989, pp. 162–163)

Although Oliver and Gershman conclude their book with a discussion of the ecological crisis, and the need to take seriously com-
munitarian thinkers and experiments, they are unable to distance
themselves from a basic premise of modernity that they claim to be
in opposition to. "Significant process transformation for both person
and culture," they conclude, "requires an environment of sustained
intimacy where people and things are genuinely known to one another, yet where there is the diversity and complexity necessary for
spontaneity and creativity" (p. 237). Like other modern thinkers,
they are able to sustain this generalization about a universal human
potential by ignoring the influence and diversity of cultures—
particularly those cultures that value the wisdom of their elders.

The "reality is process" metaphor is given a more mechanistic
interpretation by educational psychologists and philosophers. As
trans-generational communication, including the processes of encoding the intelligence and experience of past generations, are dependent upon memory, it would be useful to see how Harvard educational psychologist, David N. Perkins, combines a mechanistic
interpretation of memory with a process view of reality. While the
mechanistic image central to Perkins' way of understanding would
be rejected by Oliver and the followers of Dewey, Perkins shares
their assumption that each generation must construct its own
knowledge and moral codes. Note how his explanation of memory
could just as easily be found in a discussion of computers. More
importantly, what is to be remembered is incidental to the use of
memory as part of the thought process:

The problem is that working memory has a rather limited capacity, usually said to be about seven chunks of information plus or minus two in an adult, with considerably less available capacity in children. This implies a bottleneck in learning a thinking frame. A freshly acquired frame of any complexity will occupy considerable space in working memory. The learner may have stored the words or images that make up the frame in long-term memory, but not typically the patterns of action needed to apply the frame. When putting the frame to work, the learner must laboriously remember what the frame says to do and do it piecemeal with great attention. At the same time, the learner must also hold the problem to which the frame is being applied. (1987, p. 49)

Francis Schrag, an educational philosopher at the University of Wisconsin, manages to combine both the modern image of individual autonomy and the "Information Age" vision of computer-mediated thinking in his formulation of the challenges that lie ahead. After acknowledging that the potentialities of new technologies are still unknown, Schrag observes that "if we consider thinking to be an important educational goal and activity, and we need not do so, we will need either to invent new technologies, new 'objects' to think with, as Papert calls them, or to reverse the current trend toward standardized compulsory curricula (1987, p. 485).

What is important about these educational theorists is that while they might not share the same views about what constitutes the most effective procedure to be followed in the classroom, they would all agree with Robert J. Swartz's statement that "nothing is immune from critical thinking . . . Nothing is immune from the search for good reasons" (1987, p. 273). *The assumption that change is inherently progressive when guided by critical, creative, or procedural thinking (or a combination of all three) allows these theorists to avoid taking responsibility as elders for passing on to the next generation what they have learned from previous generations and renewed through their own experience.* If their own thinking were not so deeply grounded in the myth of progress they undoubtedly would have framed their discussions of intelligence and the content of the curriculum in an entirely different way.

When compared to the technicist orientation of many educators, their way of understanding the interactive and connected nature of experience seems both enlightened and compelling. But when the individual is recognized as a cultural being, and the culture is understood as interactive and dependent upon ecosystems now exhibiting signs of increasing stress and even decline, their emphasis on change and process seems both escapist and morally bankrupt. This criticism takes on greater meaning when we step outside the main stream anthropocentrically-oriented culture that frames their way of thinking. This criticism applies, I would argue, even to thinkers like Dewey and Oliver who understand that the natural world is an integral aspect of human experience.

Ironically, the educator's emphasis on change and process is interpreted quite differently by elders of other cultures where survival is understood as contingent upon not destroying the environment. Many of these elders understood human/nature relationships in ways quite similar to the cosmologies of Dewey and Whitehead. At the same time, they interpret the interconnectedness of the world as having radically different implications for the forms of knowledge humans should value. For example, the statement by a contemporary elder living in the Xingue River watershed of central Brazil does not reflect the spectator view of knowledge that Dewey was so adamantly opposed to, nor the mechanistic world of Descartes that Whitehead and Oliver find so problematic. Nor does the elder tell the younger generation of Kayapo that empowerment comes through learning to question everything handed down from previous generations, and that "within process the emergence of knowing and the emergence of being happen simultaneously" (Oliver, p. 135). As elder and educator of the younger generation who are experiencing the destruction of their bioregion by Western values and technology and the mesmeric effect of the new consumer culture, he states his responsibility in the following way: "I am trying to save the knowledge that the forest and this planet are alive, to give it back to you who have lost the understanding" (Suzuki and Knudtson, 1992, p. 137).

The elders of the Six Nation Iroquois Confederation take an even more direct stance in telling the younger generation, as well as everyone else who has strayed from the path of wisdom, what should be the basis of an intelligent, moral, and sustainable existence. As part of the Haudenosaunee Declaration of the Iroquois, which was published in 1979, they state:

> Brothers and Sisters: We point out to you the Spiritual Path of Righteousness and Reason. We bring to your thought and minds that right-minded human beings seek to promote above all else the life of all things. We direct to your minds that peace is not merely the absence of war, but the constant effort to

maintain harmonious existence between all peoples, from individual to individual and between humans and other beings of this planet. We point out to you that a Spiritual Consciousness is the Path to Survival of Humankind. We who walk about on Mother Earth occupy this place for only a short time. It is our duty as human beings to preserve the life that is here for the benefit of the generations yet unborn. (quoted in Moody, 1988, p. 77)

These are not the words of progressive educators or process philosophers like Whitehead and Rorty. Nor are they the words that advocates of critical thinking would be comfortable with. And they are not the words of a group of older people who gathered together for the purpose of making a public statement on what they as individuals perceive as the latest threat to their existence as a cultural group. Rather, their words encode fundamental knowledge about the interdependence and fragile nature of the web of food, information, and spirit that we now call an ecosystem. The knowledge of how to live in harmony with "the other beings of this planet" is different from the form of knowledge that Dewey would recognize (that is, a hypothesis to be tested within the experience of the social group), or that would arise in a classroom where everything is subjected to critical examination (if that romantic idea were indeed a real possibility, given the taken for granted nature of most of our cultural knowledge). In contrast to the modern view that represents individuals as expressing their own knowledge and value preferences, the elders who wrote the Declaration were giving expression to the distillation of a community of memory about what is absolutely essential to sustaining life. Rather than being authors themselves, the writing of the Declaration represented the fulfilling of their responsibility as elders to communicate the accumulated wisdom that clarifies and rectifies for the next generation their moral connections to the past and future. The challenge that the elders face is in renewing the wisdom by expressing it in ways that account for the current distractions from an ecologically-centered life (today, the modern vision of individual self-determination and consumerism), as well as the changes taking place within the environment itself. *The Declaration, in essence, is the codification and renewal of core understandings of a community of memory.* It might lead to critical reflection and even the politicization of taken for granted patterns seen to be in conflict with the communal wisdom expressed by the elders. But the wisdom itself is not put forward as the series of propositions to be judged in terms of the limited experience and subjective mood of the individual—though this may happen with increasing frequency as the modern emphasis on individually-centered thoughts and values becomes more widely taken for granted.

It would be wrong to assume that only tradition-oriented cultures have elders who possess ecological wisdom. Although he was not part of a community of memory in quite the same way that the Iroquois elders are, Henry David Thoreau's careful observations of the life systems around Walden Pond led him to express understandings that should have elevated him to the stature of an elder within the dominant culture (he was instead seen as an oddity by the people who were embracing a technologically-based view of progress). In *Walden,* he observed that "the indescribable innocence and beneficence of Nature—of sun and wind and rain, of summer and winter— such health, such cheer, they afford forever! . . . Shall I not have intelligence with the Earth? Am I not partly leaves and vegetable mould myself?" (1966 edition, p. 93).

Aldo Leopold learned to think and communicate as a genuine elder as his own experiences evolved through a growing recognition of the hubris embedded in the human-centered environmental management mentality that had been the basis of his early professional career. In *A Sand County Almanac,* published after he died fighting a fire on land he was attempting to restore to its natural state, we find the wisdom of an elder who was attempting to share the insights of a small group of ecologically-oriented scientists with the general public. Leopold codified the moral implications of these insights in the form of a "land ethic" that was clearly at odds with the conventional thought that represented the land either as a natural resource or as empty (worthless) space. Today, with the exception of public school classrooms and schools of education that "train" teachers in ways that reinforce the strange ideological mix of a rational management mentality and individually-centered learning (and continue what often appears as a deliberate conspiracy of silence about the ecologically problematic nature of the curriculum), Leopold is increasingly being recognized as an elder who has something vitally important to say about how to ensure a viable future for all. In his writings we find another example of ecological wisdom being expressed in a way where the form of moral insight and knowledge of essential characteristics shared by all members of an ecosystem (e.g., long-term survival of each species—including humans—depends on a limited resource base, to paraphrase Capra) are not presented as tentative personal insights. Indeed, his statement of the land ethic takes the almost Biblical form of a commandment that is to guide all human behavior: "A thing is right when it tends to preserve the integrity, stability, and beauty of the biotic community. It is wrong when it tends otherwise" (1966 edition, p. 262). Unlike contemporary process philosophers and constructivist-oriented educators, Leopold does not give primacy to the intellectual and moral autonomy of the individual.

We have many other elders in the mainstream culture, as well as minority cultures, who are attempting to help the younger generation understand and value the wisdom and, increasingly, just plain common sense knowledge that has enabled them (in the case of minority cultures) to survive. Although some of these elders who are doing the difficult work of trans-generational communication achieved national prominence (Black Elk, Martin Luther King Jr., Rachel Carson, Gregory Bateson, Maya Angelou, Wendell Berry, Barry Commoner, etc.), most are engaged in the less visible areas of face to face communication. Scott Russell Sanders, the author of *Staying Put: Making a Home in a Restless World* (1993), recalls what he learned from a farmer who took the time to share his understanding with a young boy:

> As a boy in Ohio, I used to help a farmer named Sivvy collect buckets of sap from his grove of maples. We emptied the buckets into a barrel that rode on a sledge pulled by twin draft horses. Mr. Sivvy preferred using horses, he explained to me, because the noise of the tractor would have disturbed the trees. It would certainly have disturbed Mr. Sivvy, who spoke to the team of dappled gray Percherons with clicks of his tongue and soft words. As we worked, he told me tales about the horses, about the maples, about the river that muscled through his farm, about the clouds, the frogs, the thawing dirt. Here is what the soil needs, he told me, here is what the rains do, here is what dogwood and larkspur say about the condition of the woods. All his actions, from plowing to pruning, were informed and constrained by what he knew of his place. 1993, p. 8)

Sanders notes that the way in which Mr. Sivvy was connected to the land was stored and passed on to him through narrative. And Sanders continues the process of trans-generational communication by telling his readers: "So might we marry ourselves to a place, commune with other creatures, make ourselves at home through stories." Television and other popular distractions, of course, may well prevent

Sanders' print-based mode of trans-generational communication from coming to the attention of youth.

The purpose here is not to identify all the people who have remained centered and largely selfless in fulfilling their responsibilities to tell the stories of good and evil essential to participation in a community of memory, and to remind the next generation of the differences in consequences between a long-term moral perspective that is ecologically-centered and the short-term perspective that is individually-centered. Rather, it is to examine the ideology that continues to influence educators as well as others involved in mediating the cultural messages that help establish for youth what their priorities in life should be. Clarifying how the language of an ideology misrepresents both the nature and sources of empowerment (to use a word now in vogue in educational circles) will help us understand the mutual responsibilities of elders and youth in the process of trans-generational communication made more complex by the power of the media and the short range perspective of most adults. This part of the discussion, it is hoped, will help establish a basis for discriminating between the trans-generational communication of the older people who are attempting to further the tradition of modernity, and elders who are centered on the interconnected nature of individual, culture, and ecosystem. Lastly, the examination of how ideology influences the efficacy of trans-generational communication will help illuminate the role that elders should play in the educational process, particularly in the area of curriculum.

Trans-generational Communication within the Context of Modern Ideologies: The Problematic Discourses

The influence of Dewey should not be considered as the primary reason for the decline of the importance of trans-generational communication in mainstream American culture. A strong case can be made that Dewey was embraced with varying degrees of enthusiasm over the years because he articulated in a more comprehensive way than most other thinkers the already widely held belief that social and individual progress required that the old ways be forgotten. He certainly was not embraced because he was a particularly clear thinker or a gifted writer. As immigrants and, most importantly, their children experienced personal opportunities that seemed impossible to imagine in the more class conscious country/

culture they left behind, they saw little reason to hold on to the old traditions. One consequence was that the elders who attempted to keep alive the traditions were increasingly viewed as irrelevant. Of course, not all immigrants chose to assimilate by declaring their individuality and freedom to make themselves—and to move away from the ethnic enclaves that still have a strong base in some American cities. However, for the Americans who continued to speak two languages, the language of their primary culture and the English essential for participating in the upward mobile culture of modernism, Dewey would have been viewed as a threat to the heritage of their primary culture.

The people who embraced Dewey were already well on their way to becoming converts to the interlocking set of cultural mythologies that we now refer to as modern culture. The experience of rapid technological change that was part of America's industrial development, the ability to achieve success in education, politics, and business to a degree well beyond what their parents could imagine, the fragmentation of the family and ethnic community made possible by the automobile and the demands (opportunities) of the workplace, and, finally, the secularizing and commercializing of the symbolic foundations that were previously associated with deep communal sources of meaning and legitimation, were all essential experiences of becoming a modern American. The symbolic underpinnings of these palpable experiences were further reinforced through the multiple languages of architecture, music, art, as well as the spoken and written language that was continually being updated by academics, artists, scientists, technocrats, and the business community who were all committed to advancing the frontiers of progress.

Indeed, the mythic nature of the beliefs upon which modern culture was mostly based made it impossible to give any serious consideration to the importance of trans-generational communication. The myths thus served as a basis for denigrating the ethnic groups who could not be integrated into the mainstream for reasons of skin color, or resisted for reasons relating to their own viable cultural traditions. The central core of this mythic belief system, that progress is furthered through modernization, made concern about the fate of the seventh unborn generation seem totally unnecessary. The key metaphors that helped to guide the early stages of modernization that the immigrants experienced, and which still guide the contemporary individual, include: individualism, critical thought, technology, progress, science, success, and, now, data.

These metaphors encode earlier analogs dictated by the experiences, successes and meta-narratives of the dominant cultural group. And these metaphors have continued to be viewed within mainstream culture as essentially nonproblematic. For decades educators have used these metaphors to justify a curriculum that has helped, along with the media and shopping malls, to limit the symbolic world of youth to what can be immediately experienced.

This brief overview of how deeply modernism is rooted in the experience of people who willingly accepted the trade off of separation from their community of memory for the promise of freedom in a work and consumer-oriented culture is intended to establish three points. These points are critical to the analysis of how modern ideologies, particularly as they are expressed in educational settings, have de-legitimated the need for trans-generational communication. The first point that needs to be established is that while cultural patterns of everyday life are based on deeper and often unconsciously held assumptions about the nature of reality and humankind's place within it, the ideology being promoted as a guide for future cultural change often fails to take account of the hidden and complex nature of these cultural patterns. The inability of modern ideologies to fully account for the complexity of human/cultural/ecosystem relationships can be seen in the ideology that guided Dewey's recommendation for a type of society that would be continually reconstructing itself. Dewey's view of the grand synthesis of democracy, the method of intelligence (scientific method applied to social problem solving), and education as the ongoing reconstruction of beliefs and values fit what many people already took for granted. For them, the explanatory power of his ideology did not need to be tested against the actual complexities of everyday experience. It was enough that it represented an elaboration of the already taken-for-granted myths that modern consciousness was based upon.

The second point relates to the hallmark experiences of the individuals (including liberal educational theorists) who were able to position themselves on the escalator of modern material progress. For them, tradition became increasingly reduced to a metaphor that had no place in the vocabulary of the progressive and liberal thinker. With tradition increasingly represented as the antithesis of progress, words and phrases like "elders," "community of memory," and "wisdom," were also relegated to the margins of ceremonial life and, in recent years, to the gulag reserved for the politically incorrect.

The third point is that the current vocabulary for identifying different ideologies creates a great deal of confusion—particularly in terms of how ideologies relate to reinforcing the assumptions that underlie the latest expression of modern culture. Within the field of education, the terms "liberal" and "conservative" are often used as context free metaphors that serve primarily as a way of labelling whether a particular group is for or against the latest educational reform. For example, self-proclaimed radical educators who want schools to foster an even more individually-centered approach to knowledge and values pin the label of "conservatism" on business leaders and politicians who want schools to train adaptable and tradition-free individuals for a work environment that is constantly undergoing change. Educators who are advocating that the folk knowledge of the community be given a more central place in the curriculum, and increasing awareness of the ecological crisis (both of which have a strong conserving orientation), point to Dewey's ideas as legitimating their reform proposals. Indeed, the confusion surrounding the vocabulary used for designating different ideologies that frame how educational and cultural issues are understood underscores Wendell Berry's warnings about the misuse of language.

Why the concern about the correct use of political metaphors? The question may appear even more bizarre in an era in which we have become increasingly unclear about whether words stand for (represent) events and objects in the real world or are to be used for the political purpose of shaping pulic opinions. Wendell Berry understands more clearly than most other contemporary thinkers the connection between the use of language and ecologically destructive patterns of life. "My impression," he writes in *Standing By Words* (1983), "is that we have seen, for perhaps a hundred and fifty years, a gradual increase in language that is either meaningless or destructive of meaning. And I believe that this increasing unreliability of language parallels the increasing disintegration, over the same period, of persons and communities" (p. 24).

His understanding that language, in its most fundamental sense, has to do with relationships—that is, with the quality of relationships that constitute the character of the community—can be seen in his explanation of a healthy culture. Observe in the following statement how his use of words designates activities and values that make sense only in terms of contexts and relationships that are the basis of human experience. Also observe how his use of language illuminates the moral dimensions of these relationships:

> A healthy culture is a communal order of memory, insight, value, work, conviviality, reverence, aspiration. It reveals the

human necessities and human limits. It clarifies our inescapable bonds to the earth and to each other. It assures that the necessary restraints are observed, that the necessary work is done, and that it is done well. (1986 edition, p. 43)

The responsible use of language, according to Berry, must meet three conditions: first, "it must designate its object precisely"; second, "its speaker must stand by it, be accountable for it, be willing to act on it"; third, "this relation of speaker, word, and object must be conventional; the community must know what it is" (1983, p. 25). Much of our face to face communication, insofar as personal memory and direct experience holds the participants to a degree of accountability not present in print based communication, often meets these conditions. But much of the more ideologically driven language used to frame both the problems we face as a society and the course of action we should take in the future seem increasingly to ignore the need for any sense of accountability—and thus moral responsibility. The ideological frameworks used by educational theorists and classroom teachers to legitimate changes in teaching style and curriculum are particularly noteworthy for their lack of accountability. And it is this lack of accountability that makes the guiding ideologies so critical to our discussion of the role of transgenerational communication in the education of youth and the larger community.

Part of the reason for the confusion that now exists in modern culture concerning the responsibility of elders can be traced to the emergence of powerful ideological frameworks created by intellectuals and theoretically oriented technocrats who wanted to base future change on abstract ideas, theories, and data. Before the emergence of a print-oriented culture made it possible for these theorists to establish in the thinking of their readers that abstract representations of future cultural possibilities were more real than experience itself, ideologies and culture were identical. That is, an ideology (which is a modern word) was synonymous with the cultural beliefs and practices of the people. The anthropologist, Clifford Geertz, explains the status of this modern word in premodern cultures:

Cultural patterns—religious, philosophical, aesthetic, scientific, ideological—are 'programs'; they provide a template or blueprint for the organization of social and psychological processes, much as genetic systems provide such a template for the organization of organic processes. (1973, p. 216)

That is, before the modern idea that cultural change should be guided by abstract theory, an ideology was part of the explanatory framework that guided daily experience.

In the West, philosophers were initially responsible for creating a separation between ideology and the lived cultural patterns Geertz refers to. In using the abstract medium of print to communicate their rational formulations of how reality was to be understood, and the form of subjectivity and social arrangements that would be consistent with their rational blueprints, the philosophers broke from the main pathway of human development—which involved renewing the cultural templates through face to face communication. From Plato to Rorty, Western intellectuals were able to communicate their abstract formulations for changing the patterns of cultural life to readers who were already conditioned to accept the authority of the printed word. Indeed, the growing dominance of print-based theory has become, within certain sectors of society, an essential cultural trait. That actual culturally-based experience often remains separate from the theoretical frameworks formulated by philosophers and educational theorists, particularly in its face to face patterns of communication, has resulted in the acceptance of a deep form of schizoprenia—or, in Berry's terms, a lack of moral responsibility on the part of the theorist.

Educational theorists have been culturally conditioned, like other highly print-oriented groups, to treat abstract representations of a more ideal form of individualism and social relationships as the primary guide for reforming education and, by extension, society. Different groups of educational theorists have been educated to think in a variety of theory-based ideological frameworks; and they are now attempting to make these maps of reality the basis of the students' taken-for-granted world. As these ideological frameworks represent competing models of cultural reconstruction a complex and even confusing vocabulary is now being used to identify friends, enemies, alliances, geneologies, basis of legitimation, and so forth. The rectification of names for these ideological frameworks will help us move closer in the discussion of trans-generational communication to a more accountable language. It will also help clarify why certain educational interpretations of an ideology make it nearly impossible to consider how elders might play a more vital role in the process of evolving more morally and ecologically coherent cultural patterns.

Sorting out and clarifying the symbolic boundaries of the main ideologies now used to legitimate different approaches to educational reform can best be achieved by dividing them into the two competing traditions of political discourse that have been dominant in the West since the rise of modern, industrial society. Although these two genres of political discourse, which can be represented in terms of liberalism and conservatism, are often seen as being in fundamental opposition to each other, certain forms of conservatism (or what I shall argue are incorrectly labelled as conservative) support the most extreme and ecologically destructive aspects of modern culture. It can also be argued that liberal traditions that emphasize constant experimentation with new ideas and values are also oriented toward conserving these nihilistic traditions. As an earlier book, *Elements of a Post-Liberal Theory of Education* (1987), contains an extensive discussion of the different forms of educational liberalism and conservatism, the discussion here will be limited to summarizing how the essential characteristics of each ideological position relates to being open or closed to seriously considering the role of elders in how cultural knowledge is accumulated, communicated, and renewed.

In short, the task is to identify the tradition of ideology that can best serve as a guiding symbolic framework for extending our sense of accountability to the rest of the biotic community we share this planet with. Modern ideologies have put us in a double bind where our form of progress requires the destruction of life systems. Given the nature of this double bind, we cannot at this point declare that the use of a theoretically-based ideology as a source of clarification, criticism, and reform is now to be regarded as passe. When the cultural patterns are ecologically destructive and when the dominant ideology legitimates the deep symbolic foundations of these daily patterns, the need for an alternative ideology becomes even more acute. The challenge is to evolve a guiding ideology that takes account of the complexity of how individuals, culture, and ecosystems are connected.

Forms of Educational Liberalism

The three dominant expressions of educational liberalism—technicist, neo-Romantic, and emancipatory—share a common set of cultural assumptions that have their origins in the thinking of the founding fathers of Western modernism. Although the proponents of these distinct interpretations of liberalism are often critical of each other, with the emancipatory liberals often labelling the technicist liberals as reactionary conservatives (which is intended as the ultimate form of denigration), they all share the assumption that change is progressive in nature, that individuals or participatory groups of individuals are the basic social unit, that science is the highest expression of human progress and source of empowerment, and that some form of rational thought (purposive rational for the technocrats, critical rationality for the emancipatory educators, and creative constructivism for the neo-Romantic educators) provides the basis for determining which ideas and values are to be the basis of individual experience. In short, they all subscribe to the main cultural assumptions that are the hallmarks of modernity.

What is distinctive about these assumptions, according to Stephen Toulmin, is that they represent a sharp break from the path of development followed by traditional cultures. It should be added that many of these traditional cultures are still resisting the pressures of modernization. Toulmin summarizes this break in terms of the proclivity of modern (liberal) thinkers to establish a number of polarities. These included privileging print (and now electronic) based discourse over oral discourse, the universal over the particular, the general over the local, and the timeless over the timely (1990, pp. 30–35). These polarities, as we shall see, are critically important to understanding why all three traditions of educational liberalism have been silent about the most important issues we now face: how to educate a culturally diverse society without engaging in hidden forms of cultural domination; how to recognize, value, renew, and reform the myriad traditions that are part of daily life; and how to avoid destroying the environment future generations will depend upon.

The three traditions of educational liberalism appear as distinct, even antagonistic to each other, because each position foregrounds a different combination of assumptions about how to achieve the promises of a modern society. While what they share in common is the most relevant to understanding why the various expressions of educational liberalism have not addressed the cultural aspects of the ecological crisis, the following seem to be the basis of their distinct identities.

Technocratic Educational Liberalism. The technocratic educators who promote classroom management techniques, behavior modification, mastery teaching, outcome-based education, computer-mediated learning, as well as a number of lesser educational fads, foreground the power of procedure thinking by experts to create techniques and programs that will enhance the teacher's ability to predict and control certain educational "outcomes." While they share with the other forms of educational liberalism the assumptions that equate change with progress, and represent the world in terms of the interests and needs of humans, they separate themselves from other educational liberals in terms of their view of human nature. For the technocratic liberals, human nature is malleable; that is, it is shaped by the environment. Any inappropriate or inefficient behavior is thus a matter of a badly engineered environment. That critical thought essential for democratic participation might be a valid educational goal is not part of their view of a society ordered by experts. This tradition of educational liberalism has little use for the type of curriculum that might encourage students to think critically about where technology, and the cultural assumptions upon which it is based, are leading us. Rather, their emphasis is on learning the social skills and forms of technically-based knowledge seen as essential to an adaptable work force.

Neo-Romantic Educational Liberalism. This form of educational liberalism has been highly visible at different times over the last century. The child-centered phase of the early progressive education movement that became a model of educational enlightenment for many middle-class parents, the open classrooms of the sixties and early seventies, and the constructivist approach to learning now being widely promoted, represent the recurring discovery of the child's natural propensities to learn, to be creative, and, in a word, to express freedom. Indeed, the freedom of the individual is the basic assumption foregrounded by neo-Romantic educational liberalism. This assumption, in turn, requires that other aspects of liberal thought be taken for granted: that human nature is essentially good, that all change is progressive, that this is a human-centered world, and so forth. It also requires that the silences and sources of cultural domination that characterize the liberal/modern agenda be codified in their language and classroom practices. Technology, experts, behavior modification, and the coupling of education to the needs of a work force and economic competitiveness are all anathema to them.

Emancipatory Educational Liberalism. While this tradition of educational liberalism is more theoretically based than either the technocratic and neo-Romantic educators (it draws heavily on the ideas of Dewey, Freire, Frankfurt School of Critical Theory), it has had little direct influence on classroom teachers. It continues, nevertheless, to exert an influence on the more socially conscious departments in colleges of education, and to provide the metaphorical language used to legitimate a wide range of educational practices—such as the technocratic educator's argument that computers foster "empowerment" and "cooperative decision making." Unlike the neo-romantic educators, this group of educational liberals do not start with the assumption that freedom is a given of the human condition. Nor do they subscribe to the technocratic educator's hierarchical and work-oriented world. The view of progress in a human-centered world (which they share with the other forms of educational liberalism) is to be achieved by an approach to education based on raising and transforming consciousness, and thus the social action of an increasingly autonomous individual (or group of individuals). What education is to emancipate individuals and groups from are the traditions that embody various forms of unequal relationships. That tradition exists prior to the individual is, by itself, an expression of an unequal and oppressive relationship. Ironically, these educational liberals argue for teaching a specific set of modern values and ways of knowing, but they represent them as universals— indeed, as essential to fulfilling the universal need of all individuals, regardless of cultural background, to realize the freedom that is basic to their humanness.

Like other forms of metaphorically based thinking, ideologies encode earlier expressions of analogic thinking that illuminate (foreground) certain aspects of social life, and hide others. They also encode and carry forward metaphorically-based misconceptions of the past—like viewing human beings as machine-like.This applies to all three streams of educational liberalism. When Locke and Descartes were establishing a new set of analogs for understanding the nature of thinking, the role of language, and the nature of the individual (which were largely derived from developments in scientific knowledge), group differences were not understood in the way we now understand cultural differences. Also encoded in the fundamental assumptions that are still shared by all three streams of educational liberalism is the anthropocentric view of the world that prevailed during the sixteenth and seventeenth century. Today, the technicist liberals represent nature, which Francis Bacon wanted "bound into service," as a natural resource to be managed by the application of scientific and technological knowledge. The emancipatory liberals are either totally silent about the biome being part of human experience or represent it as part of the physical context that needs to be reconstructed in ways that fit the ideas and values of the social group. The neo-Romantic form of anthropocentrism takes the form of children projecting onto the environment their playful images and scenarios. Even when liberal classroom teachers attempt to incorporate recycling and a scientific approach to environmental education, which usually takes the form of studying local ecosystems, their continued emphasis on an individually-centered view of intelligence and moral decision making overwhelms the possible emergence of an ecologically centered way of understanding the connections of self, culture, and natural systems.

The three educational expressions of liberalism also encode the earlier analogs that led successive generations of liberal thinkers to associate the word tradition with privilege, resistance to change, and other structural sources of injustice and inequality. Indeed, the history of liberal thought has been so centered on injustices and excesses associated with the European legacy of feudalism that this complex and vitally important aspect of human experience has still not been adequately theorized, in even preliminary form, by most liberal educators. Among educational liberal theorists—including the entire spectrum from technocrats like Seymour Papert and Madeline Hunter to emancipatory educators like Dewey and Richard Paul, tradition is still associated with anti-modern, anti-egalitarian, and anti-intellectual forces.

If these areas of silence are matched against the characteristics of modernity that Toulmin identified, we can also see other parallels between modernism as the contemporary expression of cultural colonialism and the attempt by liberal educators to impose their modernistic understanding of the nature of the person as an autonomous individual, intelligence and values as individually-centered, and experimental ideas as progressive in nature, on all cultural groups— even as they proclaim the importance of respecting cultural differences. In lacking a deep understanding of the nature of culture, anthropocentrism, and tradition, they are thus able to use the metaphorical language of liberalism as the basis for creating a modern, universal culture.

Forms of Conservatism

Conservatism is both more complex and more misunderstood, even on a surface level, than the various forms of liberalism. As liberals have viewed themselves as providing the conceptual framework for analyzing social problems and the vision of progress that is to guide social reform efforts, conservatism has long been a source of suspicion and used as a convenient category for labelling (and thus dismissing) anybody who questioned liberal efforts to further the modernization process. The lack of interest on the part of liberal academics in sorting out the different forms of conservatism, which parallels their disinterest in a more fully theorized understanding of tradition, often resulted in extremists being seen as the archetypal conservative—like the Jesse Helms and Rush Limbaughs of American political life. Educational liberals of every persuasion have shared a similar stereotypical view of conservatism, which has prevented them from even considering how their own lives involve the reenactment of several forms of conservatism. This tendency to respond in terms of stereotypes was a predictable part of a moral education class in which I had students read William J. Bennett's essays on moral literacy (along with selections representing other cultural approaches to moral education). Although I have deep disagreements with much of Bennett's thinking (Bowers, 1993, pp. 35–71), his understanding of the role that narrative plays in moral education seemed to challenge in fundamental ways the liberal assumptions that are the basis of values clarification and Kohlberg's theory of stages of moral development. Because Bennett was immediately identified as a conservative, otherwise bright and articulate students would experience a mental block when discussing his argument about the use of exemplary people such as Harriet Tubman and Martin Luther King, Jr. to help them understand how a particular virtue has been expressed in difficult circumstances. His examples, which would be embraced by most social groups concerned with racism and other forms of oppression, became an invisible part of the pages they were reading and discussing. The mention of the word "tradition" and, now, "elders" elicits the same reductionist response from liberal educators who associate these terms with the reactionary practice of "telling students what to think."

Our political maps (ideologies) might represent the territory more accurately if they were held more accountable in terms of meeting Wendell Berry's three criteria for the responsible use of language—as well as a fourth criterion Berry did not recognize: that our political vocabularies should enable us to think and communicate about the complexities of living as members of cultural and biotic communities. Indeed, our political language needs to take account of the different ways the lives of individuals, the patterns of cultures, and the autopoietic processes of all living entities reproduce (conserve) existing patterns—even as they undergo renewal and change. These conserving processes continue regardless of whether the current political language takes them into account. Our political language also needs to be held more accountable for recognizing the geneology of our political traditions. For example, many liberals categorize as conservative the beliefs and activities that are really the expression of Classical Liberalism. Again, it must be emphasized that the following discussion is intended to challenge the conventions of modern thought that continue to prevent a serious discussion of the role and responsibilities of elders.

Temperamental Conservatism. This form of conservatism is a basic aspect of human life. It is such an integral part of daily experience that it has generally gone unnoticed and thus un-named by most people. Yet our choices and sense of meaning are grounded in it. Basically, we are all temperamental conservatives in the sense that we reenact (conserve) taken for granted patterns in our form of greetings and other social interactions, what we wear and eat, and what we talk about, and so forth. Our self-identity is also rooted in this form of conservatism. It is part of the experience of the the truck driver, store clerk, college professor, high school student, and unemployed worker. It is also expressed in the taken-for-granted patterns of the person (like Dewey and Freire) who argues that everything is (or ought to be) in a state of change. Its specific form of expression may vary widely, from the rock singer and rapper to the technologist who is working to create more efficient and controllable systems. As it is partly a psychological phenomenon, it cannot be identified with a specific social, economic, or religious agenda. Nor does it lend itself more to being for or against an ecologically responsive form of behavior. If the individual's cultural way of knowing and interacting stresses that everything should be understood and valued in terms of a human perspective, the natural (conserving) attitude will tend to reproduce these patterns. And if the culture is based on a different set of meta-narratives or if individuals have worked out alternative ways of understanding and behaving they are more comfortable with (like Aldo Leopold's personal transformation), their temperamental conservatism will be expressed accordingly.

It is thus important to recognize that cultural changes, like the shift away from a patriarchal orientation that we are now experiencing in the dominant culture, will gradually become part of people's natural attitude. While this form of conservatism helps ensure the continued existence of important political achievements; it can also act as a source of resistance to change—as can be observed with people who want to continue basing economic practices on their own immediate sense of self-interest. As temperamental conservatism is part of everybody's experience, it should be taken into account as part of any ideology that adequately represents the connections between cultural change and human experience. It is particularly important for educators to take this form of conservatism into account when they are promoting the efficacy of critical reflection as the basis of change.

Cultural Conservatism. Cultural conservatism is rooted in the language and communication patterns of the culture that awaits the birth of each new member. And like temperamental conservatism, cultural conservatism may take many forms of expression—from aboriginal cultural groups who have lived within a bioregion for hundreds, even thousands of years, to capitalistic and thus highly experimental cultures that survive only by exploiting resources on a world wide scale. The distinctive nature of cultural conservatism is rooted in the way the language systems of a culture (spoken, written, kinesthetic, musical, architectural, etc.) encode and reproduce (conserve) in the present the patterns handed down from the past. Put simply, as members of a culture learn to think and communicate within the language systems that sustain the "reality" of the group, they in turn reproduce the patterns—even as they struggle to modify patterns regarded as especially outmoded. The use of the cultural language systems thus involves individuals quite literally being thought (that is, the language thinks us as we think within the language) and reenacted by the living patterns that have their roots in the past. Like temperamental conservatism, what is conserved depends upon the meta-narratives and root metaphors that explain the most fundamental relationships, including how humans are to think of themselves and act within these relationships. The critical issue, particularly in terms of our discussion of the need to recover responsible communication between generations, has to do with the nature of the beliefs, values, and practices that are to be conserved.

Economic Conservatism. The essential beliefs and practices of highly visible groups who are mistakenly labelled as conservatives are, in fact, rooted in the assumptions of Classical Liberalism. People who hold these beliefs are conservative only at the level of temperament and in the more general sense of reproducing (conserving) the cultural patterns encoded in the language systems of the culture. But even these aspects of individual/cultural experience are based on assumptions about individual competitiveness, market forces, rewards going to the strong and deserving, the progressive nature of change, the need for minimal governmental involvement beyond the enforcement of contracts and the protection of individual freedoms. Libertarian principles and the credo of nearly every business organization continue to restate the Classical Liberal emphasis on how the pursuit of self-interest contributes to the well being of the entire society. Although this mislabelled ideological position recognizes the importance of the family and religion, it readily embraces every form of technological innovation—even those that threaten to undermine the cohesion of the family and the authority of religious belief. Economic growth rather than self-limitation for the sake of others (including the biotic community) is the central value of this position. While it has its own pantheon of elders (John Locke, Adam Smith, Henry Ford, Ronald Reagan, etc.), its message to the next generation is that everybody's self-interest is enhanced through economic (and intellectual) competition and technological advancement.

The nihilism fostered by this ideology is often obscured by the hype that announces the introduction of new technologies, the exploitation of new markets, and the building of new shopping malls. But the destruction of personal lives, traditions that were the center of community life, and ecosystems are becoming increasingly difficult to hide—particularly as the myth of unending progress becomes more difficult to sustain. One of the great ironies is that this group of economically oriented ideologues would view the recovery of ecologically-centered trans-generational communication in the same way as would the followers of Dewey, Freire, and other contemporary constructivist educational reformers—as an impediment to the discovery of new ideas, values and forms of experience.

Religious Conservatism. This form of conservatism is becoming an increasingly visible part of public life. No longer willing to accept the liberal convention that represents the public domain as secular (and under the control of rationally based experts) and the religious as centered in the judgment and experience of the individual, religious conservatives have increasingly organized themselves into powerful political networks. Their goal is to achieve a closer alignment between the beliefs and values that guide life in the secular domains (primarily education, health care, and the media) and their own religious tenets. As nearly a fourth of the American population is estimated to have some form of religious affiliation, and as these groups vary widely in their interpretation of how their religious beliefs relate to the issues now being contested in the political process, any generalizations about their views of the ecological crisis and the role that elders should play in evolving a more ecologically sustainable culture would have little merit. All that can be suggested here is that this form of conservatism, in all its varied expression, needs to be more fully understood. Important characteristics of recent Western cultures, particularly their way of understanding humankind's relationship to the environment and in influencing how indigenous cultures have been treated, have been directly influenced by religious beliefs. A study of indigenious cultural groups who have learned to live within the limits of their surrounding ecosystems also reveals that their cosmologies can also be understood as religious belief systems.

Philosophical Conservatism. The essential features of this form of conservatism can only be introduced here. That a fuller examination of this complex position is not possible, given the focus of this chapter, is particularly unfortunate since this is a form of conservatism that provided in the past a basis for a critique of modern assumptions taken for granted by different interpreters of educational liberalism and economic conservatism. As I have pointed out elsewhere (1980, 1987) this form of conservatism does not take progress and the efficacy of abstract theory for granted. Rather it represents a more dialectical way of thinking about the tensions and complexities of human experience. This dialectic is understood as the need to continually work out the appropriate balance between the interests of the individual and community, the authority of abstract rational thought and the knowledge gained from direct experience, the promise of progress and the proven benefits of living traditions. The philosophical conservatives even view human nature as expressing tendencies that vary widely: intelligence, altruism, and community mindedness, as well as egotism, selfishness, and cruelty. It is this more complex view of human nature, which they use history to document, that leads them to argue for checks and balances (separation of powers) in the political system.

What is distinctive about philosophical conservatives is that they will argue for the side of the dialectic that is about to be overwhelmed. For example, when communities become too oppressive they will argue for protecting the rights and freedom of the individual; and when individualism is carried to an extreme they attempt to articulate how individual lives are embedded and enhanced by responsible community membership. The following statement by Alasdair MacIntyre (he still rejects being labelled a conservative) is

typical of how philosophical conservative thinking attempts to restore a sense of balance:

> But the key question for men (and women) is not about their
> own authorship; I can only answer the question 'What am I to
> do?' if I can answer the prior question 'Of what story or stories
> do I find myself a part?' . . . Deprive children of stories and you
> leave them undescribed, anxious stutterers in their actions as
> in their words . . . For the story of my life is always embedded in
> the story of those communities from which I derive my iden-
> tity. I am born with a past; and to try to cut myself off from that
> past, in the individualistic mode, is to deform my present rela-
> tionships. (1984 edition, pp. 216, 221)

Michael Oakeshott's (1962) critique of "technical knowledge"
and argument for "practical knowledge," Ivan Illich's (1970) defense
of mentor/pupil relationships and his criticism of the destructive-
ness of institutionalized education, and Hannah Arendt's (1954)
warnings against treating conservation and renewal as unrelated human activities are all representative of how philosophical conservatives understand the continuities and interdependencies of human
life. As the dialectical nature of these thinkers suggests, philosophic
conservatism is a nondoctrinaire way of thinking about social problems, including the limitations of modern technology for engineering a more adaptable and predictable individual, than it is a set of
guiding poltical and educational prescriptions. Indeed, thinkers associated with other political traditions, such as democratic socialism,
have exhibited an increasingly unique ability in contemporary political and educational discourse to frame issues in ways that demonstrate the influence of the philosophic conservative's more dialectical
way of thinking about the individual's relationship to the larger community. The writings of Robert Heilbroner, John Berger, and Michael
Harrington come easily to mind. While this form of reflective conservatism and renewal represents within mainstream culture a form
of political discourse that is particularly receptive to elders taking
responsibility for telling the stories essential to a balanced community of memory (balanced in the sense of accounting for evils
done to others and expressions of community enhancing beliefs and
practices), it has been totally silent about human/environment relationships. In short, its weakness is in the deep anthropocentric bias it
shares with the liberal traditions of political and educational
thought.

Cultural/Bio-Conservatism. This somewhat awkward political label may appear new, but the range of beliefs and values that it encompasses are not. Ecologically-centered cultures that occupied Turtle Island before it was discovered by Europeans and renamed America had, over thousands of years, evolved belief systems and practices that could best be described as expressions of cultural/bio-conservatism. Primal cultures in other parts of the world that adapted their symbolic systems, including the refinement of their technologies, in ways that allowed for understanding the distinctive characteristics of their bio-regions must also be seen as examples of the complex range of expression that cultural/bio-conservatism has taken. That many of these cultures have survived for hundreds, even thousands, of years without destroying the intricate interdependence of their local ecosystems suggests a powerful reason for taking seriously the shared characteristics of these cultural/political/ educational schemata. In terms of meeting the ultimate test of long-term survival, cultures based on the metaphorical constructions of modern liberalism have fallen far short of many of these other cultures.

There are also many contemporary ecologically-oriented thinkers who understand both the forces contributing to deepening the crisis, as well as changes we must be prepared to make if we are to avert its full impact. They can also be described as cultural/bio-conservative thinkers. E. F. Schumacher, Gregory Bateson, Wendell Berry, Wes Jackson, Dolores La Chapelle, and Masanobu Fukuoka are just a few of the thinkers who recognize that the primary relationships essential to long-term sustainability require conserving and renewing knowledge rather than embracing every new technological innovation and then hoping that the even newer technology will enable us to cope with the unanticipated consequences of experimenting with the cultural/ecosystem networks. Other prominent thinkers who combine elements of cultural/bio-conservatism with the liberal assumption about the primacy of individual freedom include Arne Naess and Warwick Fox.

The core beliefs and values shared by both primal cultures and contemporary thinkers include the following: (1) *Cultural/bio-conservatism involves a way of understanding time that is more attuned to the cycles of the different elements in the biome.* The cycle of life of a California sequoia, a salmon, a geological formation, and a human being are fundamentally different from each other. When the modern individualistic sense of time is imposed on other systems of life that have longer time cycles the consequences are often disastrous—as we are now witnessing with the loss of topsoil, the depletion of aquifers, and the destruction of primal forests. Cultural/bio-conservatism also has a longer view of human time: one that encompasses both past and future generations rather than a sense of time framed by the immediate interests of the supposedly autonomous individual. (2) *Cultural/bio-conservatism is oriented toward a deep knowledge of place: that is, a knowledge of the life supporting characteristics of local natural systems.* Cultural practices that do not undermine the integrity of these systems are, in essence, conserving in two ways: they do not disrupt the self-reproducing (conserving) characteristics of plant and animal life, and they conserve the knowledge and value frameworks built up over generations of living in interdependent relationships with local systems. (3) *Cultural/bio-conservatism is non-anthropocentric.* That is, it involves a more inclusive understanding of community as encompassing humans (including past and future generations), as well as the other forms of life that collectively makeup the biome. Thus, this view of community as an ecology helps avoid the more limited way of understanding where special interest groups reduce complex systems to the one or two elements that have immediate interest to them—such as the forest industry's practice of reducing forest ecosystems to the few species that have economic value. (4) *Cultural/bio-conservatism is dependent upon elders to carry forward the accumulated knowledge of local systems, as well as the human practices and ceremonies that have been renewed over generations.* This includes ways of encoding and renewing knowledge of relationships through ceremonies, song, dance, narratives, and modelling how to live an ecologically-centered life. Dolores LaChapelle's *Sacred Land Sacred Sex: The Rapture of the Deep* (1987) provides an unusually insightful analysis of why Western thinkers have denigrated the importance of traditional ways of encoding and renewing wisdom about life sustaining relationships. The book is also a storehouse of knowledge about the nature of sacred ceremonies and other traditions practiced by ecologically-centered cultures. Her book, in effect, helps clarify why the modern emphasis on instrumental knowledge and personal entertainment makes elders appear out of touch with the times and thus irrelevant, and why cultures oriented toward undestanding and living sustainable relationships within the interconnected communities of life value the role and knowledge of elders. In *Look to the Mountain: An Ecology of Indigenous Education*, Gregory Cajete explains the power of the oral tradition carried on by elders:

The techniques of oral poetry (developed in indigenous societies over countless generations) are designed to *discourage* critical reflection on the stories and their contents, and instead 'enchant' the hearers and draw them into the story. This process of enthralling the audience, of impressing upon them the reality of the story, is a central feature of education in oral cultures. Their social institutions are sustained in large part by sound, by what the spoken or sung word can do to commit individuals to particular beliefs, expectations, roles, and behaviors. Thus the techniques of fixing crucial patterns of belief in memory, rhyme, rhythm, formula, story, and so on, are vitally important. (1994, p. 129, italics added)

In contrast with this view of communication where memory, wisdom, and a sense of long-term responsibility for maintaining life sustaining relationships are highly valued, the expert knowledge encoded in software programs is predicated on the assumption that the reflective individual must decide what is relevant in a continually changing world. In addition, it is expected that data and technical systems can be the basis of policies and practices that can be imposed on local systems. Unlike the top-down approach to knowledge so characteristic of modern consciousness, a deep knowledge of the nature and consequences of cultural practices is derived only over generations of experience with local plants, animals, and other elements of the bioregion. This form of contextual knowledge cannot be learned by individuals when they confront a problematic situation—as Dewey and the more recent constructivist learning theorists assume. For example, a cultural group (such as Tiruray of South East Asia) who depend on the wild flora of the forest for food and other necessities, and have a knowledge of some 223 basic plant types that can be utilized for various purposes, are dependent on the process of trans-generational communication for this knowledge to be passed on through a variety of teaching and learning relationships. Indeed, computer stored knowledge, and the self-discovery method of learning, both of which presume the irrelevance of elders, cannot duplicate the complex interaction of communal memory, judgment, and moral centeredness of an elder whose sense of responsibility is based on a sense of connectedness to the cycles of natural systems (including past and future generations of the culture), and a knowledge of the characteristics of different species at different stages in their life cycles. To put this another way, knowledge of local environments and the moral relationships essential to long-term sustainability are too complex to be learned in the time frame of the modern individual. Loggers in the Northwest, for example, are beginning to discover that forests include other plants that can be harvested on a sustainable basis. Would their communities have remained more viable if elders had been able to share the knowledge accumulated over generations of how to sustain themselves economically and spiritually by harmonizing their activities with the cycles and diversity of plant and animal life of a forest ecosystem? Alan Drengson's observations on the vital connection of elders and ecosystems seems especially relevant here. He writes that:

> In human communities meaningful stories are held together by the elders; they are the continuity the group has with its past, just as the children are with the future. They define a community's relationships to time. The community's wisdom is fully embodied in them. Even though an elder might be silent, their mere presence speaks eloquently of the community's traditions. The accumulated wisdom of the elders prepares it for facing extreme conditions, and weathering storms and trials. How elders are treated reveals the community's spiritual condition. (1993, p. 147)

Before taking up the questions of how to be an elder in the modern world, how to recognize an elder, and how to learn from an elder, it is first necessary to make a vitally important point about the hold that liberal ideologies have on the taken for granted patterns of thinking of even the most ecologically sensitive thinkers. Two prominent examples come to mind that reflect the inability of many in the environmental and deep ecology movements to recognize that we cannot begin to address the cultural aspects of the crisis if we continue to base our thinking on the key element of the liberal ideology that has contributed to sustaining the twin myths of an anthropocentric universe and progress through technological innovation. The first example involves the eminent historian of environmental thought, Roderick F. Nash. In *The Rights of Nature: A History of the Environmental Movement* (1989), he observes that environmental ethics cannot be reconciled with the traditional liberal emphasis on the rights of the individual. But instead of acknowledging that Leopold's land ethic, with its imperative on self-limitation for the sake of the biotic community and future human generations, leads to an emphasis on conserving ecologically sustainable cultural practices, he asserts that it signals a new beginning for liberalism. As he puts it: "a biocentric ethical philosophy could be interpreted as extending the esteem in which individual lives were traditionally held to the biophysical matrix that created and sustained those lives. It can be understood, then," he concludes, "as both the end and a new beginning of the American liberal tradition" (p. 160).

Arne Naess, the Norwegian philosopher who coined the phrase "deep ecology," argued for using the platform principles of deep ecology as a guide for technological and economic practices, as well as other patterns of community life. But he retains at the core of his thinking the center piece of liberalism: the primacy of individual freedom. Note how the following statement foregrounds the authority of individual judgment, and ignores how culture is the primary source of influence on thought and behavior—including the idea of individualism that Naess takes for granted:

> We study ecophilosophy, but to approach practical situations involving ourselves, we aim to develop our *own* ecosophies. In this book I introduce one ecosophy, arbitrarily called Ecosophy T. You are not expected to agree with all of its values and paths of derivation, but to learn the means of developing "your own systems" or guides, say, Ecosophy X, Y, or Z. Saying "your *own*" does not imply that the ecosophy is in any way an original creation by yourself. It is enough that it is a kind of total view which you feel at home with, "where you philosophically belong." Along with one's own life, it is always changing. (1989, p. 37, italics added)

As both Nash and Naess demonstrate, even ecologically-oriented elders are not always able to free themselves from the more problematic aspects of modern culture. Their ideological ambivalence raises the question of the role elders can play in today's youth and change oriented culture. A second question relates to how education can help students discriminate between older people who are promoting the modern mind-set and the elders with whom they need to enter into dialogue.

THE DIALECTIC OF THE ELDER/STUDENT RELATIONSHIP

When we put aside the ideological lenses that illuminate the cultural patterns central to modernism (technological change, individual choice and values, the false sense of plenitude communicated in stores and through the media, etc.), it becomes easier to recognize that various types of elders are already part of a process of trans-generational communication that occurs in even the most modern sectors of society. The experience of previous generations in such highly technological domains as piloting a jet airliner involves passing on knowledge gained over generations of flying—knowledge which may go counter to a new pilot's common sense understanding, such as how to perform a banking turn when there is no visible horizon. Elders have been influential in other sectors of society, such as education, politics, religion, and so forth. Although the various expressions of educational liberalism foreground either an individually-centered view of the world or an expert/technological model, trans-generational communication is part of the complex communication process that sustains the culture's diverse ways of knowing and forms of relationship. Even the design of buildings and cars, insofar as they encode the thought processes of earlier generations, can be understood as part of the process of trans-generational communication that serves as the background against which more explicitly conscious concerns and interests are individually pursued.

The problem is not the lack of trans-generational communication within the multiple cultures that make up American society. Rather, it is more a matter of distinguishing between the forms of trans-generational communication that are based on an anthropocentric world view and the myth of progess through technological innovation, and the forms of trans-generational communication that are based on the wisdom of how to live symbolically meaningful lives without destroying the environment. In terms of schools where different liberal frameworks of understanding more directly influence which aspects of culture students will encounter and the interpretation that teachers will reinforce, the problem is even more complex. But as students are in the more formative stage of their individual/cultural development, and thus more receptive to complex interpretations and critical reflection about the taken for granted aspects of the culture, it is absolutely essential that the recovery of ecologically responsible trans-generational communication be made a primary goal of curriculum reform, and the education of teachers. This recommendation also has implications for the graduate programs that grant the advanced degrees (too often certificates of ideological correctness) in education.

The word "recovery" might seem an inappropriate term here, as many readers might argue that we have to go back too far in the history of the West to find a dominant tradition of elders who were ecologically centered. I use the term as a way of suggesting the need to reconnect with the main line of development in human history, which involved cultures that took into account the characteristics of the bioregion that sustained them. Cultural groups that ignored the ecological imperatives did not survive—unless they conquered and subjugated other peoples and bioregions. Recovery is also the right word in terms of elders who have existed on the margins of the dominant culture, and at the center of minority cultures. Although public schools and universities helped to make these elders invisible by privileging the abstract forms of knowledge deemed essential to the exploitation of "natural resources," and to expanding the power of the state, elders have nevertheless continued to exist as a highly attenuated tradition. Indeed, folk traditions and the kind of knowledge that Scott Russell Sanders received as a boy growing up in rural Ohio from Mr. Sivvy continue to be sustained by elders who serve as connecting links between generations.

The recovery of a more receptive, even reflective, awareness of the contextual knowledge and wisdom of elders as part of the educational process must be based on several important distinctions. Perhaps these distinctions can be put into sharper relief by identifying the characteristics of two prominent educators who have influenced the direction of reform within two different traditions of educational liberalism. Madeline Hunter's mastery teaching model has become widely adopted as the basis of teacher decision making in the classroom. Paulo Freire, the other "elder," has become a cult figure for a generation of educational theorists committed to using the educational process as a means of furthering the emancipation of the individual. Hunter, the technocrat concerned with the universal application of a set of classroom procedures, and Freire, the advocate of each generation becoming empowered to rename the world, are both elders in the sense of being older and in being able to articulate the connections between widely acknowledged social and educational problems and strategies for solving them. Also, they both use the legitimating metaphors taken for granted within their respective traditions of educational liberalism: Hunter emphasizing the connections between rationally managed classrooms and observable outcomes, and Freire emphasizing the connections between critical thought, empowerment, and social progress. In effect, both are spokespersons for different aspects of modernity. While their followers view them as exemplary elders, I would argue that they are simply popularizers (cultural amplifiers) of the very cultural patterns that are contributing to the ecological crisis. Other groups within the dominant culture also have their misdirected elders who are promoting the economic growth of large corporations, a more rigid adherence to the principles of Classical Liberalism, and religious beliefs that continue to hold out the promise of salvation to people regardless of their impact on the environment.

For educators who understand the importance of Gregory Smith's (1992) warning that the main educational challenge is learning how to live with limits, the problem of trans-generational communication is twofold. There is, first, the question of how to recognize elders who are part of the solution rather than representatives of the problem. Second, there is the question of how to involve elders in the educational process when students are being conditioned to associate success and meaningful experiences with consumerism and immediate excitement. As we shall see, the answers will require that educators begin to recognize: (1) the connections between the various streams of educational liberalism and the ecological crisis; (2) that modernization is a historically and culturally specific phenomena; and (3) the impact that modern cultures are having on the Earth's ecosystems. This is a tremendous responsibility for teachers to assume, especially when even more highly educated groups are dedicating their talents and energies to advancing economic and technological practices that are ecologically destructive. But teachers have demonstrated that they can be at the forefront of cultural change. With some prodding from outside groups, they have worked to eliminate gender biases from much of the curriculum. As important interpreters of the culture to the next generation, it is hoped that they will begin to recognize how modern culture also encodes a set of biases toward human/nature relationships, and that elders, like women and other marginalized groups, have an important, even essential, contribution to make in passing on both practical knowledge and wisdom of how to live a sustainable existence.

Because we have so many false elders who are promoting modern myths, the problem of recognizing ecologically responsible elders is even more daunting and complex than the recent problem of identifying women artists and scientists when only male achievers were represented in public school and university curricula. The following characteristics, however, may help in recognizing the essential differences. *First,* an ecologically-centered elder understands the linkages between human experience, culture, and ecosystems—and can communicate this understanding through narratives, song, and dance. A central feature of the elder's way of understanding is the ability to frame immediate experience in terms of the taken for granted cultural patterns that are being reenacted, and to situate these culural patterns in terms of their long-range consequences for the environment.

Second, an ecologically-centered elder speaks and models behavior (including moral values) in ways that help the new generation recognize and experience the connections between their own lives and the accumulated wisdom being handed down from the past. The elder thus must possess a special sensitivity to the temporal aspects of how individuals, culture, and ecosystems are connected. This means understanding the complex nature of tradition. Indeed, this is a critical point of difference between older people who are promoting the relativizing beliefs and values of modernism, and ecologically responsible elders. The advocates of modernism, which were cited earlier as promoting the idea of individually-centered intelligence and creativity, view tradition in overly simplistic terms. That is, they represent it as the expression of backwardness, as static, and whatever else is seen as obstructing the new and experimental—which they automatically associate with progress. In order to be ecologically-centered, the elder must understand that tradition is *everything* that is handed down from the past, and that without this more complex view of tradition it is impossible to understand the connections between the ecological crisis and the loss of the community of memory—which is really the storehouse of proven knowledge, technologies, moral understandings, modes of thanksgiving and celebration, narratives and communal practices that enable us to understand and experience the connectedness of life forms. Edward Shils, who is an example of an elder who understands the complexities of tradition but fails to recognize that ecosystems are the source of human life, provides an explanation of tradition that avoids the modern error of representing it as something abstract and disconnected from people's lives—like a force from the past that reaches into the modern present in order to obstruct progress and pull us backward. According to Shils:

> Traditions are not independently self-reproductive or self elaborating. Only living, knowing, desiring human beings can enact them and reenact them and modify them. Traditions develop because the desire to create something truer and better or more convenient is alive in those who acquire and posses them. Traditions can deteriorate in the sense of losing their adherents because their possessors cease to present them or because those who once received and reenacted and extended them now prefer

other lines of conduct or because new generations to which they were presented find other traditions of belief or some relatively new beliefs more acceptable, according to the standards which these generations accept. (1981, pp. 14–15)

The awareness that some traditions become outmoded while others are the basis of innovative developments, that traditions may become attenuated or even forgotten in the life of the community, that lost traditions cannot be recovered in their original form, that they are an essential aspect of everyday life (use of paper, language, patterns of driving down a street, etc.), and that not everything new in language, dress, and technology will become a tradition—all seem essential to understanding how we are connected to the past and future. In understanding that traditions encode and thus are a form of collective storage of earlier forms of cultural intelligence, the elder can help clarify how taken for granted traditions involve being controlled by earlier ways of thinking that may now be problematic— like our currrent reliance on cars that utilize nonrenewable forms of energy. This understanding of tradition may also enable the elder to help the next generation consider the long term consequences of technological innovations, such as computer-based monitoring of the workplace.

In effect, this sense of connectedness and dependency (through stories, ceremonies, and instruction) makes it possible for the young to enter into an expanded symbolic world that would otherwise remain beyond what they can attain through their own direct experience. The dialogue with tradition that the elder helps to sustain and keep properly framed has to do with the challenge of conserving the quality of community life by keeping the most enhancing relationships clearly in focus. Gregory Cajete's observation about the ideal upheld by American Indian traditions of always striving to think the highest thought seems relevant here. "Thinking the highest thought means thinking of one's self, one's community, and one's environment 'richly.' This way of thinking," he continues, "is essentially a spiritual mind-set in which thinking in the highest, most respectful, and compassionate way systematically influences the actions of both individuals and the community" (p. 43). I suspect that this attribute is learned in the same taken for granted way that speakers of English learn to use the subject, verb, object pattern of thought and communication. Thinking the highest thought within an individually-centered view of the world is fundamentally different from learning to think the highest thought when self is understood and experienced as connected to culture (living traditions) and eco-systems. The stories, explanations, and modelling of elders represent one of the primary ways the next generation learns to discriminate between the two forms of highest thought.

A *third* characteristic of responsible elders is their ability to serve as a connecting link between the living and the past by keeping alive communal ceremonies and folk practices that involve develop-ing personal values and skills, as well as community practices that do not have an adverse effect on the environment. If we add to Ivan Illich's idea of "master" the moral and practical dimensions of ecological-centeredness, the following statement pretty well sum-marizes both the forms of knowledge that are shared through trans-generational communication and the attitudes essential to this en-larged sense of community:

> The relationship of master and disciple is not restricted to intel-lectual discipline. It has its counterpart in the arts, in physics, in religion, in psychoanalysis, and in pedagogy. It fits mountain-climbing, silverworking and politics, cabinetmaking and personnel administration. What is common to all true master-pupil relationships is the awareness both share that their relationship is literally priceless and in very different ways a privilege for both. (1970, p. 100)

The mutual awareness that it is a special relationship, indeed a priv-ilege for both participants, is what, in Illich's view, separates the relationship from the type where older people act like demagogues, charlatans, and in other self-serving ways.

This discussion of how elders help renew and carry forward knowledge of essential human/natural system relationships, which represents only a beginning effort to understand the responsibilities of elders, is not meant to be used as a basis for dismissing the vitally important role of elders in holding together a sense of cultural iden-tity and spiritual centeredness of social groups who have been under-mined and marginalized by the more extreme forces of moderniza-tion. The efforts of elders, including African-American, American Indian, Hispanic-American, and Asian-American communities, to tell the stories and to keep alive the ceremonies and other forms of trans-generational communication essential to their sense of cul-tural identity have been absolutely vital to their survival. The added challenge these elders face today is to recognize that the modern Eurocentric culture that is now ambivalently viewed both as offering possibilities for economic advancement and as a threat to their cultural traditions is also exposing them to a deadly amount of toxic wastes. That is, elders in these cultural communities need to address more directly the ecological consequences of modern beliefs and technologies, and to begin asking which of their own traditions might represent, in renewed form, ecologically viable alternatives to mainstream practices. The elders in American Indian cultures, who are also powerful examples of cultural/bio-conservative thinkers, have been addressing this issue in their own communities, and are now beginning to communicate their concerns to the larger society.

Introducing trans-generational communication into the classroom is not like introducing a new computer technology into the market place. Rather, it involves making adjustments in a whole series of cultural templates that influence the student's taken-for-granted attitudes. In some communities it might be possible to bring elders into the classroom, or to take students out into the community where the context might be more appropriate to the knowledge that is to be shared by the elder. In other educational settings teachers may have to provide the most elementary background knowledge that will enable students to recognize the importance of learning from an elder. It might take the form of enabling students to undertand how individuals are nested in culture, and culture in ecosystems, and in directly teaching about the complexity and dynamic nature of traditions. This background preparation might also take the form of examining more critically the characteristics of modern culture, including the forms of knowledge that are privileged as well as those that have been marginalized, how privileged forms of knowledge are revised and passed on, whether these forms of knowledge take account of human dependency upon natural systems, and so forth. Clarifying the differences between modern and ecologically-centered cultures, including the dangers connected with borrowing from other cultures, might help students recognize the difference between responsible elders and famous people who allow themselves to be used for the purpose of promoting a product or the cause of a limited political group. In traditional cultures where the moral wisdom and practical knowledge of elders is valued, the background understandings essential to being able to listen, learn (including renew), and carry forward the communal wisdom and knowledge is reinforced through the multiple channels of communication that sustain daily life.

As suggested earlier, in order for an elder to tell a coherent story the listener must know how to participate in the relationship. Knowing how to participate, in turn, involves knowing when the elder is being accountable for communicating what the essential relationships are and how to live them. One of the more difficult challenges facing educators, from elementary grades through graduate level classes, is in preparing students to be knowledgeable and respectful participants in this process of carrying forward (which means both to conserve and renew) the community of memory that will help serve as a guide to the future. The other challenge that faces all cultural groups, but particularly the dominant culture, is for the older generation to learn how to transform themselves from being apologists of modernism to becoming ecologically-centered elders. Learning how to recognize an elder and how to participate in the process of trans-generational communication is preparatory for later taking on the responsibility of being an elder themselves—and this is one of the ways that schools can help recover the tradition of elders that modernization has undermined.

SEVEN

EDUCATIONAL MODELS OF COMMUNITY AND ENVIRONMENTAL RENEWAL

On one level American education is highly dynamic and reform oriented. Along with the economic and technological sectors of society, public schools and universities continually renew and expand the symbolic foundations of modern consciousness. Professional careers depend upon the advancement of knowledge and the discovery of new techniques, and the consciousness of students is similarly "modernized." The dislocations and stresses that accompany the growth of modernism have resulted in the emergence of three distinct approaches to educational reform. One approach is driven more by competing ideologies. These include the various approaches to modernization taken by liberal educators, as well as the efforts on the part of religious conservatives to wrest control of schools from what they perceive as secular thinking. Ironically, this latter group has not made the connection between secularism and modernism. The impetus for the second approach to educational reform is the frightening growth of urban youth violence and drug use, which has served as a wake-up call for many parents and educators who are now cooperating for the purpose of refocusing the attention and allegiance of urban youth. The third approach to educational reform is driven by powerful spokespersons for the economic and technological sector of society. The argument for a work force able to adapt to the increasing rate of technological change as America attempts to reclaim the lead in an increasingly globalized economy is gaining in prominence as more middle class people experience the increasing uncertainties of employment. All three approaches to educational reform, however, fail to address the deeper sources of the crisis of modernism. Indeed, if each of these approaches to educational reform were to succeed, including the efforts of the religious conservatives, the basic assumptions of modernism would remain intact and the consumer growth orientation of the economy would not be altered.

But on another level, educational reform is tragically superficial and short sighted. At the root of the deeper crisis not being addressed by any of these approaches is the fundamental fact that, as Herman E. Daly puts it, "the economy grows in physical scale, but the ecosystem does not" (1991, p. 180). Like E. F. Schumacher and Ivan Illich who both grasped the essential issue put out of focus by the myth of progress, Daly recognizes that a modern based economic system cannot grow indefinitely—as though the only constraints are the lack of human inventiveness and the technological backwardness of certain sectors of the world's population. By framing the problem in terms of the second law of thermodynamics, Daly is able to identify the double bind in achieving unlimited economic growth:

> We do not create or destroy (produce or consume) anything in a physical sense—we merely transform or rearrange. And the inevitable cost of arranging greater order in one part of the system (the human economy) is creating a more than offsetting amount of disorder elsewhere (the natural environment). If "elsewhere" happens to be the sun, as it ultimately is for all of nature's technologies, then we need not worry. There is nothing we can do about it in any case. But if "elsewhere" is somewhere else on earth, as it is for all terrestrial sources of low entropy, then we must be very careful. There is a limit to how much disorder can be produced in the rest of the biosphere without inhibiting its ability to support the human subsystem. (p. 24)

This line of analysis leads Daly to see the Industrial Revolution as representing a real break from the mainstream of human history, which involved the development of technologies based on the use of energy seasonally renewed by solar power. He also notes that before the Industrial Revolution economic growth was not directly experienced within the life span of most people. But with the advent of the

Industrial Revolution, and the messianic ideology of modernism that evolved as a source of its legitimation, the expectation became widely held that every person who possessed certain values and personal attributes could expect to experience directly the benefits of economic growth. Indeed, it has become part of the modern individual's natural attitude to equate their own personal success with advancing economically beyond what their parents had attained. This expectation, and the impact it has in turning low entropy forms of energy into waste that disrupts the viability of natural systems, is what Daly refers to as "hyper-growthmania" (p. 183). His argument is that we need to return to the principles of a steady-state form of energy use if our society is to maintain relative balance with the cycles of energy renewal that occur in ecosystems. Growth in our ability to more rapidly deplete the pool of ecosystem energy must be replaced by growth in the symbolic areas of culture that enrich human understanding, meaning, and the participatory dimensions of communal life.

Daly's observation that cultural life runs on energy and that we need to move toward a more sustainable relationship with the sources of energy has direct relevance to any discussion of whether current educational reforms are short sighted. It also raises the question of whether success in achieving the reforms as now conceptualized would further contribute to the cultural double bind where economic progress is achieved at the cost of depleting resources that cannot be renewed at a rate that fits the human's scale of time. For example, success in educating students to view all traditions as relative and to look to technological change as the dominant feature of human experience (which reflect the emancipatory and technicist agendas) will leave them without the symbolic means necessary for evolving a form of community not centered on consumerism and waste producing technologies. Success in aligning schooling with the workplace through apprenticeships and more work-related curricula will similarly leave students conceptually unprepared for thinking critically about an economic/technological system increasingly driven by considerations of efficiency and cost effectiveness. Nor are they likely to be able to articulate alternatives to the present approach of designing into the technology the expert knowledge and skills that, in the past, had been the possession of the workers. With the growth of smart technologies that can improve the problem solving and work efficiency, and transfer them to future generations of technology, human workers become increasingly expendable. Even success in increasing the academic performance of inner city youth, and contributing to their joining the college educated middle class, will contribute to the double bind of improving the material conditions of life by undermining the environmental prospects of future generations.

The increased media attention given to the various approaches to educational reform is noteworthy for the total silence on the connections between educational reform and the daily news coverage of contaminated water supplies, the rapid decline of bird and fish populations,unemployment caused by over cutting forests, the rising incidence of cancers resulting from exposure to chemicals being put into the environment, and so on. All of the participants in the current debate on educational reform (reporters, T. V. pundits, citizens, academics) appear to share the same conceptual categories and myths that serve to maintain the illusion that educational reform issues and the growing evidence of environmental abuse are unrelated. Even educational theorists who have been writing for the last twenty years about how schools continue to reinforce economic and political disparities between social classes have ignored the impact of the dominant economic and technologial practices on the environment.

Indeed, the earlier discussion of how mainstream educators represent the nature of individualism, creativity, and intelligence indicates that David Orr's insight that all education is a form of environmental education still goes largely unrecognized. A recent series of conversations I had with educational historians while attending a national conference in Chicago brought home to me just how radically compartmentalized the ecological crisis is in the thinking of those who claim responsibility for documenting and clarifying the significance of past educational trends, ideas, and achievements. In the course of a dinner conversation I asked the educational historians sitting around the table about the work being done by educational historians that addresses how schooling has contributed to or been a countervailing force to the cultural patterns contributing to the ever increasing demands being made on the environment. Although historians like Roderich Nash and William Cronin have made environmental history an important field of inquiry, my question to the educational historians made as much sense as if I had spoken in Latin. They knew how to frame historical studies of education in terms of theories that illuminated the connections between schools and social class, bureaucracy, gender, race, and, now, biographies of influential educators. But they acknowledged that they did not know what questions would help frame and thus guide historical studies of how schools have contributed to ecologically destructive cultural practices. Nor could they recognize the importance of questions relating to how schools have helped marginalize and subvert ecologically viable cultural traditions that represented alternatives to the approach to modernization taken by the dominant culture.

The lack of interest in my questions was further reflected in the fact that of the over ninety papers presented at the conference mine was the only one that addressed an educational issue related to the ecological crisis. The yearly professional conferences of the American Educational Research Association, the American Educational Studies Association, and the meeting of the more radical curriculum theorists (the yearly Bergamo Conference) involve literally thousands of papers on the educational aspects of nearly every major problem facing American society: drug abuse, de-skilling of the work place, computer empowerment and information highways, gender and racial equality, spirituality, educational assessment, and so forth. But papers dealing with the cultural/educational aspects of turning the environment into a wasteland for future generations were nearly nonexistent. The response to a proposal for a session involving a series of papers that would explore the implications of the Deep Ecology Movement for curriculum theory is typical of the level of understanding and receptiveness to addressing what is the most crucial issue facing humankind. In turning down the proposal that would have brought together for the first time a leading Deep Ecology thinker and curriculum theorists, the chairperson of the session cited as a basis for rejecting the proposal a series of questions and concerns raised by the reviewers of the proposal. One of the more coherent concerns about the merits of the papers was expressed as follows:

> I don't understand the last sentence of the first paragraph on 'Implications of Deep Ecology.' . . . What does it mean to identify aspects of deep ecology thinking, 'particularly the aspects of culture . . . most resistant to the self-limiting characteristics of an ecologically sustainable culture? The connections between concepts are unclear to me here.

Another reviewer wrote that "my reservations are that the proposed papers could easily take the form of political/theoretical posturing" (evaluations that accompanied correspondence from Jean Erdman, 1993). This lack of open mindedness and superficial understanding of the curriculum issues they were asked to evaluate, is not limited to a few pedantic members of the educational establishment. A request submitted to the Spencer Foundation for support that would have enabled me to reduce my teaching load to two courses a term and thus to devote more time to writing this book resulted in a rejection letter from the Vice President who stated that "we . . . regret that we cannot encourage you to develop a full proposal . . . Our review . . . leads us to believe that the project outlined would not receive an ultimately favorable response" (correspondence from John H. Barcroft). The indifference, even hostility, shown toward bringing questions about the cultural patterns contributing to the ecological crisis into educational discussions is such an important issue that I shall return to it later in this chapter.

THREE CURRICULUM MODELS OF COMMUNITY AND ENVIRONMENTAL RENEWAL

Not all educational reform efforts blindly reinforce the destructive forms of environmental education that are part of the anthropocentrically (humanistic) oriented curricula of public schools and universities. The small number of educators interested in developing a postmodern critique of contemporary classrooms, and in illuminating the limitations of current educational theory at both the public school and university level, is slowly growing. And increasingly, classroom teachers, even entire schools, are attempting to make the issue of ecological sustainability a more central aspect of the student's education. Generally, these efforts are based on a scientific model of studying local ecosystems, but the cultural impact on ecosystems is beginning to receive more attention. The problem facing ecologically-centered reform efforts, in addition to their potential of becoming focal points of controversy in the community, continues to be the lack of understanding of the encoding and reproductive patterns of culture that are a taken for granted part of the communication and learning processes occurring in classrooms. This results in a mixture of factual understanding of how technologies and other human practices impact local ecosystems, the fostering of a deep concern that we have to change environmentally destructive cultural practices, and the continued reinforcement of the very core anthropocentic beliefs and values now contributing to the problem. But even these mixed efforts must be viewed as a hopeful sign that educators, however tentative, are beginning to grasp what should be the fundamental priorities in making curricular decisions.

Three especially important models of curriculum that address (or have a unique potential for addressing) the connections between community and environmental renewal are the Foxfire Curriculum, the Common Roots Program, and the Ecoliteracy Project. While the three curricula represent very different approaches, they all share the common characteristic of having evolved outside schools of education. The Foxfire Curriculum is the most widely known, and is now being adopted across the country. It is even being incorporated into university teacher education programs. The Common Roots Program began in rural Vermont and continues to have a rural community focus—including rural poverty as an aspect of community renewal. The Ecoliteracy Project was started in the Bay Area of California, and continues to evolve within the context of urban, cultural diverse communities. We shall consider all three models as examples of the diverse approaches that can be taken to addressing the ecological crisis. We shall also consider the unique strengths, as well as limitations that need to be taken into account as these models of curriculum reform undergo further modification and more widespread adoption.

Foxfire Curriculum

Readers already familiar with the Foxfire Curriculum may be surprised to see it included in a discussion of ecologically-oriented models of learning. Indeed, the sense of surprise is partly justified, given the curriculum's strong emphasis on documenting only the human aspects of local communities, and its grounding in Dewey's principles of learning. Except when science teachers adopt a Foxfire approach, any chance that the focus of student interest would be on the environmental consequences of community practices is entirely fortuitous. The insightful writings of Eliot Wigginton, and the use of Dewey to further legitimize learning principles that emerged from years of experience in refining the Foxfire approach to learning, reflect the humanistic orientation that Deep Ecology supporters have cited as one of the chief sources of our cultural hubris. The three most important efforts to lay out the guiding principles and justifications for the Foxfire Curriculum—*Sometimes a Shining Moment* (1985), "Foxfire Grows Up" (1989), and "The Foxfire Approach: Perspectives and Core Practices" (1991)—do not even mention the ecological crisis. Yet this curriculum (which is more an approach to learning and documentation than a set body of knowledge) has evolved an approach to using the cultural practices of communities as the basis of student learning that, with further modification, could become an educational model that would connect community, which it now addresses, with environmental renewal.

The Foxfire Curriculum had its origins in the late sixties when Eliot Wigginton acknowledged to his first period English class at Rabun Gap-Nacoochee School in rural Georgia: "Look, this isn't working. You know it isn't and I know it isn't. Now what are we going to do together to make it through the rest of the year?" (1985, p. 32) The failure of the traditional curriculum that dictated what students should be interested in learning led to the collaborative use of the talent and experience of the students themselves, as well as local community personalities and folk practices, as the essential elements in the learning process. The beginnings of what eventually became known as a cultural journalism approach to curriculum started in 1967 with a student produced magazine that was given the name of *Foxfire*. The name was borrowed from an organism that glows in the dark as it subsists on decaying organic matter in damp, dark groves of trees. In subsequent years, student interviews, documentations, and photographs of the folk traditions of local communities were collected together and published as *The Foxfire Book*, which has grown into many volumes ranging from how to build a log cabin to the collection of local folk stories and the documenting of folk technologies. Later was to come, for Wigginton, the discovery that Dewey's *Experience and Education* articulated within a more comprehensive philosophical and educational framework the principles of learning that had emerged from efforts of Wigginton and the students to work through the many problems connected with their community based approach to learning. National acclaim, foundation grants, and a national network for the promotion of the Foxfire approach to education were to follow.

As Wigginton's writings indicate, successes were mixed with failures and disappointments, including the ever present danger of the Foxfire approach being turned into a set of rigid routines dictated by the teacher. Our concern here, however, is not with the history of this reform movement, but with the strengths and weaknesses of the principles that are supposed to guide students and teachers who take a Foxfire approach to classroom learning. Sorting out how some of the principles contribute to a renewed sense of community that is more in balance with itself and its surrounding environment, and how other principles reinforce a modern human-centered focus, deserves book length treatment. The following discussion should thus be viewed as both introductory on my part and as an invitation to the members of the Foxfire community to begin thinking of the distinctions between a curriculum that documents existing cultural practices, contributes to the renewal of community, and renewal of community traditions that are ecologically sustainable over the long haul—that is, renews community traditions that will help sustain the seventh unborn generation. The following "Core Practices" were published as part of the current Foxfire outreach program:

1. *All the work teachers and students do together must flow from student desire, student concerns.* It must be infused from the beginning with student choice, design, revision, execution, reflection and evaluation.
2. Therefore, *the role of the teacher must be that of collaborator and team leader and guide* rather than boss. The teacher monitors the academic and social growth of every student, leading each into new areas of understanding and competence.
3. *The academic integrity of the work must be absolutely clear.* Each teacher should embrace state- or local-mandated skill content lists as 'givens' to be engaged by the class, accomplish them to the level of mastery in the course of executing the class's plan, but go beyond their normally narrow confines to discover the value and potential inherent in the content areas being taught and its connections to other disciplines.
4. *The work is characterized by student action,* rather than passive receipt of processed information.
5. A constant feature of the process is its *emphasis on peer teaching, small group work and teamwork.*
6. *Connections between the classroom work and surrounding communities and the real world outside the classroom are real.* The content of all courses is connected to the world in which the student lives.
7. *There must be an audience beyond the teacher for student work* . . . it must be an audience the students want to serve, or engage, or impress. The audience, in turn, must affirm that the work is important and is needed and is worth doing.
8. As the year progresses, *new activities should spiral gracefully out of the old.*
9. As teachers, *we must acknowledge the world of aesthetic experience,* model that attitude in our interactions with students,

and resist the momentum of policies and practices that deprive students of the chance to use their imaginations.

10. *Reflection*—some conscious, thoughtful time to stand apart from the work itself—is an essential activity that must take place at key points throughout the work.
11. *The work must include unstintingly honest, ongoing evaluation for skills and content, and changes in student attitude.* (Foxfire Fund, 1990, p. 2)

Participatory decision making on the part of students, as well as the other guiding principles relating to active learning in "unfamiliar territory," and to insuring that the outcome of the students' work is judged by the community as important, are all strengths of the Foxfire approach. Indeed, these principles represent an insightful application of key aspects of Dewey's educational ideas that are essentially sound (Bowers, 1987, pp.116–125). But there are other strengths that relate more directly to the characteristics of a sustainable culture discussed in earlier chapters. The breakdown in the factory model of education led Wigginton to invite students to identify what they would be interested in learning. Ironically, this new direction was actually a return to the ancient pathway of human development where learning was centered in the activities of the community and face to face communication, rather than through the abstract medium of the printed word. The students' interview of Luther Rickman, an old timer in the community who had stories to tell about his years as sheriff, served to reestablish the linkage between orality and learning that modern schooling had broken. Wigginton and the students had the good sense to recognize that this approach to curriculum not only had benefits for students but for the community as well. The Foxfire books that followed were based on student documentation of oral accounts of how various folk traditions were learned, performed, and passed on to the next generation. In making spoken discourse centered in a community of memory a core part of student learning, the Foxfire approach provided an opportunity for a profoundly different experience than what is encountered through technologically mediated learning—such as encountered in textbooks, the television screen, and, increasingly, the prepackaged data and simulations of the computer.

A second strength of the Foxfire emphasis on learning from face to face communication within a real community made up of different generations (as opposed to face to face communication within a community of students who share essentially the same perspective) is that it helps to revitalize communication between the generations. The interview with Luther Rickman and other older people who were keepers of community memory involved an entirely different way of framing trans-generational relationships than what characterizes the older person who appears in a television commercial for the purpose of selling a product that promises to restore its user to youthful vigor and beauty. When students frame the relationship in a way that allows the older members of the community to tell their stories or to share their special craft with dignity and a sense that they have useful knowledge, they are not being put into a position where they feel they must apologize for being out of date and thus an anachronism in the modern world. Rather the relationship becomes a matter of respectful learning from a person who is being recognized as an elder—someone who has experiences, special knowledge, and perhaps even wisdom students want to learn about and document for future generations. In a real sense the Foxfire approach combines both the conserving aspects of trans-generational communication, as well as the renewing of community traditions through its emphasis on reflection. Incorporating into the curriculum "some conscious, thoughtful time to stand apart from the work itself" provides students the opportunity to bring their own perspectives and thus to renew the traditions that are to be passed on to the next generation.

But the emphasis on the student as journalist, and the change in the coding and storage process from the spoken word and memory to the printed word, books, and, now, CD ROM limits the character/moral forming possibilities of the student/elder relationship. The ethnographic orientation can easily lead to an emphasis on accuracy in the documentation of the knowledge of elders. But accurate documentation is very different from mastering the skills essential to being able to reproduce them for the next generation. The question that needs to be asked is: Do the students make the traditions they are learning about part of their own lives? What viable aspects of the community of memory will they be able to pass on to the next generation? Will the process of trans-generational communication they participate in be limited primarily to explanations of how to use various technologies that are part of the complex process of cultural journalism? These concerns do not, however, negate the fact that the Foxfire approach to learning makes trans-generational communication a central part of the curriculum, and thus represents a radical shift away from the type of curriculum intended to provide students the value orientation and skills that will make them more reliable workers and consumers.

A third strength is that the combination of participatory learning and local community focus represents a genuine break with the modern tradition of using techniques and learning packages designed by experts. These classroom techniques and learning packages socialize students to a technological pattern of thinking that de-emphasizes context while stressing procedural problem solving. The participatory and community focus also represents a break from the experimental approach to knowledge and values that characterize the more individual constructivist approaches to education now being advocated in many teacher education programs. The emphasis on a community context that ties together a number of the guiding principles of the Foxfire approach helps to avoid the routinization of the learning process—which is the first step to turning a process into an abstract technique that can be applied in classrooms that are disconnected from the life of the larger community. Wigginton's personal observations about the constant danger of the Foxfire approach being reduced to a series of techniques indicates a sensitivity both to the dangers of imposing expert forms of knowledge on the learning process and the routinization that often results from mental laziness—which were also concerns of Dewey. Dewey's writings simply provided the theoretical legitimization for the insights that Wigginton and his co-workers arrived at through long years of experience.

A fourth strength is that the Foxfire approach, when it is carried out in accordance with its guiding principles, introduces students to thinking, valuing, and forms of experience that go some distance toward framing the world in terms of processes, interactive relationships, and networks that are essential aspects of an ecological paradigm. The word "ecology" has its origins in the Greek word "oikos," which meant family household and its daily operations. Later, Ernst Haeckel combined "oikos" with the "ologie" and "oecologie" became the word for the study of environmental conditions of existence (Worster, 1977, p. 192). Although the modern meaning of ecology is still being re-metaphorized, the part of the essential meaning that connects with the Foxfire approach is that the individual is understood as part of the larger household we call "community." Learning how the activities that sustain community life are connected in multidimensional ways (through family connections, through stories told over time, reenacted in individual experience, and so forth) represents a shift away from the Cartesian/modern way of thinking where the student is an outside observer, and knowledge of the world is represented (encoded) as factual, objective and thus as independent of cultural traditions.

But I would stop short of suggesting that the Foxfire approach represents an ecological model of learning in the deep sense that Bateson, Maturana, and Varela understand it to be. Wigginton and his collaborators are anthropocentric thinkers. That is, their understanding of community is framed in terms of human activities: how members of human communities use the local resources of their environment, how they pass on various traditions, and so forth. The idea of humans being part of a larger biotic community (indeed, being dependent upon it for continued well being) has not been part of their thinking. That some followers are extending the guiding principles into the teaching of a scientific way of understanding local ecosystems, and even studying patterns of environmental degradation, indicates how easily this approach to curriculum can be adapted. But the absence in its theoretical foundations of Deep Ecology principles is clearly present and is responsible for a number of weaknesses still needing to be addressed if the Foxfire approach is to achieve its full potential in contributing to an ecologically sustainable form of learning.

The weaknesses can be identified under two headings: (1) the teacher's lack of an ecological perspective, and (2) the lack of a deep understanding of culture, particularly the encoding and storage characteristics of the languages used to sustain the communicative patterns of everyday life. We shall first consider the contribution an ecological perspective would make to the Foxfire approach to teacher decision making, the content of the curriculum, and the interpretative frameworks that would enable students to recognize new relationships and to pose new questions.

An ecological perspective can exist at many levels: as an explanation in the writings of Bateson and Capra, as an interpretative framework that a person may recall and bring into play when talking to other people who are concerned about environmental issues, and as a taken-for-granted way of thinking and experiencing. In suggesting that the Foxfire approach needs to incorporate an ecological perspective, I am aware of the danger that it might not become part of the teacher's taken-for-granted way of making sense of the world. If the ecological perspective has to be deliberately recalled, like when trying to remember what an author wrote, or becomes a viable explanatory framework in specific social settings, it will simply be like the rest of the intellectual baggage acquired as part of institutionalized learning and certification. Therefore, it is important to keep in focus that the following changes in the orientation of the Foxfire approach will result *only* when an ecological perspective becomes part of the teacher's taken for granted patterns of thought and language usage. *Learning to think and experience from within a new conceptual framework or paradigm, rather than just being able to think about it, is one of the most difficult challenges facing those who want to bring about fundamental reform of teacher education.* I suspect it will be one of the most difficult challenges the advocates of the current Foxfire approach will face.

Before addressing how an ecological perspective would enable teachers to help students reframe the questions that guide their inquiry, it is necessary to restate two important points relating to an ecological model of thinking. The first is that all life systems are now understood as ecosystems. This is summarized in Capra's statement that was cited earlier: "All living systems have a dual nature. They are integrated wholes and, at the same time, parts of larger wholes. Because of this dual nature, each living system has two basic tendencies: a self-assertive tendency to preserve its individual autonomy as an integrated whole, and an integrative tendency to function as part of a larger whole" (1993, p. 7 Guide). The second point is that an ecological way of thinking about how individuals are nested in culture, and culture in natural systems, requires a radical shift in our conceptual/cultural maps. To quote Capra again, "we need a new way of seeing the world and a new way of thinking—thinking in terms of relationships, connectedness, context" (1993, p. 6). This means a taken-for-granted way of understanding that individual practices are simultaneously expressions of culture and interactions that set in motion perturbations that trigger changes in the organisms and natural processes that collectively constitute an ecosystem.

Framing the Foxfire approach to learning in terms of an ecological perspective would keep the fundamental human/ecosystem relationship more clearly in focus. Instead of learning beginning with "student choice, design, revision, execution, reflection and evaluation," which is likely to reflect the anthropocentric orientation of the dominant culture, the students' collaborative efforts might be directed more toward an ecological way of thinking if the teacher could pose questions such as: "Which local traditions are most compatible with the sustaining characteristics of local natural systems?" "Which traditions are sustainable for the long term, and which foster anomic individualism and a consumer orientation?" I have listened to many student-led discussions about what they want to learn and how they want to go about it. Their ideas about the direction their own education should take are almost never framed by questions about how human/cultural expectations are to be brought into balance with the Earth's ecosystems. Asking these questions, and bringing into the discussion the theory framework (an ecological model of understanding) that illuminates the importance of the questions, is the responsibility of the teacher. To put this another way, the knowledge accumulated over generations about community/ecosystem renewal should be part of the trans-generational communication that bond teachers and students together, and this knowledge (hopefully, communal wisdom) should be brought into the discussion of which questions should guide the inquiry process.

The teacher should thus be able to help students recognize other aspects of community traditions that can become the focal point of research, documentation, and reflective class discussions. For example, the concern about ecological sustainability might lead to a more comparative study of community traditions: What traditions are essential to sustaining a group's sense of cultural identity, and what impact do these traditions have on local ecosystems? What traditions in urban and suburban settings are not dependent upon environmentally damaging technologies and consumerism? What are the traditions in the more high technology and economically affluent sectors of society that are ecologically sustainable? What traditions are in danger of being lost in rural communities as Wal-Marts and the information highways advocated by business leaders, university presidents and other promoters of the "Information Age" spread across the land? I strongly suspect that if student inquiry were framed more in terms of how cultural traditions impact the environment they would not see the teacher as being an "authoritarian boss." Furthermore, the students' efforts to document the cultural traditions of various communities would make an important contribution to understanding the diversity of ecologically sustainable cultural practices. Many of these folk traditions are being marginalized and even subverted by technologies that promote forms of entertainment connected with consumerism. These more traditionally-oriented traditions, as opposed to what Shils refers to as the antitradition traditions of modernism (science, technology, consumerism, individually-centered views of creativity, intelligence, and so forth) are also under heavy pressure from the high status/technologically-oriented forms of knowledge promoted throughout institutionalized education. Just as modern culture threatens species diversity, it also threatens cultural diversity. And what is most at risk are the traditions (indeed, ecologies) of meaning, identities, and shared memory sustained through generations of face to face communication. Foxfire learning projects that lead to the documentation of these threatened traditions might help to preserve them by enabling us to understand and thus appreciate the many expressions of ecologically sustainable cultural practices that now exist— assuming of course that they meet other expectations of what constitutes a moral ecology. Particularly relevant here is Wes Jackson's observation that we cannot know the real value of the new knowledge that is part of the information explosion until we fully take stock of the forms of knowledge that are being displaced (1987, p. 12).

The second weakness in the Foxfire approach shows up in how the teacher's responsibilities are defined in the guide to "Core Practices." The first principle states that *"all the work teachers and students do together must flow from student desire, student concerns."* Other principles represent the teacher as a collaborator, as responsible for insuring the academic integrity of the learning process and for assessing the skills and understandings of the student. While these guiding principles are noteworthy for their sense of balance, there is no reference to what is perhaps *one of the most fundamental responsibilities of a teacher—namely, the responsibility for making explicit and helping to put into historical and comparative perspective the hidden aspects of culture that are part of every learning process.* Dewey's lack of a deep understanding of culture, particularly the different cultural ways of knowing, resulted in this responsibility being ignored in his theory of education. And Wigginton, according to his own critique of what he learned in the Cornell University teacher education program, does not even mention its failure to ground classroom theory and practice in an understanding of how the language processes of a culture are integral aspects of the primary socialization process that teachers exercise control over— even in the Foxfire learning process. In effect, the omissions in Wigginton's own intellectual development, combined with his reliance on Dewey's culture-free epistemology, are reproduced in the principles that frame the Foxfire teachers' responsibilities.

As I have already explained in a number of books how culture is the symbolic medium in which all aspects of teaching and learning are embedded, I shall summarize only a few of the culturally based decisions most Foxfire trained teachers will be unconsciously making. The process Foxfire teachers are not likely to understand relates to the "structural coupling" of cultural patterns and natural systems: cultural patterns continue to be reproduced and even modified through the processes of communication that sustain the patterns of everyday life—even when the participants are unaware of them. To make this point more directly, even though the guiding principles of the Foxfire approach to learning make no reference to the teacher's special responsibility for knowing how pedagogical and curricular decisions mediate the cultural learning process, cultural patterns and processes will be part of the implicit and explicit learning that occurs. Although teacher education institutions should have the primary responsibility for educating teachers to understand the complex role of language in reproducing the patterns of cultural groups, educating teachers to the Foxfire principles should be expanded in ways that address what is now a serious area of professional malpractice that should be laid at the doorstep of teacher education programs and graduate schools of education.

A deep knowledge of culture would enable Foxfire teachers to recognize that they have pedagogical and curricular responsibilities that go well beyond the collaborative relationships advocated by Wigginton and Dewey. But exercising this responsibility in a knowledgeable manner requires an understanding of several specific aspects of culture. The first aspect is best illuminated by the Peter Berger and Thomas Luckmann interpretation of the sociology of knowledge: how language processes introduce new members into a shared symbolic universe of taken for granted meanings and typifications, and how the shared belief system and languages of expression (verbal, kinesic, proxemic) become part of the individual's intersubjective self.

As one of the characteristics of taken for granted cultural knowledge is that it is unrecognized, students are just as inclined as everybody else to bring this form of knowledge to new learning situations. Thus, teachers need to be able to recognize when to make the implicit understandings explicit and how to assist students in the process of acquiring the language essential to expressing an alternative interpretation. This requires a knowledge of how people (including students) acquire and reproduce cultural patterns at the taken for granted level of awareness—even when they are claiming to be autonomous thinkers. It also requires a deep knowledge of several different cultures; otherwise teachers might not recognize fully the culturally specific nature of the taken-for-granted traditions that are part of the extended Foxfire classroom.

Another aspect of culture that teachers need to understand is the metaphorical nature of the language/thought process, including how metaphorical thinking is encoded in cultural objects such as buildings, cars, clothes, computers, and so forth. Student learning is largely dependent upon the process of analogic thinking framed by the deep root metaphors of the culture, and they could not think or communicate without using iconic metaphors. But few are able to recognize how their thoughts, language, behavior (as well as cultural objects they interact with) are expressions of a metaphorically con- structed reality. To put this another way, few students, even the most perceptive, recognize that they are being thought by the epis- temic patterns encoded in the language systems they use to express themselves. Most teachers contribute to this form of cultural blind- ness by reinforcing a conduit view of language and the cultural con- vention that holds that words represent real things. The argument here is that *all teachers, including Foxfire teachers, should have a general understanding of the role that analogic thinking plays in providing the initial schema for understanding new situations and ideas* (Bowers and Flinders, 1990, pp. 30–60). They should also un- derstand how the analogs are largely dictated by the root metaphors (anthropocentric view of the universe, a mechanistic model of life processes, progress, etc.) of the cultural group, and how iconic meta- phors encode earlier processes of analogic thinking. These funda- mental processes that nest individual intelligence in the different forms of cultural intelligence encoded in the languages of everyday speech, architecture, and the different modern discourses, were elab- orated more fully in the chapter on an "Ecological View of Intel- ligence."

As I have learned from introducing education students to an understanding of the culture/metaphorical language/thought con- nection, it takes considerable time and many concrete examples of how the use of metaphors frame the process of understanding before students fully grasp the constituting role of metaphor. Only then are they able to recognize the pedagogical decisions related to know- ing when to point out that the analog used to understand a new situation or idea may involve differences that are more important than the similarities between the analog and new situation (e.g., the use of the computer may enable us to understand certain aspects of human intelligence, but the differences may be more profound than the similarity of both "processing data"). The general understanding of the metaphorical foundations of thought also leads to recognizing that iconic metaphors like "individualism," "creativity," "data" and so forth, encode the earlier process of analogic thinking that prevailed over other analogs that were being considered. That is, iconic metaphors have a history that can be traced back to the root metaphors of the cultural group.

Foxfire teachers should also be able to help students understand how metaphorical thinking, including the prevailing root metaphors, are encoded in material culture such as the design of buildings, the layout of communities, clothes, and even computers. What was the image of the person that served as the basis of the metaphorical thought process that went into the design of something as mundane and inconsequential as a sidewalk? When we discovered that the image of the normal person who uses a sidewalk did not include people who are physically challenged in different ways, the sidewalks were modified to reflect a more complex image of the "pedestrian." What are the metaphorical messages encoded in the design and placement of a doorway? What are the metaphorical images of intelligence and language encoded in the design of a computer, and are these images culturally specific? How do such material aspects of different cultural groups as the design and arrangement of buildings reflect basic differences in their root metaphors?

While the second guiding principle states that the teacher should be "*collaborator and team leader and guide* rather than boss," the teacher who lacks the background understanding of culture, specifically the metaphorical dimensions of culture so essential to recognizing the basic differences that exist, is incompetent in the same way that a lawyer who does not understand the Constitution would be judged incompetent. Becoming professionally competent does not mean the teacher has to become authoritarian and hierarchical like a boss. But it does involve a recognition that the curriculum should enable students to understand the complexities of their own culture, as well as the culture of other groups. The theorists and practitioners who are explaining the Foxfire approach to others need to address the challenge of providing this background knowledge if teachers are going to make a contribution to students' understanding of the interactive relationship of culture and ecosystems.

Common Roots Program

The Common Roots Program now being adopted in rural Vermont elementary schools reflects the cultural/bio-conservative orientation so clearly summarized in the following observation by Wendell Berry:

A healthy culture is a communal order of memory, insight, value, work, conviviality, reverance, aspiration. It reveals the human necessities and the human limits. It clarifies our inescapable bonds to the earth and to each other. It assures that the necessary restraints are observed, that the necessary work is done, and that it is done well. (1986 edition, p. 43)

Although Berry's insights could well have served as the guiding principles for what truly is an ecologically-centered educational reform movement, the person primarily responsible for working with administrators, teachers, and community members who decide to adopt the Common Roots Curriculum is Joseph Keifer. As Executive Director of Food Works, a nonprofit foundation started in Montpelier, Vermont in 1987, he along with Jeff Teitelbaum, the principal of Barnet School, pioneered an approach to school restructuring that addresses the fundamental connections between food, community, and ecological stewardship. These themes now serve as the basis of an integrated curriculum that is the focal point of student learning and community involvement from grades one through six.

In schools with names like Barnet, Duxbury, and Warren, the Common Roots Program demonstrates to teachers, students, and members of local communities that learning about the multiple dimensions of the students' local bioregion, including the vitally important activity of how to grow, prepare, and share food with the community, is an engaging and highly valued form of education. It is also seen as combining the best of recent educational innovations with community renewal and teaching the principles of ecological citizenship. Hands on learning, critical thinking, multiple assessment, empowerment of teachers, and parent/community involvement are combined with outdoor and indoor theme gardens that serve as the focal point for learning how different groups over time adapted agricultural and cultural practices to the characteristics of the local bioregion. The Common Roots curriculum also provides students with contemporary knowledge of sustainable agricultural and community practices.

The teachers develop their own integrated curriculum of seasonal projects that take account of the needs and cultural resources of the local community, but these projects are organized around "historical theme gardens" that are the focal point of the curriculum for each grade level. The theme garden is also used as the basis for learning both practical skills and an integrated approach to history, literature, mathematics, science, folklore, art, and so forth. The theme gardens are ordered in a way that introduces students to the agricultural/cultural practices of the earliest known inhabitants, with each succeeding grade level introducing students to a more recent stage in the historical development of the bioregion.

Grade K—Kinder Garden:
The Earth-friendly 'Kinder Garden' is planted in sunflowers, carrots, and pumpkins.
Grades 1 and 2-Native American Garden:
Students plant corn, pole beans and squash in a Native American garden. Under the 'Wickiup' gardeners discover a great place to sit and watch the world.
Grade 3-Community Heritage Garden:
In the Community Heritage Garden elders and students work together planting and harvesting crops from the community's past.
Grade 4-Historical Garden:
In the Historical Garden students grow heirloom varieties of crops once planted by the region's first settlers, such as wheat and oats, and experiment with antique gardening tools.
Grade 5-Organic Kitchen Garden:
Herbs, flowers, and kitchen vegetables that were popular in early America are grown in the raised bed intensive garden.
Grade 6-Sustainable Garden Ecosystem:
Students apply sustainable garden practices with eyes toward answering the question: 'How do we feed six billion people by the year 2000?' (Food Works, 1992)

In addition there is a Market Garden that is maintained through the summer months by students and members of the community, with the produce either sold to the community or donated for use in emergency situations.

Part of the curriculum of each grade level is connected with the Ecology Action Research Station located in an adjacent outdoor setting where students study different types of ecosystems. For example, kindergarten students observe and record the seasonal changes in the trees. In grade two the "Meadow Thicket Ecosystem" is the primary focus of study, while in grade four students investigate the interdependence of life systems in local streams and ponds, test and evaluate water quality, and share their findings with other students and the community. In effect, this is the part of the curriculum where students learn how natural systems work, and how human activities alter these systems. Their understanding of ecosystems, in turn, is integrated into the more historical and cultural parts of the curriculum.

The main strength of the Common Roots Program is that it is based on an inclusive ecological model that enables students to understand the many ways individuals, cultural practices, and natural systems are connected. For example, the study of cultural practices distinctive to a particular historical period also involves considering the characteristics of the biotic community that sustained the cultural group: the population and distribution of different animal species, the characteristics of the land—including the types and distribution of trees and other plant life, weather patterns, and so on. More importantly, the inclusion of an historical view of cultural traditions is linked directly to the student's own experience of "place," thus providing a sense of how each student is part of a "communal order of memory"—to recall Berry's phrase. The study of cultural practices within the context of local ecosystems also reinforces a radically different way of understanding primary relationships that are too often taken for granted to be noticed. As Berry so eloquently summarizes them:

> The definitive relationships in the universe are thus not competitive but interdependent. And from a human point of view they are analogical. We can build one system only within another. We can have agriculture only with nature, and culture only within agriculture. At certain critical points these systems have to conform with one another or destroy one another. (1986 edition, p. 47)

Interdependence not only serves as the root metaphor for understanding how energy is exchanged within the connected web of ecosystems but also provides students a radical alternative to the individually-centered view of moral responsibility. Unlike the modern view that equates individual progress with the attainment of greater autonomy and freedom, the Common Roots curriculum provides both the experience of being an interdependent member of a human/biotic community and an understanding that interdependence is the basic relationship that connects past, present, and future generations.

A second strength of the program is the emphasis on communal approaches to growing, preparing, and sharing food—and expressing gratitude in the form of seasonal celebrations. In effect, this curriculum engages students in the most basic human activities ignored in curricula that reinforce de-contextualized knowledge and the values associated with a consumer oriented culture. The study of human/ natural system relationships, as well as the deliberate embedding of students in community renewal activities (e.g., student/community participation in maintaining the summer garden, recovery of folk knowledge, participation in a food distribution program) shifts the emphasis away from individually-centered goals that characterize the different genres of educational liberalism. As a result, the Common Roots Program comes closest to socializing students to an ecological model of intelligence where the emphasis is placed on understanding and responding to the information communicated through the interactions of living systems.

A third strength is that its strong community orientation achieves more of a balance between face to face and print based communication and learning. The phrase "spoken discourse" tends to present a limited image of this basic difference by foregrounding speaking as the principal difference. But the most fundamental distinction between face to face and communication mediated through various forms of print technology (books, newspapers, computers, etc.) is that the former utilizes context, use of the entire body as both sender and receiver of culturally encoded messages (use of body, voice, and social space to communicate about relationships), and a form of memory that is, to a degree, accountable to the other participants in the conversation. Print based discourse, as we discussed earlier, reinforces a form of thinking that is based on de-contextualized and supposedly "objective" information. The main thrust of educational reform today is to integrate computer mediated learning, which means print based communication and thinking, into more areas of the curriculum. Advocates of this approach to educational reform view the challenge of students "navigating" their way through massive amounts of information stored on CD ROM disks as essential to becoming a contributing citizen in the emerging Information Age. The metaphor of the learner as "navigator" encodes the modern way of representing the individual as a culture-free being. When viewed in relation to the bandwagon phenomena of adapting education to the limited forms of cultural knowledge that can be processed through computers, the moral and ecological education that students in rural Vermont are experiencing seems far more relevant to becoming a contributing member of a sustainable community—which is a problem that advocates of computer-mediated learning continue to ignore.

For all of its merits, the Common Roots Program has a number of weaknesses that need to be addressed before it becomes more widely adopted. The most obvious question surrounding its future is whether it can be transplanted successfully to urban settings. How the curriculum, with its focus on historical theme gardens and an ecology research station, could be adapted to the concrete and congestion of people, buildings, and traffic of cities (and even suburban areas) has still to be addressed. There are assurances in the literature outlining the nature of the Common Roots Program that it can be done, but it may be difficult in getting urban teachers to recognize how the themes of food, community, and ecology could be the primary focus for integrating other curricular topics. However, this is not so much a weakness in the conceptual underpinnings of the program as it is a serious concern about its prospects for being adopted by urban people who have had no direct experience with growing food, or being connected directly with the land. The weaknesses with the program have more to do with the aspects of culture that students at Barnet and other Vermont schools will not learn about.

Regardless of how educationally significant it is for students to experience inter-generational gardening within the life cycles of ecosystems, they are not likely to acquire an understanding of the most essential aspects of how language encodes and reproduces earlier patterns (analogs) of thinking. In effect, the main weaknesses found with the Foxfire approach to learning are also one of the primary shortcomings of the Common Roots Program. The locally taught graduate course designed to introduce teachers to the conceptual themes that serve to integrate the curriculum does not provide for an in-depth understanding of culture and of the role that language plays in reproducing cultural patterns. Nor are teachers given a basis for understanding the metaphorical nature of the culture/language/thought connection. The failure of the teacher education programs that originally certified teachers as professionally competent is also ignored in the Common Roots teacher education course. And the consequences of not understanding the primary medium that influences every aspect of the teaching and learning process are genuinely significant for students.

The most immediate consequence becomes evident when students encounter aspects of traditional culture, as well as the most advanced expressions of modern culture—for example, when they use computers to store data and interact with the "reality" shaping processes associated with cars, television, and other forms of consumerism. To put the problem in the form of a question: Would students at Barnet School be able to recognize and understand the cultural assumptions encoded and communicated through various forms of modern culture (such as the architecture of buildings, the way consumer items are packaged and displayed, the use of print-based communication, the exhibit at a local art gallery)? Would they be able to understand the connections between the ecological crisis and the modern ideals of progress, individual creativity, and how our cultural approach to doing science relativizes the traditional foundations of moral authority?

I suspect the education they obtain at Barnet School provides a better foundation for grasping the essential cultural/ecosystem issues than what is provided students who are exposed to the anthropocentrically-oriented curriculum found in most public schools and universities. But the framing of fundamental differences between traditional and modern expressions of culture does not seem to be part of the Common Roots curriculum. Encouraging students to consider the differences between ecologically sustainable and modern cultures, between folk and modern technologies, and between rural and urban life styles, could easily be introduced without undermining the integrity of the existing curricular themes. Understanding these differences would better prepare students for recognizing how the various expressions of modernism constitute and sustain taken-for-granted attitudes toward the importance of expanding the choices of the individual, the plenitude of consumer items, and the primacy of personal excitement and meaningfulness. Not understanding the differences that separate traditional from modern cultures may leave the students who continue to live in rural areas unnecessarily vulnerable to the modern pressures of keeping up with recent technological and consumer fads. Being a temperamental and cultural conservative, like we all are in our respective experience of place, may not be enough of a basis for resisting technological developments represented as synonymous with the emergence of a new reality. For example, an understanding of the differences that separate traditional ecologically sustainable cultures from modern cultures is essential for recognizing why the information superhighways that are to be based on the merging of television, telephone, and computer technologies is more likely to accelerate the processes of technological innovation and consumer spending. The appeal of having the rural school included in the free access computer network now being promised by the telecommunications industry may overshadow the ecological consequences of this interactive technology—such as making electronic shopping available on a scale where time and distance (and perhaps the Wal-Marts now spreading across the land) become irrelevant.

In the event students later should find themselves living in urban areas of the country, the lack of a comparative focus on culture, particularly the ecological differences that separate rural from urban life styles, may also become a problem. Theoretically, it could be argued that students should address some of these critically important cultural issues in the later stages of their education. But few middle and high schools, even universities, have curricula where learning about community and environmental renewal are as fully integrated as they are in the Common Roots curriculum. Addressing the problems and concerns raised here would help ensure that students acquire a basic understanding of the essential characteristics of modernity, including the ways in which metaphorical thinking are encoded in material culture, patterns of thinking and valuing, and the cultural amplification characteristics of different forms of technology. If the Common Roots curriculum could be expanded in ways that introduced students to these questions, as well as to an understanding of how the languages of a culture encode and reproduce the metaphorical constructions of pre-ecological ways of understanding, it would become a more complete and relevant curriculum. It would also provide a foundation that students can later build upon.

Ecoliteracy Program

The Elmwood Institute's Center for Ecoliteracy has taken on the task of helping schools reorganize themselves into collaborative learning communities. The principles that are to guide the interactions of all the participants in the learning community, as well as the design of the curriculum, are derived from the characteristics of natural ecosystems. The origins of this unique approach go back to the Ecoliteracy Project initiated in 1991 when Fritjof Capra was invited to help teachers at Madison High School in Portland, Oregon, conceptualize a new environmental studies program. But the deep conceptual foundations for the Center's approach to ecoliteracy can be traced back even further to Capra's *The Tao of Physics* (1975) and *The Turning Point* (1982). These two pioneering books introduced a large reading audience to the ecological implications both of the

Newtonian/Cartesian paradigm upon which Western technological progress was based, and to the emerging new physics/systems model of thinking. In effect, the Center's efforts to restructure schools in ways that foster ecological literacy represent the educational extension of Capra's earlier efforts to explain the nature of the paradigm shift that must occur if we are to avoid our own destruction through ignorance of basic life sustaining principles.

As the Center is still in the developmental phase of organizing the Alliance for Ecoliteracy in the San Francisco Bay Area, and in working with faculty, administrators, students, and community members to develop patterns of communication and cooperation, as well as approaches to student/teacher learning, the focus here will be on the conceptual underpinnings of the Center's approach to ecoliteracy. The effectiveness of an ecoliteracy curriculum in altering the everyday patterns of a culturally diverse, heavily populated, and technologically dependent urban area will have to wait until after the Alliance schools have achieved self-sustaining ecoliteracy programs. Consequently, the focus here will be on how the principles of systems theory, which Capra frames in terms of the interactive nature of ecological systems, are used as the basis for a radically different approach to education. The central issues raised by this effort to conceptualize an approach to education in terms of an ecological model is whether it takes adequate account of the symbolic nature of culture. That is, can educators address the ecological crisis by relying primarily upon a scientifically based model of how ecosystems sustain themselves and evolve?

Careful consideration of the Center's efforts to predicate their approach to education on the characteristics of viable ecosystems, rather than use cultural themes as the basis for illuminating the interdependence of human culture with ecosystems, which characterized the Common Roots Program, may help frame the larger questions surrounding other efforts to use a scientifically based model for the purpose of altering the current direction of cultural development. That is, should the metaphor of an ecology or process, which the followers of Whitehead want to use, become the guiding framework for reconstituting the deepest symbolic foundations of the dominant culture? Or does the use of ecology as a guiding metaphor have the more limited potential of providing a basis for identifying which cultural beliefs, values, and forms of technology have to be radically modified, and which aspects need to be reinforced? I suspect that a symbolic archeology of the taken for granted patterns of any number of cultural groups—the competitive emphasis on the style of performing Rap, the expression of machismo, the organization of time shared by members in the dominant culture, and so forth—would reveal that patterns derived from the distant past are encoded and reenacted as part of present experience. These questions simply restate the problem that every rationally-based approach to reform has encountered: namely, why cultural traditions persist in the face of rationally based alternatives. Perhaps part of the answer will turn out to be that we have not understood the complexity and resilience of cultural patterns, and that we have consistently over estimated the efficacy of rationally-based reform efforts. These issues may seem abstract and thus unrelated to the discussion of the Ecoliteracy program. But the program's success, as well as that of the Foxfire and Common Roots curricula, will depend upon whether rationally based theory leads to fundamental changes in the cultural patterns of diverse groups that go back in some instances hundreds, even thousands of years.

The answer Capra gives to the question "What is Ecological Literacy?" provides the guiding conceptual framework for the educational mission of the Elmwood Institute. "At the Elmwood Institute," he writes, "we define ecological literacy as consisting of three components: (1) knowledge of the principles of ecology; (2) systems thinking; (3) the practice of ecological values" (1993, p. 3). The characteristics of natural systems (which includes the human organism) should thus be mirrored in learning communities. The differences between learning communities based on systems thinking and the machine/industrial model of education that still prevails in most schools (now hidden by the rhetoric of participatory decision making required in post-industrial work settings) are immense. One of the essential characteristics of the machine/industrial model of education is that the attributes of the autonomous individual are emphasized. This allows educators to think of the learning process in terms of delivery systems, educational inputs and outputs, prepackaged lessons and teaching procedures, and, most of all, engineering the optimal learning environment. Student learning (variously referred to as behavioral outcomes, outputs, products) is to be evaluated and recorded as part of a cumulative record that will influence future educational and work opportunities. The teacher's primary task, particularly at the high school and university level, is to transmit a specific body of subject matter to groups of students who appear before them for a limited period of time. Students are expected to work for grades just as later they will be expected to work for money. They are also expected to subordinate their own psychological sense of time to the form of mechanical time that governs the workplace, and to learn to perform tasks dictated by a higher authority who also evaluates their performance. The content of the curriculum, in turn, reinforces the high status knowledge and patterns of thinking upon which modern social and mechanical technologies are based. The recent shift from the industrial machine to the microchip has softened these patterns. But the patterns are still visible beneath the veneer of group dynamics and the ever changing professional jargon. The continued dominance of the machine model of education can also be seen in the increasingly widespread acceptance of thinking as "information processing."

The principles of ecology lead to a radically different set of guiding educational principles. The following extrapolations by Capra are meant only as a partial list:

Interdependence
All members of an ecosystem are interconnected in a web of relationships in which all life processes depend on one another. The success of the whole system depends upon the success of its individual members, while the success of each member depends upon the success of the system as a whole.

In a learning community, teachers, students, administrators, parents, businesses and community members are interlinked in a network of relationships, working together to facilitate learning.

Sustainability
The long-term survival (sustainability) of each species in an ecosystem depends on a limited resource base.

Building learning communities around the issue of sustainability means that teachers see the long term impact they have on students.

Ecological Cycles
The interdependencies among the members of an ecosystem involve the exchange of matter and energy in continual cycles.

The teaching does not flow from the top down, but there is a cyclical exchange of information. The focus on learning and everyone in the system is both a teacher and a learner.

Energy Flow
Solar energy, transformed into chemical energy by the photosynthesis of green plants, drives all ecological cycles.

Learning communities are open communities where people are moving in and out, finding their own niches in the system.

Partnership
All living members of an ecosystem are engaged in a subtle interplay of competition and cooperation, involving countless forms of partnership.
All members of the learning community cooperate and work in partnership, which means democracy and empowerment because each plays a very crucial role.

Flexibility
In their function as feedback loops, ecological cycles have the tendency to maintain themselves in a flexible state, characterized by interdependent fluctuations of their variables.
In a learning community, there is dynamic change and fluidity. Daily schedules are fluid; each time there is a change of theme, the learning environment is recreated.

Diversity
The stability of an ecosystem depends on the degree of complexity of its network of relationships; in other words, on the diversity of the ecosystem.
Experiences that encourage students to use diverse modes and strategies of learning are essential in learning communities. Diverse learning styles are appreciated for the richness they bring to the learning situation. Cultural diversity is critical to establishing the school as a true community.

Coevolution
Most species in an ecosystem coevolve through an interplay of creation and mutual adaptation. The creative reaching out into novelty is a fundamental property of life, manifest also in the processes of development and learning.
As businesses, community groups and parents work more in partnership with the school, each better understands the needs of the other. In a true, committed partnership both partners change—they coevolve. (1993, pp. 24–25)

These principles, in turn, are built into the criteria that must be met by schools selected as pilot sites for developing an Ecoliteracy curriculum. Ed Clark, a key collaborator in the Ecolitercy project and the person who coined the word "ecoliteracy" in a 1981 paper on "Ecosystem Education," explains the relationships and activities of a learning community in the following way:

> In Ecoliteracy, students, teachers, administrators, and parents work cooperatively to design curricula and programs that reflect their unique interests, concern and requirements. The participative strategy empowers participants to full ownership and responsibility. (1993, p. 28)

Although each learning community is expected to have its own overall vision and set of educational objectives, the Center for Ecoliteracy provides definite guidelines for organizing the content of the curriculum in ways that foster an understanding of how basic ecological principles operate in daily experience. What are referred to as "focus questions" (to be selected by teacher and students at each grade level) are to guide the selection of the subject matter and how it will be studied. In addition, the vertical integration of the curriculum is achieved by using a different principle of ecology as the basic conceptual framework for each grade level. In the first grade the students and teacher might explore the focus question "How am I part of many families?" in relation to the ecological principle of "flexibility." If "How big is my neighborhood" is the focus question in grade two it would be investigated in terms of the principle of "sustainability." Grade three would frame the inquiry process in terms of the principle of "partnership." As students progress through the rest of the grade levels they would study various aspects of their world of experience in relation to the ecological principles of "coevolution," "diversity," "energy flow," "cycles," and "interdependence" (1993, p. 34).

In effect, ecological principles are used to illuminate how the patterns of cultural life exhibit the same systems characteristics found in the natural world. Understanding the world in terms of factual information and discrete events, or in terms of the constructivist inclinations of the student, is replaced by an ecological model of thinking where relationships, interdependencies and coevolutionary patterns are foregrounded. Moreover, learning in terms of ecosystems helps to make moral education an integral part of the curriculum. That is, the ultimate reference point for understanding aspects of the cultural/natural world is the question of whether human practices contribute to sustainable relationships within the larger system they are dependent upon. The moral language used to communicate and think about the relationships that are the central focus in the learning process, including how students understand their relationship to what is being studied, encodes the root metaphor of life being part of an ecosystem, rather than the anthropocentric and mechanistic root metaphors now encoded in so much of the language used in classrooms.

A major strength of the Ecoliteracy approach to learning communities is that the institutional aspects of the schools (roles and rules that govern the behavior of all participants) are to conform to the principles of ecology. This leads to placing the emphasis on all participants, as members of interdependent systems, contributing to the viability of the system through the free communication of their interests, perspectives, needs, and understandings. In traditional schools, even those with an interesting and challenging curriculum, the bureaucratic rules and roles determine who can make certain decisions about what constitutes relevant knowledge. Learning who has the right to exercise certain forms of power, and adapting one's intersubjective self to the prescribed patterns, is the real curriculum. While few students are thrown out of school for not learning the curriculum of books and classroom discussions, they can be both ejected from school and burdened for life by a cumulative record of their transgressions of the school's covert curriculum. The ecology-oriented learning communities stress, instead, the opening of channels of communication between all the participants.

A second strength is that the use of ecological principles as the basis of the curriculum helps to illuminate the symbolic world of self-identities, thoughts, behaviors, technologies, and the like, in a radically different way. Even the systematic study of culture at most universities fails to represent how cultures can be understood as exhibiting the same principles that govern the behavior of ecosystems. By making the principles of ecology the basic interpretative framework for learning about different aspects of culture, the Ecoliteracy curriculum helps lay the foundation for understanding connections and interdependencies rather than discrete events and objective facts. It also foregrounds the problems that emerge when a culture becomes dependent on scarce rather than abundant sources of energy. This approach, in effect, helps to insure that the study of cultural practices and patterns (curriculum units on technology, historical events, literature, biology, computers, etc.) are not framed in terms of the anthropocentrism that characterizes the curricula in most public schools and universities.

The use of ecological principles represents one possible way of avoiding the problems identified in the earlier discussion of how teachers reinforce the cultural bias toward interpreting moral education, creativity, and intelligence as individually centered. The emphasis on process and interdependence more accurately represents the contextual nature of human experience. But the emphasis on process also raises fundamental questions that will need to be addressed as the Ecoliteracy approach to education further evolves. The following questions stand out as particularly important.

The first question relates to the concern mentioned earlier about whether a scientific understanding of the principles of ecological systems can serve as an adequate basis for addressing the cultural aspects of learning. The followers of Dewey and Whitehead easily could claim that their approach to learning also is based upon a systems way of thinking where there is no fixed and objective body of knowledge to be mastered. To recall Oliver's summary of a Whiteheadean approach: "We assume that every act of coming to understand, feel, and know, is novel. Each act of knowing comes out of relationships . . . Students and teacher learn by being part of an occasion that itself is novel, one which demands that certain aspects of the person participate and consequently change" (1989, p. 163). Even the constructivist learning theorists claim that everything should be understood as evolving relationships, and that learning is a matter of constructing ideas on the basis of information acquired through the direct experience of these changing relationships. There are, however, differences that separate the Ecoliteracy emphasis on an ecological model of governance and curriculum from the process orientation embraced by the current followers of Dewey, Whitehead, and Piaget. As the latter approaches to "process"-based learning are likely to be represented in future publications as also preparing students to live more ecologically balanced lives, the advocates of the Ecoliteracy program will face the challenge of clarifying the exact nature of the differences.

A more serious concern about the efficacy of the Ecoliteracy program has to do with its under theorized view of culture. The use of ecological principles to illuminate common features of cultural experience framed by the focus questions (e.g., "How Big Is My Neighborhood?" is used to foreground the processes connected with the principles of sustainability) is not culturally specific. That is, the principles of ecology can be used to illuminate how all cultural systems function as ecosystems interconnected with other ecosystems. *But this science-based framework does not address the possibility that the metaphorical constructions of cultural groups may be based on profoundly different meta-narratives.* These differences may be expressed in terms of how relationships within a family are understood and acted out, what foods are eaten, what constitutes the ultimate basis of authority for moral values, how time is understood, how success is defined and expressed, which members of the cultural groups are perceived as having useful knowledge, and so on. While people from different cultural groups may share taken for granted patterns in certain social settings with members of other cultural groups (the work place, centers of entertainment, consumer emporiums, transportation systems, etc.), there will be a point in their experience of being a modern person where their more deeply held cultural orientations will take over and dictate the patterns and forms of authority that separate them as members of a distinct cultural group. The nature and preparation of food, or the social setting that involves a Christian prayer may represent the point of cultural separation for the Jewish American; while the stress on competitive individualism in the classroom may cause the American Indian student to experience a sense of alienation from patterns the Anglo middle-class students take for granted. Hispanic American, Chinese American, Christian fundamentalists, and so on, also have their distinctive traditions that the process of modernization has not entirely homogenized. Recent changes in the political environment have led to more overt expressions in school settings of these previously hidden and even repressed cultural differences. These cultural differences will continue to be expressed in schools that adopt the Ecoliteracy approach to school governance and curriculum. How these differences are to be acknowledged and constructively reconciled with the new cultural way of knowing and valuing dictated by a scientifically based ecological model seems not yet to have been addressed.

An example of a specific cultural orientation built into the Ecoliteracy program can be found in how Ed Clark explains intelligence as an attribute of the individual. In the article "What Is the Nature of Intelligence?" Clark writes that "What we need most today are the creative skills to select, organize, and apply information widely—in short, to turn information into meaningful, relevant knowledge" (1993, p. 16). He also quotes approvingly Peter Russell's statement that "Intelligence is an organizing principle *within* consciousness," and Michael Polanyi's observation that "knowledge is a *personal* skill that enables an individual to integrate experiences and observations into a unified, cohesive system of understanding" (p. 17, italics added). This view of learning as individually centered, and as grounded in the immediate context of the learner, is fundamentally different from that of cultural groups who sustain their sense of identity and traditions through forms of trans-generational communication where the knowledge of elders is valued and thus renewed in the lives of the next generation.

The under theorized understanding of culture is apparent in other aspects of the Ecoliteracy program. Like the Foxfire and Common Roots Programs, there is no mention in the *Guide to Ecoliteracy* of the need for teachers to understand the metaphorical basis of language and thought—and such other expressions of cultural coding as the design and use of clothes, buildings, and mechanical technologies. Without this powerful entry point into understanding the symbolic foundations of cultural beliefs and practices, it would be difficult for Ecoliteracy teachers to recognize when the metaphorical frameworks that are the basis of a cultural tradition need to be made explicit. It is also likely that students would not learn about the constitutive role that metaphorical thinking plays either in the dominant or minority cultures. This silence about the role of language is particularly critical in the Ecoliteracy program because its primary focus is on learning to think and make value judgments in terms of an ecological root metaphor.

The tendency to fit culture to the thematic structure suggested by the characteristics of ecosystems, rather than to start with the distinctiveness of the cultural traditions now found in urban settings, will make it more difficult to identify and incorporate into the curriculum the traditions of cultural groups that are already grounded in meta-narratives that represent humans as interdependent with nature. Similarly, the Ecoliteracy teacher will be less likely to recognize that an ecologically oriented approach to the Foxfire curriculum would broaden the students' ability to be eco-literate in terms of recognizing the traditions of different cultural groups that have a benign impact on the sustaining characteristics of local ecosystems. For example, the identification of the traditions of different cultural groups that contribute to an expanded sense of communal participation and meaning, such as festivals, ceremonies, musical performances, forms of play, sharing of craft knowledge, family gatherings, and so forth, should be considered part of an ecoliteracy survey and documentation process of cultural practices that do not degrade the environment. An understanding of these traditions should lead, in turn, to an examination of developments within the technological/consumer-oriented mainstream culture that threaten their continued viability. To frame the challenge facing the

Ecoliteracy curriculum in a slightly different way: Should students be encouraged to create new community-centered traditions that reflect the principles of ecology, or should they first learn about the nature of the already existing traditions that are not ecologically destructive?

That these questions have not yet been addressed may be due to the recent establishment of the Center for Ecoliteracy. As sources of funding and the Alliance for Ecoliteracy become more established, these questions may be resolved as part of the growth process. On the other hand, the questions may not be addressed because of a double bind caused by interpreting the educational implications of the principles of ecology in terms of modern assumptions. A comparative study of traditional, ecologically-centered cultures with the form of modern, scientifically based culture promoted by our educational institutions and technological/economic sectors of society would help clarify the culturally specific nature of the metaphorical framework that currently underlies the Center's approach to Ecoliteracy. Many of these traditional cultures understood the point made by Daly that "if something is nonphysical, then perhaps it can grow forever" (1991, p. 17). And by extension, they also learned that survival requires that demands on what is physical be limited. The ways in which these two fundamental insights are encoded in daily cultural practices represents each culture's distinctive form of cultural/bio-conservatism. Whether the Ecoliteracy program's "process" orientation to thinking and valuing can be modified to take account of existing cultural practices that conserve the sources of energy that sustain ecosystems needs to be a more central part of the dialogue. As Maturana and Varela point out, the structural coupling within ecosystems involves patterns that are both conserving and open to adaptation to changes occurring in other parts of the system. The question is whether the imposition of a modernist interpretation of this dialectical process will lead to emphasizing adaptation and change over conservation of structural characteristics. If this modernist bias is incorporated into the Ecoliteracy program it will be severely limited, and will likely be resisted by cultural groups who have retained a deeper sense of connectedness with their traditions.

Concluding Remarks

The strengths of these three models of educational reform far outweigh their respective limitations. But as I have attempted to show, it would be relatively easy to address these limitations in ways that would facilitate the achievement of the distinctive educational goals of each program. That they all share essentially the same limitations raises a larger set of questions about the education of teachers in general. The teachers who undergo the special preparation required of the Foxfire, Common Roots, and Ecoliteracy programs all received their initial professional education in teacher education programs and graduate schools of education. The main responsibility for the failure to center teacher education in a deep understanding of culture, particularly the cultural encoding and reproduction processes of the languages used by cultural groups to sustain their view of reality, thus needs to be laid at the door of these institutions. The current emphasis on multicultural education provides teachers with little more than the tourist industry's level of understanding of cultural differences, and thus falls far short of preparing teachers to understand the complex process associated with their mediating role in the cultural communication process we call teaching and learning. The only real difference that separates multicultural education from the tourist industry's "appreciate cultural differences" approach is that educators frame the discussion in terms of promoting democracy and other social justice issues. This superficial exposure to culture still leaves teachers without any real understanding of the connection between a cultural group's root metaphors and the analogs selected to introduce students to new understandings, how the epistemic patterns that characterize different fields of knowledge are based on metaphorical constructions that simultaneously illuminate and hide, and how the iconic metaphors that go largely unnoticed in classroom discourse encode and reproduce the form of intelligence that prevailed in earlier processes of analogic thinking. Even though it is impossible to communicate in the classroom (or any place else) without the use of metaphor, teacher education classes continue to reinforce a conduit view of language. And the emphasis given in teacher education programs (and in graduate schools of education) to various representations of individualism prevents them from addressing the educational implications of how culture is experienced by the student— including how culture becomes part of the student's intersubjective self. If they were to acknowledge that culture is the symbolic medium within which all learning takes place, they would have to modify the current orthodoxies embraced by different groups of educational liberals—including the latest efforts to explain mental processes (the behavior of the brain) in terms of the interactions of nerve cells and molecules associated with them. As long as teacher education programs, and the graduate schools that educate the teacher "trainers," continue on the present course, reform efforts such as the three programs discussed here will be seriously hampered. In addition, the effectiveness of the growing number of ecologically conscious teachers in the public schools will continue to be limited by their inability to recognize that they control the language processes that reproduce problematic cultural patterns in every area of the curriculum.

Few graduates of teacher education programs and graduate schools of education encounter courses where there is a discussion of the cultural aspects of the ecological crisis. This collective professional silence, which is not too different from the failure of German intellectuals to challenge the silence of their times in relation to the rise of Nazism, raises the question of where the leverage points are for affecting radical change. There is a status system in teacher education/graduate programs, and from time to time prestigious institutions like Stanford University, Harvard University, University of Chicago, University of California, and so forth, appear to exert leadership in setting in motion new reform efforts. In my more optimistic moments I like to think that if the deans of these institutions, as well as the nationally prominent faculty, were to make public statements and write books addressing the educational implications of the ecological crisis, the current national debate on school restructuring might be expanded to include the critically important issue of how to educate for a sustainable future. Leadership by those at the top might also help establish new priorities in funding research and curriculum development. But so far they seem united only in maintaining the silence.

David Gabbard argues that the educational establishment has a history of controlling the discourse in ways that exclude truly radical thinkers who threaten the orthodoxies upon which professional careers (and funding) are based (1993). His study of how Ivan Illich's proposal for de-schooling society was excluded from becoming part of the educational discourse raises questions about why the ecological crisis has received similar treatment. Illich's analysis illuminated how public schools created new forms of dependencies that undermined the viability of community life while strengthening the consumer/technological orientation especially beneficial to a particular social class. In exposing how schooling promotes a technologically dependent and consumer oriented form of consciousness, Illich was challenging the deepest levels of moral and political legitimation used to justify the existence of teacher education and graduate education programs. Excluding him from the discourse is understandable within the framework of the friend/enemy approach to politics that characterizes the leadership of institutions whose very existence is being questioned. But why do prominent educators who have access to the public media not recognize that the continued degradation of the Earth's ecosystems will affect the quality of life of their own children, and their children's children. Concern with the well-being of children in general is supposed to be a moral preoccupation of the educational profession. But somehow the trend setters and "elders" of the educational establishment who are supposed to possess a broader perspective on the problems facing society seem unable to interpret the signs of the times—that is, the vast amount of scientific documentation of ecosystem decline and the more sensationalist media accounts of ecological disasters that occur with increasing frequency.

I find it hard to believe that they do not read newspapers or watch television. What accounts for their continued silence when even supermarkets are getting the message that the "greening" of their products helps customers equate consumerism with being a good environmental citizen? Are they so embedded in anthropocentrically grounded conceptual frameworks that they are incapable of recognizing the connections between environmentally destructive cultural practices and the beliefs, values, and approaches to technology taught in the classrooms of the nation? Is it rooted in the psychological phenomenon of *ressentiment* Nietzsche wrote about in the late nineteenth century? The ability of those who find their strength and moral superiority in upholding the orthodoxies of the day, while masking their conformism by giving lip service to higher ideals, must be taken into account when considering the promotion process that leads to a deanship. Perhaps the silence simply reflects the intellectual laziness and moral dullness rewarded by colleagues who do not want the foundations of their own careers challenged in any fundamental way.

The reasons for the silence, I suspect, are as complex as they are varied. A more careful study of characteristics of how fundamental educational reform has been initiated and sustained in the past might enable us to see more clearly workable strategies for bringing public education into the process of reconstituting the foundations of modern culture. Based on past experience, I suspect that if the federal grants were available to teacher education/graduate programs that made cultural/ecological relationships a core part of their programs, we would witness how quickly the silence can be broken by the sounds of another educational bandwagon. Unfortunately, this scenario would likely lead to teacher educators using their modernist assumptions about the nature of individualism and the experimental road to progress as the basis for socializing the next generation of teachers to become more aware of the ecological consequences of cultural patterns reproduced through the curriculum. A more sober assessment of the ability of the educational establishment to move in a direction that avoids this cultural double bind, which currently characterizes other university departments, leads me to believe that real change, as exemplified by the Foxfire, Common Roots, and Ecoliteracy programs will continued to be nurtured by reformers who have the ability to promote their ideas outside of institutional settings.

But the problem of real reform being limited to the margins of institutionalized education is that the mainstream institutions will continue to reinforce the very aspects of modern culture that are now devastating the environment. At times it seems that the advocates of ecologically compatible cultural changes are at about the same place in their struggle as the feminists were in the late nineteenth century. When the comparison is made with the feminist movement a sobering fact emerges: namely, that the cultural changes required by applying the principles of equality to women and men alike were minor in comparison to the deep changes that will be required in the years ahead. Not only will we need to reach a consensus on quality of life issues that relate to long-term sustainability, but we will have to counteract the impact of an increasing world population, an increasingly globalized consumer-oriented economy that reproduces the same patterns of social stratification that were part of the Industrial Revolution, and the spread of a technological/scientific world view that holds out the promise of resolving our difficulties through new approaches to engineering— including genetic reprogramming of human and other species. If we can keep the emerging information technologies in proper perspective, which we have not yet been able to do, perhaps the scientific studies of degraded ecosystems can become widely enough shared that more people will realize that their own future, including, that of their progeny, is at risk. Perhaps then they will have a personal stake in joining the reform effort—just as women and others joined to bring about changes in the patriarchal foundations of the dominant culture largely inherited from Europe. Educators became aware of gender bias in the curriculum after a concerned and articulate public reached a certain critical mass. It's quite likely that we shall have to wait until a concerned public learns to think in radically different ways than they were taught in public schools and universities before we see mainstream educators waking up to the presence of even more problematic biases in the curriculum. On the other hand the public may become increasingly preoccupied with the economic dislocations caused by the current direction of technological restructuring and the breakdowns in ecosystems. In that case we may have to settle for reform efforts such as the Foxfire, Common Roots, and Ecoliteracy programs reminding us that significant reform is *only* a possibility.

References

Arendt, Hannah. 1954. Between Past and Future. New York. Viking.

Armstrong, Thomas. 1991. "The Seven Kinds of Smarts: An Introduction to the Theory of Multiple Intelligences." Cloverdale, CA: Mind Styles Consulting Service. Unpublished manuscript.

Barcroft, John H. 1993. Correspondence

Barnes, Rob. 1992. *Teaching Art to Young Children 4–9*. London: Allen & Unwin.

Barrow, John D., and Tipler, Frank J. 1988. *The Anthropic Cosmological Principle*. New York: Oxford University Press.

Bateson, Gregory. 1972. *Steps to an Ecology of Mind*. New York: Ballantine Books.

——— 1973. "Style, Grace, and Information in Primitive Art." In *Primitive Art and Society*, edited by Anthony Forge. London: Oxford University Press. 230–245.

——— 1991. *A Sacred Unity: Further Steps to an Ecology of Mind*. Edited by Rodney E. Donaldson. New York: Harper Collins Publishers.

Bennett, William J. 1988. *Our Children and Our Country: Improving America's Schools and Affirming a Common Culture*. New York: Touchstone Books.

Berry , J. W. 1986. "A Cross Cultural View of Intelligence." In *What Is Intelligence?* edited by Robert J. Sternberg and Douglas K. Determan. Norwood, N. J.: Ablex Publishing. 35–37.

Berry, Wendell. 1983. *Standing By Words*. San Francisco: North Point Press.

——— 1986 edition. *The Unsettling of America: Culture and Agriculture*. San Francisco: Sierra Club Books.

Betts, George, and Knapp, Jolene. 1986. *The Autonomous Learner Model for the Gifted and Talented*. Greeley, Colorado: Autonomous Learning Publications.

Bowers, C. A. 1984. *The Promise of Theory: Education and the Politics of Cultural Change*. New York: Longman

——— 1987. *Elements of a Post-Liberal Theory of Education*. New York: Teachers College Press.

——— 1988. *The Cultural Dimensions of Educational Computing: Understanding the Non-Neutrality of Technology*. New York: Teachers College Press.

——— 1993. *Education, Cultural Myths, and the Ecological Crisis: Toward Deep Changes*. Albany: State University of New York Press.

Bowers, C. A., and David J. Flinders. 1990. *Responsive Teaching: An Ecological Approach to Classroom Patterns of Language, Culture, and Thought*. New York: Teachers College Press.

Broudy, Harry S. 1972. *Enlightened Cherishing: An Essay on Aesthetic Education*. Urbana, Illinois: University of Illinois Press.

Brown, Lester R. 1993. "A New Era Unfolds." In *State of the World*. Edited by Linda Starke. New York: W. W. Norton.

Bruer, John T. 1993. *Schools for Thought: A Science for Learning in the Classroom*. Cambridge: MIT Press.

Cajete, Gregory. 1994. *Look to the Mountain: An Ecology of Indigenous Education*. Durango, CO: Kivaki Press.

Capra, Fritjof. 1975. *The Tao of Physics*. Boulder: Shambala.

——— 1982. *The Turning Point. Science, Society, and the Rising Culture*. New York: Bantam.

——— 1993. "What Is Ecological Literacy?" *Guide to Ecological Literacy*. Berkeley: The Elmwood Institute. 4–8.

Cardinal, Douglas, and Jeannette Armstrong. 1991. *The Native Creative Process*. Penticton, British Columbia. Theytus Books.

Carson, Rachel. 1962. *Silent Spring*. Boston: Fawcett Crest.

Chaney, J. 1989. Postmodern Environmental Ethics: Ethics as Bioregional Narrative," *Environmental Ethics*. (Summer): 2:117–134.

Chapman, Laura. 1978. *Approaches to Art Education*. New York: Harcourt Brace Jovanovich.

——— 1985. *Discover Art* (Teacher's Edition, Grade 3). Worchester, MA: Davis.

Clark, Barbara. 1986. *Optimizing Learning: The Integrative Education Model in the Classroom*. Columbus: Merrill Publishing Co.

Clark, Edward. 1993 a. "How Do We Design an Ecoliteracy Curriuclum?" *Guide to Ecoliteracy.* Berkeley: The Elmwood Institute. 28–36.

———— 1993. "What is the Nature of Intelligence, of Knowledge, of Learning?" *Guide to Ecoliteracy.* Berkeley: The Elmwood Institute.

Cohen, LeoNora. 1990. "Theory Summit Conference on Optimal Development of the Mind: Working Papers." Portland, Oregon: Unpublished manuscript.

Colbert, Cynthia, and Martha Taunton. 1992. "Developing Appropriate Practices for the Visual Arts Education of Young Children," In *An NAEA Briefing Paper.* Reston, VA: National Art Education Association. 1–4.

Crutchfield, Richard S. 1962. Creativity and Conformity," In *Contemporary Approaches to Creative Thinking.* Edited by Howard E. Gruber, Glenn Terrell, and Michael Wertheimer. New York: Atherton Press. 120–140.

Daly, Herman. 1991. *Steady-State Economics.* Washington, D. C.: Island Press.

de Bono, Edward. 1970. *Lateral Thinking: Creativity Step By Step.* New York: Harper Colophon Books.

Dewey, John. 1960 edition. *The Quest for Certainty.* New York: G. P. Putnam's Sons.

Dissanayaka, Ellen. 1988. *What is Art For?* Seattle: University of Washington Press.

———— 1990. "Art for Life's Sake." *Currents in Modern Thought.* (April): 571–583.

Doll, William E. Jr. 1993. *A Post-Modern Perspective on Curriculum.* New York: Teachers College Press.

Drengson, Alan R. 1993. "Remembering the Ecological Wisdom of Ancient Forests and Elders." *The Trumpeter.* Vol. 10, no. 4 (Fall): 142–148.

Durning, Alan. 1991. "Asking How Much is Enough?" in *State of the World.* Edited by Lester Brown. New York: W. W. Norton. 153–170.

———— 1992. *How Much is Enough? The Consumer Society and the Future of the Earth.* New York: W. W. Norton.

Ellison, Launa. 1992. "Using Multiple Intelligences to Set School Goals." *Educational Leadership.* (October): 69–72.

Ellul, Jacques. 1966. "The Artist in the Technological Society." *The Structuralist.* No. 6: 35–41.

Elmwood Institute. 1993. "Principles of Ecology-Principles of Education." *Guide to Ecoliteracy.* Berkeley.

Erdman, Jean. 1993. Correspondence.

Estes, W. K. 1986. "Where Is Intelligence?" In *What Is Intelligence?* edited by Robert J. Sternberg and Douglas K. Detterman. Norwood, N.J: Ablex Publishing. 63–68.

Evans, Fred. 1993. *Psychology and Nihilism.* Albany: State University of New York Press.

Feldman, David H. 1989. "Creativity: Proof that Development Occurs." In *Child Development Today and Tomorrow,* edited by W. Damon. San Francisco: Jossey-Bass.

Forge, Anthony. 1973. "Introduction." In *Primitive Art and Society,* edited by Anthony Forge. London: Oxford University Press. 1–13.

Foodworks. 1992. *The Common Roots Program.* Montpelier, VT: (brochure).

Foxfire Fund. 1990. "The Foxfire Approach: Perspectives and Core Practices." *Hands On.* (Spring/Summer): 1–3.

Freire, Paulo. 1970. *Pedagogy of the Oppressed.* New York: Seabury.

Gablik, Suzi. 1983. *The Reenchantment of Art.* New York: Thames and Hudson.

Gardner, Howard. 1898. *To Open Minds.* New York: Basic Books.

——— 1993. "Multiple Intelligences Go To School: Educational Implications of the Theory of Multiple Intelligences." In *Readings and Cases in Educational Psychology,* edited by Anita Woolfolk. Needham Heights, MA: Allyn and Bacon. 64–73.

Garson, Barbara. 1989. *The Electronic Sweatshop; How Computers are Transforming the Office of the Future into the Factory of the Past.* New York: Penguin Books.

Geertz, Clifford. 1973. *The Interpretation of Culture.* New York: Basic Books.

——— 1983. *Local Knowledge: Further Essays in Interpretive Anthropology.* New York: Basic Books.

Goodenough, Ward H. 1981. *Culture, Language, and Society.* Menlo Park, CA: Benjamin/Cummings.

Gore, Al. 1993. *Earth in the Balance: Ecology and the Human Spirit.* New York: Plume.

Gouldner, Alvin. 1979. *The Future of Intellectuals and the Rise of a New Class.* New York: Seabury Press.

Greene, Maxine. 1990. "Arts Education in the Humanities: Toward a Breaking of the Boundaries." In *Artistic Intelligences: Implications for Education.* Edited by William J. Moody. New York: Teaches College Press.

Gruber, Howard E. 1990. "The Evolving Systems Approach to Creative Work." In *Theory Summit Conference on Optimal Development of the Mind: Working Papers,* edited by LeoNora Cohen. Portland, Oregon: unpublished manuscript.

Hamblen, Karen. 1988. "Approaches to Aesthetics in Art Education: A Critical Theory Perspective." *Studies in Art Education.* Vol. 29, no. 2:81–90.

Heidegger, Martin. 1977. *The Question Concerning Technology and Other Essays.* New York: Harper Colophon Books.

Highwater, Jamake. 1981. *The Primal Mind: Vision and Reality in Indian America.* New York: New American Library.

Hoerr, Thomas R. 1992. "How Our School Applied Multiple Intelligences Theory." *Educational Leadership.* (October): 67–68.

Holly, Bruce. 1992. Psychology of Creativity." *Art Calender.* (July/August): 9.

Hopcroft, John E. 1987. "Computer Science: The Emergence of a Discipline." Communications of the Association for Computing Machinery. (March): 201–210.

Huyssen, Andreas. 1986. *After the Great Divide: Modernism, Mass Culture, Postmodernism.* Bloomington, Indiana: Indiana University Press.

Ihde, Don. 1979. *Technics and Praxis.* Dordrecht, Holland: D. Reidel Publishing Co.

Ikegami, Yoshihiko. 1991. "'DO-language' and 'BECOME-language': Two Contrasting Types of Linguistic Representation." In *The Empire of Signs: Semiotic Essays on Japanese Culture,* edited by Yoshihiko Ikegami. Amsterdam/Philadelphia: John Benjamins Publishing Co.

Illich, Ivan. 1970. *Deschooling Society.* New York: Harper & Row.

Jackson, Wes. 1987. *Alters of Unhewn Stone: Science and the Earth.* San Francisco: North Point Press.

Kamii, Constance Kazuko. 1985. *Young Children Reinvent Arithmetic: Implications of Paiget's Theory.* New York: Teachers College Press.

Kamii Constance. 1991. "What Is Constuctivism?" In *Early Literacy : A Constructivist Foundation for Whole Language,* edited by Constance Kamii, Maryann Manning, Gary Manning. Washington, D.C.: National Educational Assocation. 17–29.

Kay, Alan C. 1991. "Computers, Networks, and Education." *Scientific American*. (September): 138–148.

LaChapelle, Dolores. 1978. *Earth Wisdom*. Silverton CO: Finn Hill Arts.

——— 1988. *Sacred Land Sacred Sex: Rapture of the Deep*. Durango, CO: Kivaki Press.

Lawlor, Robert. 1991. *Voices for the First Day: Awakening in the Aboriginal Dreamtime*. Rochester, VT: Inner Traditions.

Leopold, Aldo. (1966 edition). *A Sand County Almanac*. New York: Sierra Club/Ballantine Book.

Lowenfeld, Viktor. 1947. *Creative and Mental Growth*. New York: Macmillan.

MacIntyre, Alasdair. 1984. *After Virtue*. Notre Dame, IN: University of Notre Dame Press.

Maturana, Humberto R. and Francisco J. Varela. 1980. *Autopoiesis and Cognition: The Realization of the Living*. Holland/Boston: D. Reidal.

——— 1992. *The Tree of Knowledge: The Biological Roots of Human Understanding*. Boston: Shambhala.

McClintock, Robert O. 1988. "Marking the Second Frontier." *Teachers College Record*. (Spring): 345–351.

McLaren, Peter. 1989. *Life in Schools*. White Plains, NY: Longman.

Minsky, Marvin. 1988. *The Society of Mind*. New York: Simon & Schuster.

Moody, Roger, ed. 1988. *The Indigenous Voice: Visions and Realities* (Vol. 2) London: Zed Books.

Moustakas, Clark. 1967. *Creativity and Conformity*. Princeton, NJ: D. Van Nostrand.

Naess, Arne. 1989. *Ecology, Community, and Lifestyle: An Outline of an Ecosophy*. Cambridge: Cambridge University Press.

Nash, Roderick F. 1989. *The Rights of Nature: A History of the Environmental Movement*. Madison: University of Wisconsin Press.

Nietzsche, Friedrich. 1968. *The Will To Power*. New York: Vintage Books.

Oakeshott, Michael. 1962. *Rationalism in Politics*. New York: Basic Books.

Oliver, Donald, and Kathleen Waldron Gershman. 1989. *Education, Modernity, and Fractured Meaning: Toward a Process Theory of Teaching and Learning*. Albany, NY: State University of New York Press.

Orr, David. (1992). *Ecological Literacy: Education and the Transition to a Postmodern World*. Albany: State University of New York Press.

Papert, Seymour. 1980. *Mindstorms: Children, Computers and Powerful Ideas.* New York: Basic Books.

——— 1993. *The Children's Machine: Re-Thinking Schools in the Age of the Computer.* New York: Basic Books.

Paul, Richard W. 1987. "Dialogical Thinking: Critical Thought Essential to the Acquisition of Rational Knowledge and Passions." In *Teaching Critical Thinking Skills*, edited by Joan Boykoff and Robert J. Sternberg. New York: W. H. Freeman. 127–150.

Perkins, David. 1987. "Thinking Frames: An Integrative Perspective on Teaching Cognitive Skills." In *Teaching Thinking Skills: Theory and Practice*, edited by J. Baron and R. J. Sternberg. Hillsdale, NJ: Lawrence Erlbaum.

Posner, Michael. 1962. *An Informational Approach to Thinking.* Ann Arbor: University Microfilms.

Rorty, Richard. 1989. *Contingency, Irony, and Solidarity.* Cambridge: Cambridge University Press.

Rosenshine, Barak, and Carla Meister. 1992. "The Use of Scaffolds for Teaching Higher-Level Cognitive Strategies." *Educational Leadership.* (April): 26–33.

Sanders, Scott Russell. 1993. Telling the Holy." *Parabola* (Summer): 4–9.

Sapir, Edward. 1949. *Culture, Language and Personality.* Berkeley: University of California Press.

Schiller, Friedrich. 1967 (original 1795). *On the Aesthetic Education of Man.* New York: Ungar.

Schneider, Stephen H. 1993. " A Better Way to Learn." *World Monitor.* Vol. 6, no. 4: 30–38.

Scollon, Ron and Suzanne Wong-Scollon. 1991. "Mass and Count Nouns in Chinese and English: A Few Further Whorfian Considerations." In *Working Papers on China, Literacy, and American/East Asian Intercultural Communication*, by Scollon and Wong-Scollon. Haines, Alaska. Unpublished monograph. 1–23.

Shils, Edward. 1981. *Tradition.* Chicago: University of Chicago Press.

Shrag, Francis. 1987. "The Classroom as a Place for Thinking." In *Thinking: The Second International Conference*, edited by D. N. Perkins, J. Lockhead, J. Bishop. Hillsadle, NJ: Lawrence Erlbaum.

Simon, Herbert A, and Kaplan, Craig A. 1989. "Foundations of Cognitive Science." In *Foundations of Cognitive Science*, edited by Michael Posner. Cambridge: MIT Press. 1–8.

Smith, Gregory. 1992. *Education and the Environment: Learning to Live with Limits.* Albany: State University of New York Press.

Snyder, Gary. 1980 edition. *The Real Work: Interviews and Talks 1964–1979.* New York: New Directions.

Steinbright, Jan. 1992. "Artist Profile: Ross Sheakley." *Journal of Alaska Native Arts.* (January–March): 7–9.

Sternberg, Robert J. 1990. *Metaphors of the Mind: Conceptions of the Nature of Intelligence.* New York: Cambridge University Press.

―――― 1990 b. "Intellectual Styles: Theory and Classroom Implications," In *Learning and Thinking Styles: Classroom Interactions,* edited by Barbara Z. Presseisen et al. Washington, D. C.: National Education Association and Research for Better Schools. 18–42.

Suzuki, David, and Peter Knudston. 1992. *Wisdom of the Elders: Honoring Sacred Native Visions of Nature.* New York: Bantam Books.

Swartz, Robert J. 1987. "Critical Thinking: The Curriculum and the Problem of Transfer." In *Thinking: The Second International Conference,* edited by D. N. Perkins, J. Lockhead, J. Bishop. Hillsadle, NJ: Lawrence Erlbaum.

Taylor, Brandon. 1987. *Modernism, Postmodernism, Realism: A Critical Perspective for Art.* Winchester, NH: Winchester School of Art Press.

Thoreau, Henry David. 1966 edition. *Walden and Civil Disobedience.* New York: W. W. Norton

Torrence, E. Paul. 1969. *Creativity.* San Rafael, CA: Dimensions Publishing Co.

Toulmin, Stephen. 1990. *Cosmopolis: The Hidden Agenda of Modernity.* New York: Free Press.

Turner, Frederick. 1986. *Beyond Geography: The Western Spirit Against the Wilderness.* New Brunswick, NJ: Rutgers University Press.

Vygotsky, Lev Semenovich. 1962. *Thought and Language.* Cambridge: MIT Press.

Whitehead, Alfred North. 1926. *Religion in the Making.* New York: Free Press.

―――― 1936. *Modes of Thought.* New York: Free Press.

Whorf, Benjamin Lee. 1968. "Science and Linguistics." In *Everyman His Own Way: Readings in Cultural Anthropology,* edited by Alan Dundes. Englewood Cliffs, NJ: Prentice Hall. 318–328.

Wigginton, Eliot. 1985. *Sometimes a Shining Moment. The Foxfire Experience.* Garden City: Anchor/Doubleday.

——— 1989. "Foxfire Grows Up." *Harvard Educational Review*. Vol. 59 no. 1 (February): 24–49.

Woolfolk, Anita E. 1993 edition. *Educational Psychology*. Needham Heights, MA: Allyn and Bacon.

Worster, Donald. 1977. *Nature's Economy: A History of Ecological Ideas*. New York: Cambridge University Press.

INDEX